THE RISE OF
CELEBRITY
AUTHORSHIP

THE RISE OF CELEBRITY AUTHORSHIP

NINETEENTH-CENTURY
PRINT CULTURE
AND ANTISLAVERY

SARAH DANIELLE ALLISON

Columbia University Press   *New York*

Columbia University Press
Publishers Since 1893
New York   Chichester, West Sussex

Copyright © 2025 Columbia University Press

All rights reserved
Library of Congress Cataloging-in-Publication Data

Names: Allison, Sarah (Sarah Danielle) author
Title: The rise of celebrity authorship : nineteenth-century print culture and antislavery / Sarah Danielle Allison.
Description: New York : Columbia University Press, 2025. | Includes bibliographical references and index.
Identifiers: LCCN 2025003921 (print) | LCCN 2025003922 (ebook) | ISBN 9780231209700 hardback | ISBN 9780231209717 trade paperback | ISBN 9780231558075 ebook
Subjects: LCSH: Slavery in literature | Antislavery movements in literature | American literature—19th century—History and criticism | Authors and readers—United States—History—19th century | Authorship—Social aspects—United States—History—19th century | English literature—19th century—History and criticism | Authors and readers—Great Britain—History—19th century | Authorship—Social aspects—Great Britain—History—19th century | Fame—History—19th century
Classification: LCC PS217.S55 A44 2025 (print) | LCC PS217.S55 (ebook) | DDC 810.9/35552—dc23/eng/20250303

Cover design: Elliott S. Cairns
Cover image: Portrait of Fredrika Bremer, from *Nordstjernan. Witterhetsstycken och Poëmer* (Stockholm, 1844)

GPSR Authorized Representative: Easy Access System Europe, Mustamäe tee 50, 10621 Tallinn, Estonia, gpsr.requests@easproject.com

To Elsie B. Michie

CONTENTS

Introduction: Antislavery Celebrity
and the Literary Author   1

1 Cards on the Table: How Data-Driven Approaches to
Literary History Shaped This Archive   21

2 The Collectible Author: Autographs, Homes and Haunts,
and Antislavery Gift Books   43

3 White Lady Authoresses Cross the Atlantic:
Antislavery Gift Books and Travelogues   71

4 Becoming the "Real Uncle Tom":
A Textual History of the Lives of Josiah Henson   99

5 A True History of *Jane Eyre*: The Collaborative
Posthumous Creation of Charlotte Brontë   127

Coda: Refiguring Authorship   157

Acknowledgments   163
Notes   167
Bibliography   207
Index   231

THE RISE OF CELEBRITY AUTHORSHIP

INTRODUCTION
Antislavery Celebrity and the Literary Author

T*he Rise of Celebrity Authorship* is not so much a history of the author as an account of how the figure of the author emerged through competing and complementary literary forms. The anarchic enterprise of creating literary celebrity operated through a host of print forms that share an association with the author's person and work. That history has an ensemble cast, and many of the cocreators of celebrity authorship featured in this account—people who wrote biographical notices or printed collections of autographs—played ancillary roles in literary history. The history of how an author's name might function as a brand highlights a broader set of figures working in a wider range of genres and so also reveals how changes in an author's brand over time can limit how we see writers of the past: the authors whose names have come down to us as novelists or poets also wrote many other kinds of things.

In literary histories organized by author or genre, the sea of miscellaneous texts adjacent to major works has been largely invisible. Celebrity authors emerged, in part, through such miscellaneous writings—by themselves and by others; closer attention to miscellaneous forms reveals how celebrity grew from resonances across a variety of texts. As I explain in depth in chapter 1, computational studies have created the condition for a study of miscellaneousness that makes it possible to see the close connections across this particular series of texts.

The Rise of Celebrity Authorship is set in the decentralized context of mid-nineteenth-century Anglophone letters, just in and after the period Meredith McGill calls the "age of reprinting." McGill's study opens with a court decision in 1834 restricting the rights of authors and traces American letters through the early 1850s, when "the promise of a more coordinated, national market for print" emerged.[1] Superstar novelists navigated the context of mass reprinting and remediation while fighting for stronger copyright protections for their work. Joe Moran's book on literary celebrity in America is largely about the twentieth century, but it opens in the 1850s, when "the public personality of the author was sponsored by two lucrative areas of public activity which were closely interrelated—the lecture circuit and the popular press."[2] In this context, many players in the literary marketplace developed strategies to make money from authors' names, developing collections of signatures, anthologies, and biographies that created a separate revenue stream associated with the person of the author. This book pulls these other players into view, trading a focus on major figures for a better look at the wider field to illuminate the collective creation of celebrity in and through print culture.

This study of literary celebrity in nineteenth-century print culture draws many of its examples from antislavery discourse. From a publishing perspective, the history of authorship and print in the United States is imbricated with antislavery: McGill closes her study in 1853, following the release of Harriet Beecher Stowe's *Uncle Tom's Cabin* (1852) in volume form. McGill notes that the novel "galvanized readers with its compelling antislavery sentiment, but it also opened publishers' and readers' eyes to the potentially enormous market for American fiction. Recognized as an unprecedented event in the history of publishing, the novel's success tested the norms of domestic copyright and redrew the terms of debate over an international copyright agreement."[3] From the perspective of my study, antislavery discourse also weaponized cultural myths about gender and authorship through print forms that connected readers with writers. It was gendered, racialized, and, in the strain of popular and sentimental texts I draw from here, framed as a universal appeal to readers' humanity rather than toward specific reforms. In many of these texts, the figure of the author underwrote the argumentative appeal of the work. In the diffuse atmosphere of nineteenth-century literary production, antislavery literature worked like a heat map to reveal the intersection of literary form and the figure of the author.[4]

By the middle of the nineteenth century, anyone could write antislavery texts in any genre by taking up the topic. As a genre, antislavery writing was not at all based on form but rather on an endorsement of the idea that slavery was wrong: an antislavery text might be a travelogue or a short note contributed to a collected volume. Antislavery discourse drew on the full breadth of collaboratively produced print forms circulating in a transatlantic literary market. Such texts push us to reckon with miscellaneousness, revealing the limits of disciplinary subfields organized by theme and genre. They resist disciplinary patterns of attention that might focus on the "literary" production of major writers or divide travel writing from translated lyrics, political speeches from polemical novels.

To understand this miscellaneousness, I draw on book history, digital archives, and algorithmic criticism as interlocking computational approaches to genre. Computational perspectives shape the archive of this book. The meticulous historical and contextual investigation required by book history seems very different from the meticulous model building and maintaining required by large-scale textual analysis, but both reveal a more expansive literary field. Case studies drawn from the more heterogeneous set of texts examined in this study challenge disciplinary assumptions at the heart of ideas of literary celebrity and literariness that grow from the single figure of the celebrity author.

Scholars of nonfictional discourses such as biography, history, and travel writing might have an acute sense of the many literary genres; members of the Society for the History of Authorship, Reading, and Publishing often focus on a set of agents broader than the single author. Combining these approaches illuminates the relational and textual networks that produced the authors we know best. By bringing these insights to celebrity studies, *The Rise of Celebrity Authorship* asks what it means to balance such broad perspectives with the irrefutable hypersignificance of star figures and their star works. The larger literary field I consider offers a new archive of literary celebrity. The 1840s and 1850s might have seen some of the most canonical novels and poetry of the United States and Britain, but more of the book market comprised various kinds of nonfiction. Also, much of the material printed was in literary periodicals. This material can be too easy to filter out of literary history. Computational perspectives disrupt the modes of organization that literary history has developed by putting major texts by major authors in constellation with significantly less-major authors and related but unexpected kinds of texts.

Nineteenth-century Anglo-American literary culture was characterized by cultural and legal debates over the idea of the author as proprietor of their work that took place within and against a growing field of marketable print forms produced and reproduced without crediting their creators.[5] In the context of a transatlantic book market characterized by an international circulation of texts in books and periodicals, authors, publishers, booksellers, and legislators debated questions about originality, authenticity, and freedom of expression.[6] Looking at transatlantic antislavery and literary celebrity together in this period illuminates relatively minor figures writing in what now seem like marginal genres but in the context of major political and intellectual currents of their time.

A notion of copyright in which the work belongs to the creator can glamorize the idea of an original work of art. Paul Saint-Amour argues that copyright has been used in the "protection and consecration of a model of the self as original genius": "Dissevered not only from the more collective sources and modes of its own production but from the hypothetical nature of its originality, it [the original work] attains the theological rank of a 'classic,' 'a masterpiece,' a 'work of genius.'"[7] By contrast, I emphasize the "collective sources and modes" of literary production by ignoring the author's *work* in this copyrightable sense in favor of the circulation of authors' signatures and accounts of their lives. The distributed cultural marketplace of the nineteenth century, with its collections of "homes and haunts," edited letters, and autobiographies, reveals the many stakeholders who created and benefited from such author brands.

The development of copyright ultimately led to a division between the author as the owner of a work and the author as a persona, which is important for thinking about what a literary celebrity is.[8] In a discussion of corporate authorship in advertising, Catherine Fisk distinguishes between attribution and reputation, copyright and the right of publicity: "Together, attribution and reputation help to constitute a valuable persona.

The right of publicity has evolved to protect a person's right to the revenue stream associated with that persona. Like copyright, it embraces multiple versions of what it means to be a creator, including the modernist conception of the author as a unique, transformative force. To be a persona is to be an author of oneself, which has come to entitle one to be recognized as the author of one's creative work."[9]

By this light, the materials I examine here might be connected with what came to be the "right to publicity," which Fisk defines as the "right to revenue stream associated with personal attribution and reputation."[10] The nineteenth-century texts here bear not only on an author's work but also on the author's persona.

Nineteenth-century gift books, translations, and biographies turn the spotlight back on the team of people who produced the authors we came to know. This study builds on a tradition of scholarship about collaborative writing from a range of perspectives. Martha Woodmansee considers a range of writing contexts that practiced collaborative authorship in both the nineteenth century and our own: business, government, industry, the law, and the sciences and social sciences have long countered a received Romantic idea of author as genius.[11] Patricia Okker and Jewon Woo study collaborative editing in the U.S. context.[12] The contributions made by editors can be difficult to trace: Fionnuala Dillane takes up the problem of seeing George Eliot's editorial work through careful review of her letters, and Lauren F. Klein uses topic modeling to render visible the editorial work of Mary Ann Shadd and Lydia Maria Child.[13] Translation is another inherently collaborative mode of authorship. My study of cultural producers reflects the ways in which forms of collective work have long shaped the history of celebrity authorship.

The myriad genres within antislavery print, which espoused myriad political perspectives within antislavery, cohere as a single genre only from the perspective of book history, the perspective of the nineteenth-century literary marketplace. Stowe characterized the term *antislavery* as "hacknied" in a letter advising Susan F. Porter on a gift book to raise funds for Frederick Douglass's newspaper in 1852.[14] Antislavery print culture included images, poetry, novels, autobiography, biography, gift books, pamphlets, periodicals, newspapers, and travel writing as well as compendia of evidence and firsthand accounts of slavery. As an international trend organized loosely around a few star authors and texts, antislavery print culture reveals how texts such as literary miscellanies and multivolume travel narratives both drew on and helped create transatlantic celebrity authorship. Opposition to slavery was a stance available not only to major political figures such as Douglass but also to someone like the popular Swedish novelist Fredrika Bremer, who wrote an antislavery travel narrative on the strength of the popularity of her novels in English translation. As I discuss in chapter 3, Bremer's path to abolitionist discourse is clear if—and only if—the story accounts for her relationship with her best-known translator into English, Mary Howitt, and for the genre of the travelogue as a celebrity genre as well as an abolitionist one.

Literary celebrity seems, well, literary. But antislavery writing demonstrates that it can also be political. One major difference between Charles Dickens and Stowe, two often-cited celebrity authors of the period, is Stowe's public investment in the political movement against slavery. Stowe contributed to the creation of "antislavery" as a literary genre by writing a novel that prompted many responses and imitations in print culture and beyond, a phenomenon Sarah Meer calls "Uncle Tom mania."[15] Because antislavery print culture could take any form, a study of antislavery print reveals different genres of literature adjacent to one another, working together to amplify a political message—and an author's profile. Antislavery literature was defined only by thematic content, so it can allow us to see beyond the genres we often recognize today as literary to genres that were central to nineteenth-century ideas of literature, such as travel writing. Nonfictional genres emerge in their full array in relation to one another and in relation to more familiar celebrity-written novels, poetry, drama, and literary essays. The idea of "antislavery literature" is both political and formal, and texts under that rubric call forth an idea of the author that is cocreated from political and literary materials. These texts deployed the names of famous authors in calculated ways: through print, an author's personal support connected their work with their politics in a way that tied the two closely together.

If we often understand literary celebrity as a name attached to a genre (for example, Byron the poet, Dickens the novelist), we are likely mistaken—not only because Byron wrote reviews and Dickens produced *Household Words* but also because their brands emerged from a collective of individuals writing about them and engaging with their works before, during, and after they rose to fame. In Sharon Marcus's formulation of celebrity, agency is "everywhere": celebrities, media, and publics all wield power. Marcus expands the archive of public responses to celebrity—scrapbooks, fan mail, firsthand accounts of celebrity, as well as life writing.[16] My study of literary celebrity takes up texts by celebrity writers and writings about them in contexts where that celebrity is put to use. The agents I focus on here are minor figures or figures who have come to seem minor; publishers and editors who might have a less visible but important role in literary culture; and major figures working outside the forms of the novel, critical essays, and poetry. I bring marginal figures and texts to the foreground in a new, more evenly populated cultural landscape that would have been clear to many nineteenth-century readers, a landscape that shows how a singular brand could be collectively produced.

The rise in cheap print in the mid–nineteenth century worked with the global circulation of text and images to create the beginnings of celebrity culture as we know it now. From the perspective of the history of literary celebrity, scholarship on Frederick Douglass has developed a clear framework for understanding the connection between literary celebrity and transatlantic antislavery print culture in Anglophone abolitionist discourse in the 1840s and 1850s. Douglass's series of autobiographies complemented his fame as an international lecturer and antislavery advocate. The historian Manisha Sinha, whose account of the long history of antislavery activism characterizes abolition as an interracial movement fueled intellectually and politically by radical Black resistance, describes the 1840s and 1850s as a time when formerly enslaved figures such as Douglass "created an authentic, original, and independent critique of slaveholding," one that they enacted through print and in their public careers.[17] Douglass was also an important figure in the international antislavery lecture circuit. The most-photographed man in the nineteenth century used the relations among his experience, public speaking, and literary production to cultivate a stardom that furthered his political project.

Scholarship on Stowe gives another picture of antislavery literary celebrity from the time that her breakout novel set the stage for her subsequent fame as a high-profile abolitionist. As Samantha Pinto's work on Black women celebrities argues, celebrity in this era entailed a public and sustained encounter with gendered and racialized expectations.[18] Stowe was an exemplary white lady of the period. Her literary celebrity was inextricably tied to her racialized and gendered identity as a figure in nineteenth-century social reform, a broader movement that Amanda Claybaugh characterizes as inherently collaborative across Britain and the United States and manifested in print.[19] Stowe is an important figure in Margaret McFadden's study of the "golden cables of sympathy" stretching across the Atlantic—her writings circulated in Britain, and she spoke there—as an example of a celebrity whose influence exceeded her design: "Though she herself was no champion of women's rights, Stowe nevertheless contributed to that cause."[20] Stowe was a transatlantic lecturer and is featured, with Douglass, in Amanda Adams's work on the nineteenth-century transatlantic lecture tour,[21] and *Uncle Tom's Cabin* sold more copies in the United Kingdom than in the United States. Stowe's sentimental condemnation of slavery fit well with the literary production of "political poetesses" of the period, whose work Tricia Lootens reads in the context of "patriotic—and imperial—narratives of moral triumph over transatlantic slavery."[22] Stowe is the prototypical sentimental "authoress" version of the transatlantic, antislavery literary celebrity.

By drawing a wider circle around the celebrities who matter, I sketch larger-than-life figures such as Douglass and Stowe next to lesser-known figures such as Josiah Henson. One reason Henson has dropped from view is that he rose to fame in the nineteenth century as the "original Uncle Tom." Indeed, Harriet Beecher Stowe pointed to "the published memoirs of the venerable Josiah Henson," *The Life of Josiah Henson, Formerly a Slave, Now an Inhabitant of Canada, as Narrated by Himself* (1849), as a "parallel" to Uncle Tom in her *Key to Uncle Tom's Cabin* (1853).[23] The story he tells is also complicated: Clint Smith recently recovered Henson's story as one that "reflects the complexity and moral incongruence that animated the lives of enslavers and shaped the lives of the enslaved" because it was a "slave narrative in which the central protagonist makes morally dubious decisions, regrets them, struggles with them." Smith argues that it is a "loss that Henson has not been part of our collective understanding of the history of slavery. Not every enslaved person was Frederick Douglass. Not every enslaved person was Harriet Tubman."[24] Smith shows how archival rediscovery can yield new insights into collective understanding. I show how perspectives from book history and digital humanities methods can facilitate archival rediscovery and illuminate new textual connections. Henson's writings closely connect Douglass's first narrative to Stowe's novel in the narrative form that Henson's "lives" take, in their content, and through the circumstances of their publication and circulation. Henson's work might easily be read in relation to Douglass's or Stowe's. But recognizing how Henson's celebrity emerged in relation to those figures and their works without losing focus on Henson reveals the matrix of literary culture around the figures and genres we already teach and write about.

Nineteenth-century treatments of celebrity authors reveal a broader and much less centralized system of literary production than literary history might have us believe. The archive for this book was shaped by computational work that reveals a variety of genres no longer visible as "literature" and that showed me a new way of thinking about how fiction and nonfiction are mediated by genre. Chapter 1 shows how this archive, connected by perspectives on transatlantic celebrity authorship, draws together texts that make sense in specific critical contexts but don't often appear together: periodical satire, author's homes and haunts, travel writing, Uncle Tom mania, the nineteenth-century lecture circuit, and gender and literary celebrity. I have departed from the nineteenth-century practice of treating miscellany through the "anthology"—etymologically a "gathering of flowers"—by offering a bouquet of examples. I instead read hinge texts that reveal connections between subfields that are too often separated.

The first half of this book argues that nineteenth-century cultural producers used literary forms that made readers feel close to authors, such as printed collections of author signatures, homes-and-haunts collections, biographies, and travel writing to lend cultural capital to the transatlantic political movement against slavery. Texts about celebrities, as Marcus argues, both created and disseminated celebrity.[25] Metacelebrity discourse in the nineteenth century appeared in a wide variety of artifacts, such as the birthday book, author interviews, and circulating images of the author.[26] Chapter 2 sets the stage for my study of the author in a print culture characterized by anonymous reprints *and* ubiquitous popular accounts of celebrity authors through printed collections of facsimile autographs. Here, two examples of American canon making deploy the aura of handwriting in an age of mechanical reproducibility. The first, Edgar Allan Poe's series "Autography" (1836) in the *Southern Literary Messenger* and "Chapter on Autography" in *Graham's Magazine* (1841), was a hoax that satirized autograph collecting. Based off a British original published in *Fraser's Magazine*, "Autography" emphasized Poe's centrality in U.S. letters as an editor whose desk was piled with correspondence from famous writers. The second example in this chapter is also an American adaptation of a British original: William Howitt's *Homes and Haunts of the Most Eminent British Poets* (1847) was the inspiration for George Palmer Putnam's *Homes of American Authors* (1853). As Alexis Easley explains, such forms "linked literary texts to specific biographical and geographical details that could be experienced virtually, through reading periodicals and other texts, or in actuality, by handling personal relics or viewing literary shrines."[27] Nicola J. Watson's work on literary tourism and writer's houses emphasizes the importance of place in creating a sense of closeness to an author.[28] I call attention to the reproductions of authorial manuscript in volumes such as Howitt's and Putnam's to bring readers close to a scene of production.[29] The name on the cover of *Homes of American Authors* was Putnam's, an editor whose volume highlighted the most famous authors from his publishing house, and the chapters in the volume were authored by writers who would later write for his magazine. It drew on a range of literary figures, including authors of history as well as fiction.

Such forms could then, as now, be deployed to connect celebrities with causes. These forms were shared across America and Britain. Studies of literary celebrity and studies of social reform discourse take the transatlantic circulation of texts for granted. As Ann Wierda Rowland and Paul Westover have argued, this transnational literary culture reflected different local investments but also shared practices of imitation, reiteration, and remediation.[30] In mapping a set of national celebrity authors, both *Homes* books manifested print forms of author love. The antislavery gift book *Autographs for Freedom* (1854) used the fan culture behind homes-and-haunts gift books to promote antislavery feeling.

Chapter 3 explores the dynamic between celebrity and antislavery writing in the genre of the gift book and the travelogue. Miranda Marraccini's work on the woman-run Victoria Press uses archival and network analysis to argue that contributors to gift books might be valuable primarily for their names alone. Taking up that argument, I consider contributions to *The Liberty Bell* (1839–1857, edited by Maria Weston Chapman) by

Harriet Martineau, an English social theorist well known for her antislavery advocacy, and Fredrika Bremer, the popular Swedish novelist. The names "Martineau" and "Bremer" signaled international literary celebrity.[31] Antislavery gift books, often edited by high-profile figures such as Chapman, traded on authors' names and collected disparate genres into one volume. Over the years, Martineau's contributions ranged from an analysis of the American antislavery sentiment to a first-person poem on invalidism to an essay titled "Incidents of Travel" on the area that is now Sudan. A version of that essay appeared the same year in Martineau's travelogue *Eastern Life, Present and Past* (1848). "Incidents of Travel" seems at first glance to exemplify the edited-collection phenomenon we still see today, in which an editor commissions an essay from a writer on a topic connected with their previous work, and the writer obligingly sends whatever they have on hand. If the writer is important enough and the essay is close enough, that essay gets included. But this particular essay also served as a hinge: it connected U.S. abolitionist writing with a British imperial context. Chapter 3 also develops the connection between literary celebrity and antislavery through Martineau's fellow contributor, the Swedish novelist Frederika Bremer. Her contribution to *Liberty Bell* is very slight, but a few years later she wrote a travelogue of her own. *Homes of the New World* (1853)—translated by Mary Howitt, who was also a prolific writer and editor—takes the shape of a series of letters that contribute to conversations about slavery in the South and Cuba. Both Bremer and Martineau capitalized on their distance, whether positioned afar (Martineau) or *from* afar (Bremer), from the American South to make their points. By recognizing how editors deployed the names of authors, we can see how a form that might seem very American (the antislavery gift book) reveals a global perspective.

If the first half of this book recuperates a history of literary forms that decenters the novel, the second half turns back toward the novel in this expanded generic framework, specifically to the problem of fictionality as it triangulated with nonfictional works and the figure of the author. It focuses on nonfictional forms that cluster around an author, including texts about celebrity authors and celebrity-authored texts whose significance in their own time had more to do with the cachet of the author than with the content of the text. In his study of Lord Byron's celebrity, Tom Mole calls this celebrity a fascination with the "person of the poet" that results in a hermeneutic of intimacy among the author, texts, and readers.[32] In contemporary author studies, Simone Murray has documented an increasing demand for authors to write in propria persona on social media to create intimacy with readers.[33] Chapters 4 and 5 ask how novel readers drew meaning from the factual forms just adjacent to the novel, including not only "true" accounts of fictional events but also autobiographical and biographical accounts of the lives of central author figures. In the complex ecosystem of nineteenth-century literary culture, novels circulated alongside nonfictional narrative forms that included accounts of authors' lives.

For example, Frances Trollope's tremendously successful travelogue *Domestic Manners of the Americans* (1832) was to be the beginning of her career as a novelist. Trollope's work demonstrates how writers might treat similar material in nonfictional and fictional modes. By Elsie B. Michie's account, Trollope "quickly sought to give that non-fictional material a fictional form" in two novels, *The Refugee in America* (1832) and *The Life and Adventures of Jonathan Jefferson Whitlaw; or Life on the Mississippi* (1836).[34] Readers in the period were more comfortable than critics are now with the idea that the same material might inspire both fiction and nonfiction. High-profile fiction/

nonfiction pairs reveal how authors emerged not only through what they wrote but also through the interaction between things they wrote and things written about them.

The representation of truth in antislavery writings—whether through documentation, firsthand accounts, or imaginative depiction—was a central problem in the period as well as in the years that followed the legal abolition of slavery. Chapter 4 takes up the question of the appropriation and commercialization of the experience of enslavement in the "lives" of Josiah Henson, who wrote a slim narrative of his life in the 1840s to raise money for a school in Canada but then became associated with the figure of Uncle Tom after Stowe pointed to his narrative as a source for her novel; by 1880, he had become the model for "Uncle Tom" in Madame Tussaud's wax museum.[35] This encounter with literary-inflected celebrity empowered Henson to build a much bigger name. He produced two expanded autobiographies and gave public lectures in Britain before and after the Civil War. Henson used the encounter between his lives and Stowe's novel to change the way he presented himself, but he was still the same person representing the same community. The proceeds from his final lecture series in the 1870s benefited the same school as the first edition of the narrative of his life in 1849.

In chapter 5, *The Rise of Celebrity Authorship* considers what a study of antislavery print culture reveals about literary celebrity in a text that might seem to have little to say to it, Elizabeth Gaskell's biography of Charlotte Brontë. Brontë's early death meant that her work was read by many as part of a "Brontë myth" created posthumously by biographers, in particular Elizabeth Gaskell, who worked in close relation to Brontë's texts to document the "originals" of characters in *Jane Eyre*. The notion of literary celebrity emerging across genres reveals that the fictionality of *Jane Eyre* is not defined by its difference from the facts of Brontë's life but by its inseparability from them and from the central figure of Brontë. Many critics today would hesitate to draw a straight line between Brontë and a real Jane Eyre, but many nineteenth-century critics were eager to do so. In a discussion of straightforwardly biographical accounts of authors, Joe Moran has argued that these accounts not only "unmask the celebrity personae these authors assumed when they were alive, [but] they also reproduce a central premise of celebrity by satisfying our desire to know the 'reality behind the legend.'"[36] Fiction offers still another curtain to draw back. Novels by literary celebrities are always also in conversation with nonfictional forms—often ones they did not author alone. Literary celebrity is created through the idea of the author as an "original" who can be embellished upon in further writings, both their own and other people's.

Each member of the cast of characters here will be known to some readers, but few of the readers who are familiar with the contributions that George Palmer Putnam made to U.S. letters as a publisher and an advocate for international copyright will know not only that Putnam's *Homes of American Authors* (chapter 2) is a reworking of William Howitt's *Homes and Haunts of the British Poets* but also that Howitt was Mr. Mary Howitt, husband to the woman who encouraged the writing career of Elizabeth Gaskell (chapter 5), the same Mary Howitt who brought the novels of Fredrika Bremer to a broader Anglophone audience (chapter 3), and the person so connected with antislavery circles in the States that she ran a gift book for Lydia Maria Child for a few years and recruited Gaskell and Harriet Martineau (chapter 3) to write for *Sartain's Monthly Magazine* in Philadelphia.[37] Stowe, one of the best-known transatlantic literary celebrities of her own day, is likely to be known to all readers and appears with some regularity in this book but usually in other guises than as novelist: as a preface writer, poem contributor, compiler of documents, and a kind of foil to Josiah Henson (chapter 4). Ubiquitous but not quite central, this decentered Stowe reveals the many roles authors played and the diverse texts that composed "celebrity" in the period.[38]

The Rise of Celebrity Authorship traces figures of authorship through a set of texts drawn from a disparate group of nonfictional genres grouped loosely together as "antislavery writing" in this period. Though today these writings can seem unliterary and miscellaneous, in the nineteenth century they acted as the thread that stitched current political topics such as antislavery activism into the fabric of the celebrity personality. Even major works would have been read in the context of this more capacious, politically engaged version of literary celebrity.

This book methodologically underscores the connection between recent work in "big data" and long-established computational tradition in bibliography and the sociology of literature to argue that such approaches are valuable to studies of print culture precisely because they are not bound by discursive contexts such as genre and an author's nationality of origin. Although the genre of antislavery offers a productive way to draw out resonances across established disciplinary contexts, the contexts are disparate. In chapter 1, I discuss a few key ways that large-scale computational studies shaped this project—and it is best to be clear from the beginning that these practices, designed to pursue very different questions about closely related objects, do not easily fit together.

As book history, this study advances two interrelated points. The first argument is that the collective production of texts is more clearly visible in works *about* authors than in works *by* them. The idea of an "author's work" often connotes the *major* works, those texts that fall into the best-recognized literary genres now. Such a formulation can obscure the many kinds of texts authors wrote as well as the other roles they played in literary production. By contrast, the kinds of author portraits I look at here are connected by subject: they are oriented around the figure of the author. This refiguration lets us see anonymous essays "about authors" and autobiographical work "by authors" as equivalent opportunities to understand the figure of the author. Such texts often circulated in nineteenth-century material forms such as periodicals and miscellanies that were fundamentally—and obviously—collaborative in nature.

The second argument is that such texts help recuperate a broader nineteenth-century understanding of the term *literature* that gives due weight to the belletristic prose that characterized so much of print culture in the nineteenth century. In tandem with computational approaches to book history that reveal the interplay of fact and fictional genres in the literary marketplace, algorithmic approaches to literature show that same interplay within texts. Such computational perspectives are like God's—or the Author's—presence in creation: everywhere felt and nowhere seen. I borrow Flaubert's simile to suggest how profoundly findings from book history and algorithmic criticism shape the contours of the present inquiry, an approach to the golden age of the three-decker novel that focuses instead on the literary author and nonfictional forms.[39]

1

CARDS ON THE TABLE

How Data-Driven Approaches to Literary History
Shaped This Archive

The *Rise of Celebrity Authorship* affords a model for integrating data into literary history. There are no charts in this book, yet charts—and the painstaking task of transforming print-culture artifacts into manipulable numerical forms—drive the conception of every part of this project. In using published computational studies, often collectively authored, I show how such work, huge in scope, affords new ways of structuring our fields of inquiry by giving us new objects to work from. Quantitative approaches offer a kind of divinely cosmopolitan perspective on print culture that pushes us to think across the place and time frameworks of subfields. This indifference to context can result in research that deals with a miscellaneous set of books, but these modes of inquiry empower us to see past the identification between author and recognizably "literary" work to the range of texts just beside them.

I have argued elsewhere that daringly simple project design can yield startlingly fresh perspectives on complex literary problems.[1] This book takes up the seamy side of the argument: the coappearance of disparate texts on one spreadsheet can create complex problems for literary phenomena we thought we understood. The novel seems like the main event in nineteenth-century studies now in part because it grew increasingly popular over the course of the century and often ultimately took volume form. Yet publishing histories reveal a midcentury book market dominated by nonfictional forms such as travel writing, history, biography, and criticism—the forms that, we know, constituted so many periodicals, sometimes right alongside serialized novels. The first observation based on numbers this book promotes is that the novel was a relatively small portion of the "literary" landscape.

Lots of people know this. Yet this fact challenges a persistent received idea in literary studies that poetry and the novel were the dominant literary forms in the Victorian period. One outcome of this disciplinary pattern has been that literary criticism that treats texts from natural science, history, philosophy, and political economy is often pushed to return to what those discourses show about "literary forms" such as the novel and poetry. By contrast, sociological approaches to literary study contextualize imaginative fiction in a more even relation to other forms of writing. Because algorithmic approaches rely on models that are indifferent to disciplinary subfields, they can give us new purchase on the history of genres. If computational methods reveal the many people who produced the "author," they also reveal how many kinds of texts "literary" authors published. This chapter methodologically models how to treat algorithmic findings like a traditional scholarly reference.

It opens with a demonstration of how computational perspectives that emphasize nonfiction at the intersection of celebrity and antislavery connect with our perspective on fictionality in the period through a specific example of how findings from algorithmic criticism point to the complexities of Josiah Henson's narrative of 1849, *The Life of Josiah Henson, Formerly a Slave*, a text that connected closely with discussions of fictionality and literary celebrity but in a context where Henson figured as author, as literary character based on that narrative, and then as a literary character who authored a revised narrative. Whereas chapter 4 offers an extended analysis of the lives and lectures of Josiah Henson, the discussion here offers a methodological account of how I came to include Henson in the study. I then turn to quantitative work in a broader sense: the perspectives from the sociology of literature that motivated my focus on nonfictional genres. Finally, I consider what periodical studies have taught us about celebrity (in signed and unsigned articles), the collective creation of literature (through editorial intervention), and genre (the miscellaneous essays that insistently demonstrate that nonfictional forms of writing also constituted literary work in the period).

ALGORITHMIC CRITICISM: FICTION, NONFICTION, AND "HARD CASES"

Many books that derived their force from being associated with celebrity authors were not "works" by those authors. Deidre Lynch connects the importance of biography to a new relationship to imaginative literature and wryly points out that the nineteenth-century "public's appetites for writers' lives tended to outrun its eagerness to consume writers' works," as in the case of James Boswell's *Life of Samuel Johnson* (1791) in relation to the works of Samuel Johnson.[2] Richard D. Altick characterizes the novel and biography as "two major departments of narrative prose . . . in acknowledged competition throughout the [Victorian] period" and notes "the cliché that a good biography made as interesting reading as a novel—better, really, because it was true."[3] For nineteenth-century critics writing reviews, the reading experience of the two forms was (in the best case) equally compelling, and the difference between them rested largely on the truth claims of a "good biography."

How different, really, are the two forms? From a narratological perspective, they differ sharply. For Catherine Gallagher, the rise of the novel *is* the rise of fictionality: "The historical connection between the terms *novel* and *fiction* is intimate; they were mutually constitutive."[4] Daniel Defoe's *The Life and Adventures of Robinson Crusoe* (1719) alleges that it was "written by [Crusoe] himself," a claim backed up by the "editor": "The editor believes the thing to be a just history of fact; neither is there any appearance of fiction in it."[5] The novel arrived when readers stopped expecting such stories to be true—when they could read a story that seemed as if it could really happen and yet was neither libelous nor obviously a fantasy. In Gallagher's terms, the "credible" narrative became the "plausible" when fictional narratives started to follow the laws of probability despite being cut off from the accidents of history.[6] Ian Watt's version of the story explains how the novel quit making unsubstantiated claims to verifiable fact (as in the title page of *Robinson Crusoe*, which states the novel's events were written by Crusoe "himself") and started to depict a lifelike but fictional world (as in the novel *Robinson Crusoe*). Watt describes this process as the "rise" of formal realism.[7] Srinivas Aravamudan calls it the narrowing down of the nineteenth-century field of legitimate prose fiction into the texts that exhibited formal realism. Aravamudan clarifies a broader distinction between fictional modes that highlights the diversity of imaginative fiction in the eighteenth century, in particular the popularity of "Oriental tales": the provincialist narrative about the "rise of the novel" is a deliberate exclusion of "the history and theory of prose fiction in its broadest sense," which would include Oriental tales and travel narratives.[8] Literary biography can read like antifiction, working to demonstrate verifiable facts about fictional narratives.

One way to understand the relation between the novel and biography is through the reader's encounter with the figure of the author in both forms. When readers treat fictionality as a fiction—ignoring the novel's claim to be fictional in favor of tracing its history in fact—they are doing what Lynch calls "loving literature." That is, they are reading in accordance with an emerging consensus in the eighteenth and nineteenth century that "the transactions that would count as literary would involve heart-to-heart relations."[9] My question is about how forms help create this relation: How might the figure of the author emerge through novel-adjacent forms, fictional and nonfictional?

This figure certainly manifests in paratext. For Monika Fludernik, *factuality* is the nineteenth-century norm against which fiction emerged, and fiction can be many things besides a novel.[10] The key feature for Fludernik is that readers recognize the nonhistorical or nonfactual nature of a text's truth claims, so their encounter with external or extrinsic generic cues is a key part of their encounter with fictionality. Text-based approaches to nineteenth-century fictionality can use paratextual markers such as tables of contents and appendixes to mark nonfiction. But do the truth claims in biography and autobiography leave a trace in the text?

Ted Underwood says yes. At least, according to his book *Distant Horizons: Digital Evidence and Literary Change* (2019), his models learned to use a set of features that tend to characterize fiction to predict with fair accuracy whether a text is fiction or biography and with increasing accuracy over time—results were "clearer in the nineteenth century, than in the eighteenth and clearer in the twentieth century than the nineteenth." It is, he writes, as if "the novel steadily specialized in something that biography (and other forms of nonfiction) could rarely provide: descriptions of bodies, physical actions, and immediate sensory perceptions in a precisely specified place and time."[11] But to get to that finer distinction, his algorithm had to get better and better at recognizing the difference between fiction and nonfiction books, even for books that initially got confused with fiction.

This is the story of how this book that you are reading came to be, which I hope will model a way that computational work can challenge us to rethink the boundaries of literary study. My project was shaped by a precursor to the study in *Distant Horizons*: Ted Underwood's National Endowment for the Humanities Digital Humanities project "Understanding Genre in a Collection of a Million Volumes" (2014). Bibliographic at its heart, the project aimed to "use machine learning to select genre-specific collections from digital libraries."[12] Though the team would ultimately zoom in to distinguish more finely between difficult cases and distinct nonfictional genres, the project offered in the first rough sort a sketch of the literary landscape in giant piles. My story here is anecdotal—how Ted Underwood, generous and transparent, shared some early results with me—and it is also an example of the conceptual importance of project design and development. I cite a conference paper, an interim report, a blog post, and personal correspondence.

In 2014, Underwood observed that the early models he designed to work with HathiTrust texts were "good at identifying clear cases of our received categories; I found that they agreed with my research assistants almost exactly as often as the research assistants agreed with each other (93–94% of the time, about broad categories like fiction/nonfiction)."[13] Underwood and his team found that biography and autobiography are particularly difficult to distinguish from fiction at the page level. Echoing James Fitzjames Stephen's contemporaneous description of *The Life of Charlotte Brontë* (1857) as a "biography that opens exactly like a novel," the team's interim report points out that "nineteenth-century biographies that invent imagined dialogue often read exactly like a novel."[14] In the fall of 2013, they noted that they used special classifiers to capture different types of nonfiction because "nonfiction prose is a large category, containing genres like 'biography' and "autobiography' that are especially difficult to distinguish from fiction."[15] A starting point for the consideration of genre in a consolidated, digitized collection of major library holdings such as HathiTrust, then, is the simple recognition that those holdings contain a significant amount of nonfiction prose, and within "nonfiction prose" some books look much more like novels than others.

Human readers rely on structural, contextual, and generic cues to tell us what to believe and what to disbelieve, but such clues are not available to an algorithm that has access only to the text but none of the context. Fictional worlds are nothing to the tagger, as Underwood suggested in a blog post in 2014: "A statistical model of fiction doesn't care what 'really happened'; it pays attention mostly to word frequency."[16] Word frequency is helpful as long as you, like the HathiTrust tagger, are built to cope with it. Genre here is implicitly defined by a collection of features and—let's be clear—of words. Strings of characters and other textual features make an excellent starting point for many forms of analysis not only because they can be counted but also because, taken together, they can help us visualize relationships between and among texts. Word frequency is less interesting in itself than in the textual constellations it can map.

An approach based only on patterns of feature sets seems counterintuitive if you are used to thinking about words as meaningful signs. However, strings of characters and other textual features make an excellent starting point for many forms of analysis because, taken together, they can help us visualize relationships between different texts. Word frequency can capture formal features such as proper names, first-person journals, and reported dialogue—traces of the rise of fictionality from nonfiction in the eighteenth century.

Underwood and his team "read" the HathiTrust library at a large scale that ignored distinctions among texts that now implicitly structure fields of inquiry—location of publication and author affiliation in national or racialized terms. As Underwood's work developed, this approach meant training the tagger on a set of books that were more and more like novels, or—per Underwood in correspondence—were "*within* a sample where lots of obvious kinds of nonfiction (and poetry and drama) had already been excluded. So this isn't specifically a fiction versus biography model, but it's closer to fiction versus (biography and travel writing and letters, etc.) than it is to 'fiction versus everything.'"[17] The model Underwood used to generate the list he characterized as "hard cases" worked with a broader corpus than the subgenres that we might now recognize as literary categories. Among these books that shared formal features with fiction and nonfiction—enough to confuse an algorithm trained to tell the two apart—was Josiah Henson's narrative *The Life of Josiah Henson, Formerly a Slave, Now an Inhabitant of Canada, as Narrated by Himself* (1849). That is, it classified his book as a novel but within that category as having a relatively high probability of being nonfiction.

When I scanned the long list for writers and texts I recognized, with an eye to nonfiction books by or about celebrity authors, Henson's book leaped out. While most twenty-first-century literary critics familiar with the text wouldn't classify it as a novel, few would be surprised by the algorithm's confusion. I first experienced this confusion as the algorithm rehearsing a nineteenth-century proslavery skepticism about the truth status of Henson's narrative, then I reflected that the algorithm was more likely working from the deployment of documentary forms that characterized the slave narrative more generally. The imbrication of fiction with nonfiction in the history of the testimony of enslaved people—combined with the appropriation and commercialization of such testimonies in nineteenth-century antislavery literature—is an established area of critical discussion. The model noticed something that has also been well established: the form of the slave narrative looks like a novel. From a perspective of the development of narrative nonfiction, the elements of a slave narrative that to the model "read like" the novel are the elements it shared with fiction (first-person account, dialogue) but also with nonfictional forms that gave rise to the early novel.

The model may have identified Henson's text initially as a novel in part because it is related in first person and includes dialogue. In the context of nineteenth-century texts about slavery, those formal features worked to signal objectivity and factual testimony, in contrast to the novel. In *A Key to* Uncle Tom's Cabin (1853), Stowe compiled examples of first-person accounts of slavery to demonstrate the factual basis of her fiction.[18] She cited precedents for the incidents of the novel and its central figures, as I explore in chapter 4. It was not until the postbellum London edition that Henson's narrative directly traced relations between Stowe's novel and his life, and it included more claims than Stowe made. The complex afterlife of Henson's 1849 narrative in its aspect as source for *Uncle Tom's Cabin* (1852) reveals the interdependence between firsthand testimony and fiction. Henson is an ideal case study for figuring the author because of the interplay between the fictional and factual accounts of his life. The intersection between Henson's and Stowe's writings reveals the history of celebrity authorship as it emerged through interactions among different author figures, through genre, and through the intersections of race, gender, and national identity.

It isn't surprising that Henson's narrative is an object of study in a book about literary celebrity, but it was not an intuitive choice for a study of the figure of the author because his authorship was so thoroughly appropriated by Stowe. In an account of celebrity authorship as it emerges from novel/autobiography pairs, Henson would be a terrible example because *Uncle Tom's Cabin* is an obviously illegitimate account of Henson's life. Henson's literary celebrity grew from his own nonfictional writings *and* his encounter with the figure "Uncle Tom" from Stowe's novel.

An algorithm built to tell fiction from nonfiction thought Henson's lives were a hard case. The algorithm, in its indifference to literary-historical context, proves to be counterintuitively helpful for understanding literary history.

THE SOCIOLOGY OF LITERATURE AND THE NONFICTION LANDSCAPE

One of the major contributions of computational perspectives to a study of literary celebrity is a more distributed sense of the book market, but it is worth recognizing why novels have been so central to thinking about literary prominence. By contrast with nonfictional steady sellers, one marker of the novel is its potential for blockbuster sales. Not only can the novel sell, but it also creates a wave of related works that sell. In *"Pamela" in the Marketplace* (2005), for example, Thomas Keymer and Peter

Sabor consider Samuel Richardson's *Pamela* (1740) along with a continuation by Richardson as well as "the rival sequel that forced him to write it," John Kelly's *Pamela's Conduct in High Life* (1741), "counter-fictions" such as Henry Fielding's *Shamela* (1741), and Eliza Haywood's *Anti-Pamela* (1741).[19] In literary-historical terms, then, some novels make a much larger impact than others. This is still true; when the U.S. Department of Justice moved to stop Penguin Random House from acquiring Simon & Schuster in 2022, one headline highlighted the outsize impact of a "very small sliver" of books, and novel acquisition is still shaped by the perceived relation between a new manuscript and successful published work.[20] Jordan Alexander Stein's account of eighteenth-century U.S. publishing challenges the idea that only novels worked this way: his chapter on the text network pairs *Pamela* with David Brainerd's missionary journal (1745–1746) to show how both circulated in multiple editions around a single figure.[21] The brief discussion of *Pamela* here reveals three other authors who profited by the success and controversy over that novel.

If *Pamela* is a major example of a bestselling novel that spawned more books, so is *Jane Eyre*, and so is *Uncle Tom's Cabin*. The publishing history of *Uncle Tom's Cabin* in particular reveals that it facilitated big sales for many forms of nonfictional and polemical writing.[22] In reading the life of Josiah Henson, the "original" of Uncle Tom, in conversation with the life of Charlotte Brontë, the "original" of Jane Eyre, we are also reading accounts of fictionalized experience that highlight politics, race, and testimony in conversation with accounts of fictionalized experience in Britain that highlight authorship, gender, and evidence. Both texts reveal the way that extratextual ideas about authorship and authenticity created the celebrity author across fiction and nonfictional texts. It might seem as though Stowe was famous because of the novel she wrote, but the lifespan of the 1849 Henson text—which did well in its own way and was only later swept up and republished as part of the Stowe furor—reveals how Stowe's celebrity emerged in part from texts she didn't author.

The combination of algorithmic criticism and computational book-history approaches reveal an interplay of fact and fictional genres in the literary ecosystem through individual texts and in the literary marketplace. Recognizing how nonfictional genres work as celebrity genres can challenge the centrality of novels and poetry to literary celebrity. That is, in seeing past the novel, we can begin to see past the novelist. Easley's work has demonstrated how digital databases focused on novelists and poets can render invisible even major women journalists such as Eliza Cook.[23] In their introduction to their edited volume *Narrative Factuality: A Handbook* (2019), Fludernik and her coeditor, Marie-Laure Ryan, call for a comparative attention to the many "factual" genres that get lumped together under the name "nonfiction."[24]

Computational perspectives on nineteenth-century literature reveal the centrality of nonfictional genres in the nineteenth century. Genres based on how books are sold form the groundwork of my study of celebrity and antislavery writing through gift books, travel writing, and life writing. Recent work has demonstrated how fiction and nonfiction were imbricated in eighteenth- and nineteenth-century book markets.[25] The figure of the author could unite texts written in different modes.[26] My historical perspective on genre here draws on Simon Eliot's bibliometric analysis of Victorian book genres, published in 1994.[27] Computational studies of genre that draw on nineteenth-century publisher's catalogs work from fundamentally different definitions than contemporary narrative theories about fictionality and factuality because genre is keyed to the production and distribution of books—it has more to do with the cover than with the contents.

A sociological perspective such as Eliot's might also double down on the way genre is developed by publishers. Scholars working on forms such as travel narratives, history, political economy, and natural history have long drawn connections across book-length narrative forms. But to capture a sense of the broader book market, there is nothing like math. Eliot notes that across his charts of genres in the period 1800–1919, "whenever the category 'Fiction, juvenile,' increased its percentage share [of books published in England], 'Geography, travel, history, biography" decreased," a way of understanding "two broad categories" as competing forms.[28] Alison Booth—one of the many people to whom the novel's relation to nonfictional forms has long been evident—uses Eliot's bibliometric data to point out that "nonfiction still dominated the stock of the lending libraries (only 20 per cent of books were novels as late as 1850)."[29] Moreover, Eliot's nineteenth-century sources don't use the word *novel*.

Eliot's work in quantitative book history uses nineteenth-century perspectives on genre to create a computational overview of Victorian publishing. He emphasizes that his sources are not consistent: "As with all nineteenth-century sources of information about subject publishing, the *Bibliotheca Londinensis* has its own picturesque and arbitrary classification system, a system that makes comparison with other sources particularly difficult."[30] To comprehend the "Literature of Great Britain," publishers offered a range of taxonomies. One of Eliot's sources is *Bibliotheca Londinensis: A Classified Index to the Literature of Great Britain During Thirty Years Arranged from and Serving as a Key to the London Catalogue of Books 1814–1846*, compiled by Thomas Hodgson (1848). He writes:

The main subject headings used in the *Bibliotheca Londinensis* were: "Antiquities," "Biography," "Divinity," "Domestic Economy, Sport" "Drama and Poetry," "Education and Learning," "Fiction, etc.," "Fine Arts, Illustrated Works," "Geography, History, Voyages, Travels, etc.," "Juvenile Works, Moral Tales, etc.," "Languages, Ancient and Modern," "Law and Jurisprudence," "Logic, Moral and Mental Philosophy," "Mathematics," "Medical Sciences," "Natural and Experimental Philosophy," "Natural Sciences," "Naval and Military," "Political Economy, Parliamentary, Statistics, etc.," "School and College Books, Educational," "Trade and Commerce," and "Miscellaneous Books."

This list offers flashes of genres that touch novels-I-have-known ("Sport," such as *Pickwick*; "Natural Philosophy," such as *Middlemarch*), and a few major Victorian prose writers are suggested by these categories: Mill, Carlyle, Martineau, Darwin. But genres such as antiquities, poetry, and geography are well-represented in the omnibus reviews of literary quarterlies. Theories of the eighteenth-century novel predicated on its closeness to nonfictional forms can bring to light the novel's relation to other forms of prose; even in the Victorian period, the novel itself is notoriously heteroglossic. But periodicals gather together different genres that composed mid-nineteenth-century literary culture.[31]

My scholarship and teaching have prioritized the novel in prose and verse, but approaches from the sociology of literature and publishing history frame the novel as only a small part of the literary landscape, revealing the predominance of belletristic genres such as travel writing. Algorithmic criticism makes it possible to see books in new company according to new metrics—to list them not only by author or by year but also by a model's estimate of how likely a book is to be fiction or nonfiction. Such methods also illuminate the many ways texts get cocreated—rewritten, edited, and packaged—on their way to publication. Authorship attribution, an established practice of using patterns in word frequency to recognize style, can also identify texts in which an author's signature style is blurred by the work of another hand. At every turn, computational studies give us a richer perspective on the period, pointing to texts and figures that are clearly connected to familiar material but have previously lain just out of frame.

The idea of "literature" has been an important part of disciplinary histories and debates about the value of the humanities. The growing prominence of "creative nonfiction" suggests that nonfiction requires an extra qualifier to claim a place in the world of letters. In *Keywords* (1985), Raymond Williams traces "the attempted and often successful *specialization* of literature to certain kinds of writing."[32] The relevance of the term *literature* as it is often used in the twenty-first century lies both in its apparent contrast with informative writing and in the way different types of literature are distinguished from one another. The *Oxford Historical Thesaurus* gives twenty-eight entries under the heading "types of literature," including "highest class" and "inferior" as well as "satiric," "folk," "ancient Latin and Greek," and so forth.[33] That is, the word *literature* is useful in drawing distinctions not only of value but also of genre and provenance. The question about literature in the nineteenth century was often not *whether* a text was "literature" because *literature* was a less restrictive term then. Rather, the question might be what *kind* of literature a text was. Thomas Koenigs argues that in nineteenth-century American literature, fictionality often had a function other than an appeal to aesthetics—for instance, "didactic, polemical, religious, civic, and historiographical"—that reflected the openness of literature to multiple genres and contexts at the time.[34]

What if the key feature of the term *literature* has only ever been the modifier that precedes it? If *literature* is a word whose main significance might actually lie in the adjectives that qualify it, then we can usefully trace its history in terms of the company it has kept. Computational text analysis helps restore this word to nineteenth-century discursive contexts. In a presentation called "Around the Word 'Littérature': The English Case" (2016), Mark Algee-Hewitt, Ryan Heuser, David McClure, and Franco Moretti developed (effectively) a series of snapshots of discourse from the narrow perspective of a string of characters: l-i-t-e-r-a-t-u-r-e.[35] Their work lets us see what McClure characterized as "marquee-level changes in its use," which confirms, in part, the emergence of the idea of literature as specialized imaginative fiction, a story traced by Raymond Williams and others. This idea thus also interrupts a perspective on the nineteenth-century literary field that defaults to imaginative literature, instead drawing our attention to the presence of the word in the nineteenth century in discourses about classicism, pedagogy, and nationalism. That is, the language in which a text is written or the culture it hails from or the commercial or pedagogical context of its circulation might be considered a top candidate for the most salient feature of the texts we study, and a distanced perspective on the word *literature* lets us see all those uses at once. The modifiers of this word help us see past the genres we impose, if only by suggestive, implicit contrast.

The gift books I discuss in the next chapter reveal other genres that "go with" celebrity, including letters and sketches by authors—and letters and sketches *about* authors. The sketches of intellectual life in *Homes of American Authors* (1853) demonstrate a flexible understanding of who is an author and what kinds of literature "literary tastes" can accommodate. One sketch features Daniel Webster, best known as a politician, who appears as an author and a reader of classics ("Cicero continues to be his favorite author to the present day"). The poet William S. Bryant's "tastes and pursuits [lead] him through the entire range of literature, from the Fathers to Shelley, and from Courier to Jean Paul"; "he turns naturally from the driest treatise on politics or political economy, to the wildest romance or the most tender poem—happy in a power of enjoying all that genius has created or industry achieved in literature." Bryant appears not only as an "American Author" to be sketched but as a contributor to the volume. The first "general collection" of his works was primarily poetry and contained "in one volume all the poems he was willing to acknowledge," yet the sketch itself highlights the "papers" he contributed to the *Literary Gazette* and to other literary reviews as well as his work as an editor and proprietor of the *Evening Post*.[36] That is, his literary work comprises biography, books, and journalism in addition to poetry. A look across genres helps clarify the outlines of an author's work beyond a list of novels to a broader collection of genres, bound and unbound.

PERIODICAL STUDIES: MISCELLANEOUSNESS AND AUTHOR ATTRIBUTION

Linda K. Hughes argues that we should read sideways, including "analysis across genres," using nondigital methods to reckon with the glorious miscellaneousness of nineteenth-century quarterlies.[37] I also follow Anne DeWitt in suggesting we orient ourselves sideways by using computational methods to develop a picture of the landscape of nineteenth-century discourse when authorship is not signed (or known). DeWitt argues that we must understand nonfictional as well as fictional genres: recognizing "the 'large mass of facts' that constitute Victorian print culture" is especially important in light of the "well-established imbrication of novels with the periodical press." DeWitt's own study traces the "rise" of a specific genre, the "theological novel," as it was created retrospectively through periodical reviews.[38]

Quarterlies and other literary periodicals reveal both the central importance of celebrity names and the importance of unsigned articles. The convention of anonymity in early and mid-Victorian periodicals can make it difficult to trace authorship across periodicals, yet the practice of naming writers of one-off or occasional pieces can serve to make the breadth of an author's work more visible.

As the Wellesley and Curran Indices make clear, anonymous and pseudonymous publication was very common in nineteenth-century periodical culture. Periodicals offered writers the opportunity to identify with a publication rather than with their person. Oscar Maurer explains how at the beginning of the nineteenth century an important quarterly such as the *Edinburgh Review* could speak for a political or social group in an eighteenth-century "tradition of party criticism." Such a system made the signature of an individual reviewer seem "irrelevant."[39] In *First-Person Anonymous: Women Writers and Victorian Print Media, 1830–70* (2004), Alexis Easley considers the ways Victorian women writers moved between signed and unsigned works to advance their careers.[40] Anonymity and pseudonymity gave authors some degree of control over their public personae. Pseudonymity permitted the creation of authorial personae. Derek Spires shows how in the 1850s Black writers, in particular Black women writers, "used pseudonymity as a way to create and signal belonging to what was becoming a well-defined and interconnected Black print community." Unlike anonymity, "pseudonymous personae take on elements of fully-fleshed-out characters in a Black print-space."[41] Periodicals offered a range of possibilities for authors to identify themselves with their work. It is also obvious that creating a periodical is not an individual sport. In "The Death of the Author" (1967), Roland Barthes argues that the author "still reigns" only in histories of literature, biographies of writers, interviews, and magazines.[42] Paradoxically, I suggest, such forms are good at pushing us to see the other cultural producers who create literary celebrity. A corollary insight of authorship attribution—that sometimes you can't tell who wrote a text because it reflects the style of more than one person—shows how the creation of a celebrity author is a collaborative endeavor.

As the nineteenth century went on, the debate over the importance of signing articles grew—especially reviews of literature and the question of whether "the personal responsibility implied by the reviewer's signature [guaranteed] an honest and competent review."[43] The convention of not signing reviews made it possible for the editor of the *Athenaeum* in 1855–1869 to review his own books. Yet anonymity was not always very anonymous; Laurel Brake quotes an essay from 1853 that characterizes anonymity as "a graceful disguise . . . opaque enough to shelter diffidence, transparent enough to verify conjecture."[44] This transparency also caused problems. When Robert Southey wrote a critical and anonymous review of *Lyrical Ballads* (1798) by Samuel Taylor Coleridge and William Wordsworth, Wordsworth knew exactly whom to blame: "[Southey] knew that I published those poems for money and money alone. . . . If he could not conscientiously have spoken differently of the volume, in common delicacy he ought to have declined the task of reviewing it."[45]

Critics working today to recover the full oeuvre of individual writers have to contend with nineteenth-century cultural norms and editorial practice. Sometimes working to isolate a central figure illuminates a collaborative context. Coleridge, for example, wanted very much to know who blasted his volume *Christabel; Kubla Khan, a Vision; The Pains of Sleep* (1816) in the *Edinburgh Review*. Though he had opinions about who wrote the review, no one in the past two hundred years has been able to identify that person with certainty. In 2015, Francesca Benatti and Justin Tonra attempted to ascertain the true identity of the author of the review in order to discover whether it was written by Thomas Moore. They note that much of the evidence adduced to prove authorship has been external, in contrast to their approach, which focuses on "internal linguistic evidence from the text and from other texts by the authors that scholarship has identified as the most likely candidates for authorship." They recognize up front that they cannot resolve the question of authorship but offer only a set of probabilities determined by a series of decisions. The most effective supervised method ultimately tested each article by the candidate authors one hundred times and picked the author of the *Christabel* review as Francis Jeffrey 63 percent of the time, Moore 28 percent, and Henry Brougham 8 percent—all three literary reviewers for the *Review* and the first two among its founders. This result is inconclusive—but suggestive.[46]

Stylometric analysis is suited to revealing the identity of a particular individual (it might be time, for instance, to challenge the attribution of a review by Brougham that the model assigned to Jeffrey), but the results might have been befuddled by nineteenth-century editorial practice. Scholarship on this review had previously suggested that William Hazlitt was the author, yet the algorithm never named him as a top contender. Benatti and Tonra looked more closely at the algorithm's performance on articles by Hazlitt from the test set and note that the algorithm's results for —or set of probabilities regarding— the authorship of the *Christabel* review are most like a review by William Hazlitt in which "editorial intervention by Jeffrey is likely to have been extensive." Perhaps Benatti and Tonra's stylistic analysis points to an inflection point where an editor's work turns into authorship: "Jeffrey is known to have applied numerous 'retrenchments and verbal alterations' to Hazlitt's articles in at least two other occasions, and to have extended this practice to all *Edinburgh* contributors. Depending on the extent of his participation, it could be argued that any or all of the reviews in the *Edinburgh* have actually two authors."[47] Susanna Ashton's book on collaboration in the United States defines it as "textual agency that can be distinguished from editorial or compositional contributions" but notes that this line can be difficult to draw.[48] Sociological perspectives on texts from book history and from quantitative analysis work to account for the full history of how a text takes shape and the reality that more than one hand is often at work. Earlier I suggested that literary critics often find it more productive to think of an author as a concept or notion (as in Foucault's "author-function") rather than as a person. Yet the focus on the *person* of the author also generates critical questions precisely because it asks us to think about how texts get created—generated, written, rewritten, and edited—by actual people.

Specialists in nineteenth-century periodical production start from a thorough awareness that many people leave a mark on a published text. This awareness is shared by the specialists in literary stylistics who have developed software for authorship attribution. Contributors to the Curran Index, a project establishing authorship of texts published anonymously in the nineteenth-century periodical press, address the complex question of collaborative authorship by studying archival materials such as publishers' accounts and private letters; developers of the software program Stylo addressed it by developing a method of teaching the model to recognize that different chunks of a single text bear the characteristic marks of different writers.

Perhaps an unrecorded mystery author wrote the review of *Christabel*. Or perhaps the review offers itself as evidence for the way collaboration or editing is a process written into much of what we read, including the best of what we read. When computational perspectives on genre refigure the novel as a relatively small portion of the literary landscape, they reveal how strange it is to identify "celebrity" with "novelist" when, after all, many literary celebrities weren't novelists. If the model of literary celebrity accommodates many kinds of "literature," it should also encompass how many kinds of literary work such figures did in addition to original composition.

Then, as now, readers were fascinated by the relationship between an author's life and the author's work and by those things that cannot be known from a study of the text alone. Indeed, the anthologies and lives I study here are a step beyond what Gerard Genette calls the *epitext*, or materials outside a text that nevertheless bear on the text; they are at the "fringe of the fringe," where the material quits bearing on the text at all and becomes only about the author.[49] Such liminal forms add surprising contexts in the textual production around famous writers and their works. The history of authorship as a proper name is written in the outer edges of the literary field.

2

THE COLLECTIBLE AUTHOR

Autographs, Homes and Haunts,

and Antislavery Gift Books

The antislavery gift book *Autographs for Freedom* (1854), edited by Julia Griffiths for Frederick Douglass's cause, prints signatures of its contributors as one would collect signatures for a petition. Published in the aftermath of Douglass's public split from William Lloyd Garrison, Griffiths's collection of signatures functions as a proxy for political support.[1] It also takes up the nineteenth-century trend of autograph collecting to draw on the power of celebrity literary figures. One striking element of the volume from this distance is that although its title highlights the images of author autographs, it also contains original contributions, which blend what might seem like literary and political work. For example, it contains the first publication of *The Heroic Slave*, Frederick Douglass's only published work of fiction. To set the stage for the intersection of transatlantic literary celebrity with antislavery, this chapter connects nonliterary antebellum print culture with the rise of literary celebrity and fan culture through an account of three other collections of facsimile signatures: the Declaration of Independence; Edgar Allan Poe's two series on autography (1836, 1841); and *Homes of American Authors* (1852), edited by George Palmer Putnam. Each transforms holograph signatures and fragments into published texts and refigures the process by which manuscript—literally handwriting—becomes print. Instead of sending the manuscript to the printer to become type, the publisher sends the manuscript to the engraver to become a reproducible image.

The nineteenth-century fascination with reprinting signatures was owed not only to developments in techniques of copying but also to developing cultural ideas about authorial labor, copyright, and celebrity authorship. These texts about American authorship emerged in a seriously asymmetrical international market. According to Robert A. Gross, the late 1830s saw "about four books entering the United States from abroad for every one exported."[2] In the introduction to their edited collection *Transatlantic Literature and Author Love in the Nineteenth Century* (2016), Ann Wierda Rowland and Paul Westover present a transnational literary culture that is "neither smooth nor unified, one never fully achieved or organically original."[3] Collections of American author signatures by Poe and Putnam developed a nationalist argument about American literature by transforming British models. Daniel Hack uses the word *transformation* to describe the broader set of active practices that Black writers in the United States used for "framing and reframing" British literature.[4] I borrow it here to emphasize the range of transpositions of print forms into a self-consciously American context.

These collections offer a decentralized perspective on authorship. They sold the author's mark in a form that emphasized the material circumstances of its collection and reproduction. The Declaration of Independence is perhaps the quintessential handwritten document of the founding fathers' document triptych (the Constitution, Bill of Rights, and Declaration of Independence), but the version we know best is a product of early nineteenth-century U.S. print culture. The "John Hancocks" of the founding fathers present on the day the engrossed (calligraphied) copy was signed now figure a record of representational democracy. Yet Thomas Starr points out that the Declaration of Independence was sent to the printer rather than to the calligrapher when the draft was finished and signed. The signatures that appear on that first copy are only those of John Hancock, the president of the Continental Congress; Charles Thomson, the secretary; and John Dunlap—the printer. The Declaration of Independence was printed, read aloud, and reprinted in newspapers all over the colonies within days of the initial signing. Starr traces the history of the document forward to show how the widely popularized "official copy," the one still hanging in classrooms today, wasn't produced until 1821, when the material was transferred by facsimile at the request of John Quincy Adams. Starr argues that "calligraphy serves to enhance the hand of the author. It is inherently individual and hierarchized. [Calligraphy] is the medium of the few," while type is inherently plural and public.[5] John Bidwell points out that most versions of the Declaration of Independence printed in the nineteenth century reproduced the facsimile autographs at the bottom, in one form or another, as an "essential" feature. This hand-produced, *written* version of the declaration is a central part of the national mythology that displaced an earlier value on print; the legal, cultural power of the signature is clear, even in facsimile.[6]

The Declaration of Independence uses autographs to evoke a real gathering—an event. In this respect, it connects with the way people in private life collected the autographs of personal acquaintances in commonplace books with entries that served as traces of breathing individuals. As I discuss at the end of the chapter, autograph collectors in the United States gathered the autographs of acquaintances as well as of famous historical or literary figures. Some people, of course, were acquainted with major figures: Sojourner Truth kept autograph albums of people she met that were replicated and appended to the 1875 edition of the *Narrative of Sojourner Truth*. The art historian Darcy Grimaldi Grigsby observes that these autographs, taken together, compose a "form of autobiography" written through a registry of the many public figures Truth had met. The signature replaces what could be a discursive account of a meeting with an artifact. Grigsby also points out the strangeness of Truth's decision to transform these artifacts into printed text: "Truth collected the autograph, ultimate emblem of the uniqueness of handwriting, only to imagine turning it into a mechanically reproduced publication. How odd, given autographs were valued as indexical signs of the individual, registrations of the hand's unique actions applying pen to paper."[7] The reprinted signatures from what Truth called her "Book of Life" reveal the way book collections of facsimile autographs circulated as both celebrity artifacts *and* a way of organizing the figures they "contained" around either the person who collected them or the rubric under which they were gathered.

The history of collecting the traces of important figures intersects with developments in printing and illustration. Mid-nineteenth-century periodical culture was characterized by the blend of word and image, facilitated in part by the end-grain woodblock engraving process. Engraved woodblocks could integrate the author's signature with printed text. The reprinted autograph is, technologically speaking, less like the current supplanting of the legal "wet signature" by electronic signatures in some instances than it is like the little image of a signature faithfully pasted into a letter of recommendation and uploaded online as a pdf, that versatile file format that deftly captures words and images at the same time. The handwritten text has been capable of being manually copied or reproduced as an engraving as long as has any other image, but the mechanically reproduced signature emerged as a real phenomenon by the mid–nineteenth century. As Tamara Plakins Thornton points out in her history of handwriting in America, "Within a few years [of the publication of Poe's "Autography" in 1836], Americans could purchase whole albums of autograph facsimiles, mass-marketed in cheap editions."[8] Quite a few biographies that included authors' portrait or images of their home also included facsimiles of their handwriting. In the history of fan culture, collections of facsimile manuscripts build on the developing connection between authorship and tourism.

Although my focus here is on the autographs of literary figures, people collected all kinds of autographs in private collections and in volume form. In his essay "Autographs" (1881), Isaac Disraeli cites a few precedents that tended to focus on historical figures.[9] Putnam's publishing list of facsimile manuscripts includes not only *Homes of American Authors* but also John Jay Smith's *American Historical and Literary Curiosities: Consisting of Fac-Similes of Original Documents Relating to the Events of the Revolution*, which had seen five editions by 1852. Another volume focusing on literary figures appeared in 1840, *Historical and Literary Curiosities, Consisting of Facsimiles of Original Documents*, engraved by Charles John Smith.[10]

Gerard Curtis suggests that manuscript reproduction became important in the nineteenth century because "combinations of image and hand-scripted text gave the viewer a sense of being present at the moment of creative mark-making. 'Evidence' of writing, of narrative unfolding beneath the hand, also served to surmount the stasis of the image through an implied temporal action; the hand active in writing." This attempt to evoke "concrete authorial and authentic presence," he argues, was a reaction to a market-oriented mass literary culture and informed by debates over authorial labor and copyright. Curtis cites the example of Charles Dickens's signature being copied into certain U.S. editions to prove their authenticity, revealing how publishers blended graphic text and artistic print to "promote and protect the image of the author."[11] In the texts I look at here, signatures circulated apart from the author's work: they promoted the image of the author, but they did not protect it.

Autographs of celebrity writers are importantly different from those of other notable figures because writing is the author's medium. In the context of literary celebrity, Thornton argues that autograph collecting became popular because the Romantic idea of genius became associated with handwriting as a form of psychological and physiological self-expression.[12] Handwriting signals the vanished act of creation more clearly in the case of authorship because it recalls the original manuscript that became print. An artist might sign a painting years after the initial composition. Such a signature can claim the painting or mark its authenticity, but a better figure for the initial act of creating a painting is a mark associated with this art—for example, a Jackson Pollock painting that shows where he put his hand in the wet paint, leaving a physical imprint of painting.[13] As the portrait of an author at work, the author's autograph approximates those handprints.

Insofar as the author's "hand" comes to stand in for the author, copied handwriting both facilitates the development of that authorial self and compromises its uniqueness. Walter Benjamin argues that something happened to the aura of a work of art in the age of technological reproducibility: aura is not reproducible, but images are; reprinted autographs seem like an obvious bid to capture aura. Lara Langer Cohen argues that aura emerges *against* the idea of the copy. Pace Benjamin, "authenticity may not be a casualty of modernity—'that which withers in the age of mechanical reproduction'—so much as an invention of it. In other words, originality is a second-order phenomenon, which requires the idea of the copy to exist."[14] If the idea of authorship develops in part in the face of a culture of reprinting, as Meredith McGill suggests, cheaper technologies of reproduction also facilitate the fetishized manuscript.[15]

While the "aura" of writerly authenticity established by the image of handwriting seems to show the "author at work," its reproduction also reveals the work of editors and publishers. The two figures I focus on here as compilers of author autographs also loom large in discussions of copyright in the United States: Edgar Allen Poe, who appears as editor of the *Southern Literary Messenger* and *Graham's*, and George Palmer Putnam, publisher and advocate for international copyright as well as an editor and a writer. The texts they created present the author as part of a larger system in which the key "players" are publishers, editors, and the periodicals and books they publish. Edgar Allan Poe's two series on autography in *Southern Literary Messenger* (1836) and *Graham's Magazine* (1841) are a metacritical satire on autograph collections and literary figures and an extension of a series in *Fraser's*, the kind of high-end British periodical subject to cheap reprinting in the States. G. P. Putnam's edited volume *Homes of American Authors* (1853) is a literary nationalist homes-and-haunts book featuring handwritten fragments by the major authors of the Putnam catalog. Both texts look at authors working in a variety of genres, and both use signatures to foreground the business of literary production. Both reveal how the figure of the author is also constituted through the many genres that flourished on the antebellum literary scene.

EDGAR ALLAN POE: AUTOGRAPHY IN THE LITERARY-CRITICAL ESSAY

In his 1841 "Chapter on Autography," Poe argues: "Next to the person of a distinguished man-of-letters, we desire to see his portrait—next to his portrait, his autograph. In the latter, especially, there is something that seems to bring him before us in his true idiosyncrasy—in his character of scribe. The feeling which prompts to the collection of autographs is a natural and rational one."[16] Poe uses copies of the signature, proxy for the author as originary figure, to place authors in a broad literary context. McGill argues that the autography essays sold well in part because the woodcuts were too expensive for other papers to reproduce. Editors who wanted to reprint the earlier series, for example, had to apply to the *Messenger* to rent its woodcuts. McGill concludes that "the disruption Poe introduces into the system of reprinting actually *produces* this mass-produced magazine as an original" as the signature gets published in "a context that raises the question of its availability, alternately asserting and denying its susceptibility to reproduction."[17]

The autography series offer the reader a collection of facsimile copies of author signatures that, as Poe notes, "bring [the author] before us in his true idiosyncrasy—in his character of scribe" at the same time that they serve up individuals to the scorching analysis of Poe's editorial perspective, or what in part 3 of "Chapter on Autography" he calls his "hasty critical, or rather gossiping observations" about each writer.[18] For example, Poe observes that W. L. Stone, the editor of the *New York Commercial Advertiser*, has a manuscript "heavy and sprawling, resembling his mental character in a species of utter unmeaningness, which lies like the nightmare, upon his autograph"; H. T. Tuckerman's recent publications in the *Southern Literary*

Messenger may have been bad, but the writing is neat enough that "perhaps, the legibility of his MS. has been an important, if not the principal recommendation."[19] In tone, this "collection" of articles on autography has more in common with Alexander Pope's denunciation of his rivals in the *Dunciad* than it does with a collection of facsimiles of "reliques and antiquities" such as *Historical and Literary Curiosities, Consisting of Facsimiles of Original Documents*, in which the chief editorial material is a description of the plates of the documents—without the criticism.

Poe's satirical essays were adapted from an English model, "The Miller Correspondence" series published in *Fraser's Magazine* in November 1833. The British series purports to be a collection of signature-fishing letters to major literary figures, though the editors joke that the best way to obtain signatures from literary men is to discount their bills because "you might in that case be perfectly certain of retaining their autographs, accompanied by notes." The *Fraser's* series trades on the idea that autographs require direct correspondence with the unique person of letters. At the same time, that encounter—which, by "bland and agreeable artifice," is already a prank—affords the editors the opportunity to satirize authors in their responses. In one example, "Miller" inquires about a man called Campbell, offering a peep into Sir Walter Scott's domestic life with a little extra "Scottishness" and featuring a malicious in-joke about Alexander Campbell, who "collected and arranged" *Albyn's Anthology*.[20]

The *Fraser's* series plays with a version of printed authenticity older than facsimile: the publication of a private letter.[21] The signatures vouch for the authenticity of dubious letters. By contrast, Poe's constellation of signatures sparks a short critique of each writer.

XXVIII.—WALTER SCOTT.

There is only one autograph among all this batch that betrays the slightest shadow of any thing like annoyance, and that, *mirabile dictu!* is the note addressed to our friend Miller by the best-natured great man of our age, or perhaps of any age—Sir Walter Scott. But the date explains all. Alas, alas! the good Sir Walter had had at least one visitation of the mortal malady before he was honoured with the correspondence of Mr. Miller.

We are rather surprised, by the by, that Sir Walter should have said no person of the name of Campbell was ever servant to him. What, we should like to be told, was old Elshie Campbell, *alias* " Alexander Campbell, *Esquire*," the editor of *Albyn's Anthology?* Did he never actually clean Sir Walter's boots? We are sure he fulfilled many baser duties in that quarter.

SIR,
   I regret that my name has been used to mislead your benevolence; I know no such person as Duncan Campbell, nor was a man of the name of Campbell ever servant to me.

The fellow who imposed upon you deserves punishment, and, for the sake of others, I hope you will see it inflicted.

I am, Sir,
Your humble servant,

Abbotsford, Melrose, 21 *January,* 1831.   WALTER SCOTT.
I received yours of the 18th this day.

FIGURE 2.1 Excerpt from "The Miller Correspondence," *Fraser's Magazine for Town and Country* 48, no. 8 (November 1833): 635.

Source: Photo courtesy of the University of Minnesota Libraries.

Poe makes a key change to the structure of the British series: he replaces the typescript signature with a facsimile signature. "Autography" (1836) says it includes "every individual in America who has the slightest pretension to literary celebrity" in order to characterize and criticize the author's work according to their handwriting. It explicitly picks up in America where *Fraser's* left off, with one furious Joseph *. Miller (whose middle initial progresses alphabetically from A to Z in the course of the sketch) storming the editorial "sanctum" with an article from London in which he is supposed, in the service of a well-known passion for autographs, "to have indited sundry epistles, to several and sundry characters of literary notoriety about London, with the sinister design, hope, and intention, of thereby eliciting autograph replies" by inquiring after the characters of "certain cooks, scullions, chambermaids, and boot-blacks." He confesses that the letters he sent were "the result of some—of some ingenuity on the part of your humble servant," but he asserts that he has "propounded no inquiries about scullions."[22] Poe builds on *Fraser's* gag by pairing a signature copy, that marker of authenticity, with transparently inauthentic text.

Just as the *Messenger* is a miscellany of literature and criticism, "Autography" is a miscellany of the writing of *Messenger* contributors and other contemporary literary figures.[23] As Poe would point out in his second series on autography in *Graham's*, "Complete, or even extensive collections, are beyond the reach of those who themselves do not dabble in the waters of literature. The writer of this article has had opportunities, in this way, enjoyed by few."[24] Poe is not, like the "Miller" he satirizes, primarily an enthusiast. He is a member of the "literati."

As an example of an entry from the first series demonstrates, this form allows Poe to satirize major figures while emphasizing his acquaintance with them. The entry on J. Fenimore Cooper takes the form of a mock letter about the "numerous engagements" that prevent Cooper from submitting to a boring-sounding magazine, the *Humdrum*. The description of the paper the letter is written on suggests that the editor has access to a real letter—in fact, to an unidentified number of "other letters" by Cooper.

The editor here is not a fan, but an expert. The second series, published after the publication of *The Narrative of Arthur Gordan Pym of Nantucket* (1838), when Poe was editing *Graham's*, builds on this critical relation to the authors in review and registers Poe's more prominent literary profile. This three-part "Chapter on Autography" series appears headed by a byline of Poe's own

> LETTER V.
>
> St. Mark's Place, New York, ———.
>
> Dear Sir,—Your obliging letter of the ——— was received in due course of mail, and I am gratified by your good opinion. At the same time my numerous engagements will render it out of my power to send you any communication for your valuable Magazine, 'The Humdrum,' for some months to come at least. Wishing you all success, and with many thanks for your attention.
>
> I remain, sir, your humble servant,
>
> JOSEPH E. MILLER, ESQ.   *J. Fenimore Cooper*
>
> Mr. Cooper's MS. is bad—very bad. There is no distinctive character about it, and it appears to be un-formed. The writing will probably be different in other letters. Upon reference we find this to be the fact. In the letter to Mr. Miller, the MS. is of a *petite* and finicky appearance, and looks as if scratched with a steel pen—the lines are crooked. The paper is fine, and of a bluish tint. A wafer is used.

FIGURE 2.2 Excerpt from Edgar Allen Poe, "Autography," part 1, *Southern Literary Messenger*, February 1836, 207.

Source: Photo courtesy of the Book Collection, Harry Ransom Center, University of Texas at Austin.

giant autograph: "EDGAR A. POE." This time there are no hoax characters and no fake letters, just author signatures and Poe's commentary. In writing as editor able to connect the autographs with the scope of each author's literary production—in analysis that might include comparisons of poetry to essays or an overview of the periodicals they contribute to—Poe positions himself as editor and critic at the center of U.S. literary culture.

This second series also replaces the conceit of Mr. Miller's painstaking autograph collection with the image of a pile of correspondence accreted on Poe's desk. Poe suggests a certain carelessness about this heap: "We have thought it unnecessary to preserve any particular order in their arrangement." He often compares the single signature to the typical manuscript. J. K. Paulding's "signature is a good specimen of his general hand," whereas C. S. Henry's signature, "bold and decided, conveys not the faintest idea of the general MS," which varies so much that it is "impossible to say anything respecting it, except that it indicates a vacillating disposition, with unsettled ideas of the beautiful."[25] Poe emphasizes his familiarity with the author by providing a snapshot of their careers that shows how handwriting is susceptible to change over time. Kevin J. Hayes argues that for Poe "both the autograph and the personal image functioned as external indicators of personality.... When converted into images accompanying biography—a woodcut of an autograph or an engraved portrait—these external signs ostensibly validated the biography they accompanied."[26] Handwriting has the potential to reveal not only the innate character of authors but also how their experiences have shaped them. If a man's ideal hand is the "fair characters of his boyhood," his handwriting over time can only reveal degeneration, not only what Thornton calls (in her book on handwriting pedagogy) "the alienating and stultifying circumstances of contemporary life" but also a kind of *overliteracy*.[27] Poe assesses Washington Irving's hoax letter in the November 1841 "chapter" on autography as "not nearly so well-written" as older letters: "Mr. Irving has travelled much, has seen many vicissitudes, and has been so thoroughly satiated with fame as to grow slovenly in the performance of his literary tasks."[28]

Poe uses his meditations on authors' signatures in "Autography" to reflect on the relationship between natural genius and its harnessing for the market—most often by tracing the deterioration of the manuscript through work. He claims one purpose of his series is "to illustrate our position that the mental features are indicated (with certain exceptions) by the handwriting."[29] The exceptions are situations in which authors' natural genius (as represented by their hand) has been corrupted by the "haste" demanded by the "vicissitudes" of life. In *Handwriting in America*, Thornton argues that Poe's analyses privilege individuality and idiosyncrasy over the "produced" aspects of handwriting: "According to Poe, scripts that did not deviate from writing masters' models indicated nothing more than a complete lack of character," whether those models were informed by clerkship or a female boarding school. Poe draws attention to the uniformity among the letters by including a description of the paper and seal employed by the writer at the end of each letter as an indication of wealth and personal choice. Thornton argues that Poe's criticism evinces a Romantic ideal: "Poe thus attached the greatest significance to the handwriting of people sequestered from the modern world, the farther the better."[30] My focus here, by contrast, is on Poe's emphasis on his own role as editor at the heart of a literary network. Editorship has an uneasy relation to authorship in this formulation.

Editorship is a profession that, like others, wears down individuality. The handwriting of R. M. Morris "has no marked characteristics, and like that of almost every editor in the country, has been so modified by the circumstances of his position, as to afford no certain indication of the mental features." The manuscript of Jos. R. Chandler "must be included in the editorial category—it seems to have been ruined by habitual hurry." "Accustomed to the daily toil of an editor," John S. Du Solle "has contracted a habit of writing hurriedly." Poe dismisses editorial writing entirely at one point—the entry on R. W. (Rufus) Griswold notes that "he has written much, but chiefly in the editorial way, whether for the papers, or in books"—but here Poe also foregrounds the centrality of periodical editorship. Mr. Godey, for example, is "only known to the literary world as editor and publisher of the *Lady's Book*, but his celebrity in this regard entitles him to a place in this collection," and the series concludes with Ann S. Stephens, whose "excellent" manuscript is that of an editor who has "written much and well, for various other periodicals, and will, hereafter, enrich this magazine with her compositions, and act as one of its editors."[31]

Poe not only signs the second "Autography" series but also makes it an opportunity to correct the record on earlier, unsigned essays. He disavows an article attributed to him—an article on Dickens that "abounded in well-written but extravagant denunciation of everything composed by the author of 'The Curiosity Shop,' and which prophesied his immediate downfall"—and instead claims authorship of a review in the *Messenger* that predicted, "and in the most emphatic manner, that high and just distinction which the author in question [Dickens] has attained."[32] Signature in this sense reflects a growing trend toward named periodical submission; it stakes a claim for the role of the editor as critic. Rather than the "our" of the editorial desk at the *Messenger*, analogous to the "our" of *Fraser's*, Poe signs the criticism of 1841 in *Graham's* under his proper name, as a critic and a literary celebrity in his own right whose autograph and literary production should be of interest to readers.

WORKING FROM HOME: FACSIMILE MANUSCRIPT IN *HOMES OF AMERICAN AUTHORS*

If Poe ultimately writes as a celebrity among celebrities, Putnam's lavishly illustrated gift book anthology *Homes of American Authors* of 1853 foregrounds the highlighted authors at the expense of the people who wrote the volume. *Homes of American Authors* is an answer to Putnam's friend William Howitt's *Homes and Haunts of the Most Eminent British Poets* (1847).[33] Nicola Watson has theorized how the writer's house—including "rituals of contact" such as the signature—can facilitate the reader's "encountering the author as the embodied origin of his or her works."[34] In a book on how the writer's house can work as a narrative construct, Alison Booth credits *Homes of American Authors* with helping to "establish a lucrative line of biographical piecework."[35] Although the model was to prove fruitful, this particular volume was so expensive to produce that there never was a second one.[36] Scott Casper argues that "collective biographies—dictionaries, series of magazine articles, volumes of short biographical sketches—were the new nation's hallmark biographical form. . . . Although these works resembled similar English publications, American republicanism gave particular resonance to the collective form."[37] I argue here for the special significance of handwriting to literary fan culture, but a literary sociology perspective also reveals that gift books took up a wide range of cultural figures. When I described *Homes and Haunts* to Johan Svedjedal of the Section for the Sociology of Literature at the University of Uppsala, he asked, "What kinds of other books were like this?" The answer: in Putnam's list alone, several. And there is a strong formal similarity across political and literary volumes. According to Michael Winship, the "first photographic illustration in an American book was the frontispiece in *Homes of American Statesmen* [a comparable volume about politicians] published by G. P. Putnam and Company in late 1853."[38] *Homes of American Authors* reflects the business of publishing in its entrepreneurial gift-book-making spirit as well as in its treatment of authorship within its pages. A perspective from the sociology of literature, which focuses on how books move in the world, makes it possible to recognize the fundamental likenesses between illustrated gift books published with very different aims.

As a gift book, *Homes of American Authors* depicts each author's person, home, and manuscript. Putnam was a passionate collector who would wind up with "one of the larger autograph collections of his generation," and most of the author facsimiles in the book are representative manuscripts.[39] This publication adds "homes" and handwriting, not simply autographs, to Poe's list of things the lover of literature most longs to see. Putnam was both the publisher of this volume and its editor. As the introduction makes clear, the homes-and-haunts sketches of notable authors that frame the figure of the author as a person in relation to the reader also reflect the professionalization of authorship. *Homes of American Authors* combines essays about authors with images of their homes and handwriting to create portraits of the author at work. Washington Irving's manuscript sample is from the *Knickerbocker*; Daniel Webster's is from *Oration at the Capitol*. Not all the facsimiles include autographs, and even some of the signatures are not functioning as "autographs" but merely as written names: Longfellow wrote his name on the same page as part of the direction for sending his proofs of the manuscript poem, and Cooper's signature appears on a publication contract.

The introduction to the volume emphasizes the economic structure of publishing. Putnam spent his life working for an international copyright law and put money into copyrighted U.S. works. The gift book he created placed authors in the intimate domestic spaces so important to "author love," but it also explicitly took the size of their houses as a proxy for the viability of authorship as a profession. "Although there are no Abbotsfords, which have been rendered from the earnings of the pen, among our authors' homes, yet we feel a degree of pride in showing our countrymen how comfortably housed many of their favorite authors are, in spite of the imputed neglect with which native talent has been treated. Authorship in America, notwithstanding the want of an international copy-right which has been so sorely felt by literary laborers, has at last become a profession which men may live by."[40]

Putnam frames the collection of sketches with the suggestion that U.S. literature *would* be the kind of business that could produce an Abbotsford (Walter Scott's home) if its legislators would support a national literature by passing an international copyright law. As the site of writing that was paid for by the number of volumes an author sold, the author's home could represent a physical link between their labor and the money they made. *Homes of American Authors* thus documents the success of the authors it features while promoting them—creating celebrity and selling it at the same time. Many chapters contain engravings of "homes and abodes" authors had lived in at different points over the course of their careers; for example, the chapters on Webster and Cooper open with color illustrations of lonely cabins and subsequently feature a second illustration of a comfortable country house. This suggestion of progress supports Putnam's narrative of authorship as a developing profession.

In its references to Abbotsford—and to Scott, that nineteenth-century megastar—the volume also highlights the literary relationship between the United States and Great Britain and the way U.S. literary culture saw its British counterpart as a model for its own development. The relationship is evident in the form of *Homes of American Authors* and in the way it imagines the professional author. Paul Westover points out how, from the introduction to the volume on, Abbottsford serves as a "stick against which to measure American progress."[41] Booth argues that in Putnam's volume Washington Irving's home Sunnyside also "seems to personify an 'essentially American' landscape and at the same time 'a bond in letters between our own country and England.'"[42]

We can also see *Homes of American Authors* as U.S. literary history written from the perspective of Putnam's publishing list; the volume is composed largely of authors whose works already were or would be coming out of Putnam's publishing house as Putnam sought to establish himself as the "preeminent publisher of works written by the leading literary authors of the previous generation."[43] The title page attributes the book to "various writers," who are named in a list of "contributors," as if the biographical sketches of individual writers were written collaboratively. Putnam's biographer Ezra Greenspan suggests that this volume marked the beginning of Putnam's own foray into magazinery. Three writers of *Homes of American Authors* became key staff of *Putnam's Magazine*, marking the "previous generation" as past and them as the future.

In her "counterhistory of literary nationalism," Lara Langer Cohen recounts the significance of a publisher running an in-house magazine as part of the puffing system; like the Harper brothers and their magazine, Putnam ran the magazine that touted his books; occupying these "dual roles" enabled "publishers to direct readers' tastes to their own catalogs."[44] McGill frames the project in terms of the history of copyright:

> George Palmer Putnam's early advocacy of international copyright provides one measure of the shift from a market dominated by reprinting to one in which publishers increasingly regarded copyrighted domestic texts as good investments. Putnam founded *Putnam's Monthly* in 1853 as an answer to Harper & Brothers' extraordinarily successful *Harper's New Monthly Magazine* (1850–), which was made up largely of reprinted material. Putnam sought to publish only American writing that was original to his magazine, a more risky [*sic*] venture than the *Harper's*, though he stood to profit by developing a

stable of domestic authors and retaining control over their texts.[45]

The treatment of Cooper in Putnam's volume is quite straightforwardly an account of the development of American authorship in relation to the British model of Scott. The chapter on Cooper describes the composition of *The Spy* twenty years earlier, and the manuscript fragment included in the volume dates not from the novel's composition but to its reissue years later.

Homes of American Authors manifests the celebrity it also promotes, transforming writers of books and periodicals into "authors." In the collection and engraving of artifacts of authors' persons, the volume's solid expensiveness complements the more ephemeral work of periodical writing. Handwritten texts function as images of their authors in this book: the facsimile of the writer's holograph is classified as an "illustration" and concludes each chapter. *Homes of American Authors* links authors' texts with their person and their place of production by connecting the authors' handwriting with sketches of their homes. The chapter on George Bancroft begins by noting that "our present duty is not with the work, but with the circumstances which the work has made interesting," a statement that demarcates a line between criticism and biography.[46] The "circumstances" made interesting by the work include descriptions of the writing process and the trace of circumstances. Only one of the handwriting facsimiles in *Homes of American Authors* is more than one page long: William Prescott's is three. It looks as if it was written in pencil. The sketch is concerned mainly with Prescott's three houses, family history, and idyllic domestic life, but it devotes the full last page to a letter from him describing the process of composing his manuscript *Conquest of Peru*, which, due to "a disorder of the nerve of the eye" was written with a special apparatus.

Prescott's description of the writing process he used recalls the peritextual apparata of the eighteenth century—those introductory histories of the text that added value to a story by an account of its provenance. The editor appends Prescott's account of his writing process to the biographical sketch, establishing a narrative of the manuscript in which the original was already a carbon copy of the author's trace:

> The writing is not, as you may imagine, made by a pencil, but is indelible, being made with an apparatus used by the blind. This is a very simple affair, consisting of a frame of the size of a common sheet of letter-paper, with brass wires inserted in it to correspond with the number of lines wanted. On one side of this frame is pasted a leaf of thin carbonated paper, such as is used to obtain duplicates. Instead of a pen, the writer makes use of a stylus, of ivory or agate, the last better or harder. The great difficulties in the way of a blind man's writing in the usual manner, arise from his not knowing when the ink is exhausted in his pen, and when his lines run into one another. Both difficulties are obviated by this simple writing-case, which enables one to do his work as well in the dark as in the light.[47]

But while Prescott describes the text that the apparatus produces as "indelible," the facsimile reproduction gives the illusion of an erasable instrument associated with the graphic arts.

Prescott elaborates in print what cannot be reproduced in a copy of his manuscript: his method of composition in his mind and with his instruments. Instead of a pencil, Prescott writes with an indelible instrument: the harder, the better. Darkness is

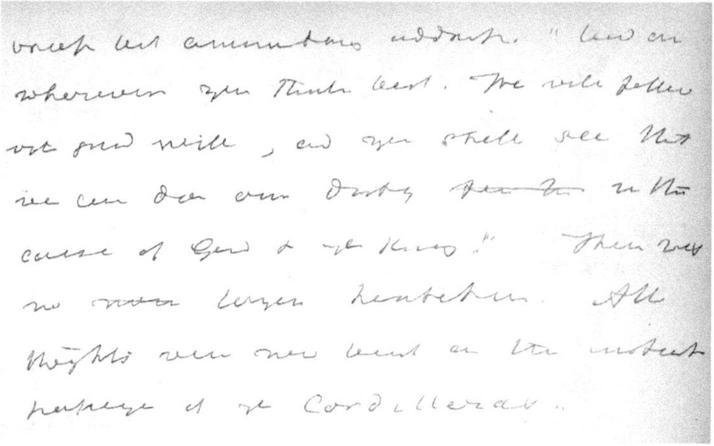

FIGURE 2.3 Sample of William Prescott's handwriting, accompanied by a description of his writing apparatus, in "William H. Prescott," in *Homes of American Authors*, ed. George Palmer Putnam (Putnam, 1853), between pp. 156 and 157.

Source: Photo courtesy of the author.

no impediment to the historian's inspiration, and the process of composition becomes internal. Because the actual writing takes place on carbon paper, the facsimile represents a copy of the initial writing—the line of the stylus, which leaves no trace. Prescott offers readers an account of writing that is all imprint—an impression that establishes a limit to what is capable of being visually reproduced, as if the manuscript requires an account of its origins. Booth argues that the writing desk and pen are at the heart of the writer's home; Putnam's volume offers the material trace of composition, but one in which the original act of writing already leaves the trace of a copy.[48] The special insight into an idiosyncratic writing process emphasizes the mediation between the author's inscription and the printed product.[49]

AUTOGRAPHS AS SIGNATURES: *AUTOGRAPHS FOR FREEDOM*

Poe used signatures to sell magazines and promote himself; Putnam paired manuscript fragments with pen-and-pencil sketches to call into being a canon of professional U.S. authors. Both emphasized the author at work in correspondence with their editor or in the proofs and contracts that made up the written trace of print publication. Here I consider another use of the autograph, a political one, when a key function of the signature is to represent personal endorsement.

Autographs for Freedom (1854) exemplifies Leon Jackson's more variegated economic picture of the antebellum "business of letters," which makes room for economies such as manuscript "gifting," a practice that, he argues, supported the *Southern Literary Messenger* for years.[50] This economy is central to abolitionist gift books, as I discuss here and in the next chapter. *Autographs for Freedom* dramatizes celebrity authorship and personal political commitments. Meaghan M. Fritz and Frank E. Fee Jr. characterize this book as a "hybrid of the highly popular autograph album and the standard gift book form" and highlight the "cultural, national, and political diversity" of contributions to it.[51] Authors contributed not only brief letters or essays to the volume but also their signed support of Frederick Douglass's cause. John R. McKivigan and Rebecca A. Pattillo argue that *Autographs* was a "cultural and political tool designed by Douglass and [Julia] Griffiths to help assemble a more powerful antislavery coalition."[52] Its connection with the autograph album is thus of particular relevance because such albums both cultivated and demonstrated a network of acquaintance.

The friendship album is an important cultural context because of the way it frames the relation among contributors—as "friends"—and because it allows the invisibilized editor/compiler to take on a more obviously central role. Fritz and Fee note, for example, that Griffiths asserts her role as editor by including correspondence implicitly addressed to her but not contributing to the volume.[53] Michael Cohen observes that another antislavery anthology, *The North Star: The Poetry of Freedom by Her Friends* (1840), "materialized political commitments with tokens of fellow activists' 'individuality as intellectual and moral beings.' *The North Star* was therefore a book of friendship: poems written by the friends of freedom and the slave [*sic*], for other friends, and put in a format, the giftbook, meant for exchange among friends."[54] Another friendship album compiled from the 1830s through the 1850s by Amy Cassey, a middle-class African American Philadelphia woman, "reveals the owner as a leader among women in free black communities" and "reflects Cassey's powerful network as it met the hands of many prominent contributors," according to Jasmine Nichole Cobb. Cobb argues that its "inclusion of White abolitionists likely facilitated Black women's work in the antislavery movement, and enabled free women to comment on gender norms in antislavery periodicals."[55] Cassey's leadership position in activist circles made new patterns of affiliation possible. By collecting contributions, the editor/owner of the album also facilitated the exchange of ideas.

Autographs for Freedom was something like an autograph album but was also a gift book that gave the bulk of its pages to its most prominent contributors. If a person with only a glancing familiarity with the antislavery movement in the 1850s got two guesses about the chief celebrity contributors to this volume and whose contributions take up the most space, that person might congratulate themselves for correctly guessing Frederick Douglass and Harriet Beecher Stowe. Douglass's *The Heroic Slave* spans almost a third of the volume. Stowe, too, is largely represented: one contribution is a letter addressed to her, and she contributes a poem and a story. In his history of the gift book and literary annual, Ralph Thompson groups *Autographs for Freedom* with other antislavery and temperance gift books—as well as gift books that represented fraternal orders or a celebration of the new president, Andrew Jackson—as volumes "intended to serve a specific purpose." Thompson's sharpest characterization of British gift books is that they "toadied to would-be aristocrats with a roster of titled contributors or caught the public eye with the names of great literary lights—who, as it turned out, had rarely anything to say."[56]

The substantial contributions by Stowe and Douglass in *Autographs for Freedom* are complemented by brief letters by others less directly connected with the cause. The volume was published by John P. Jewett, the publisher of *Uncle Tom's Cabin* and *Life of Josiah Henson, Formerly a Slave* (1858), and Stowe herself suggested possible contributors and advocated for changing the volume's title from *Autographs for Antislavery* to *Autographs for Freedom*.[57] Fritz and Fee point out that Griffiths "worked to accumulate as many celebrity contributions as possible in order both to increase consumer interest in the collection and to set *Autographs for Freedom* apart from the more traditional gift book format as seen in the [*Liberty*] *Bell*."[58] The flexibility of the facsimile autograph—a cause for satirical criticism in "Autography" but evidence of the creation of American authorship in *Homes of American Authors*—becomes in *Autographs for Freedom* the mark of an author's voluntary public support of antislavery.

In his contribution, the congressman and abolitionist Horace Mann emphasizes the limits of signing his name—"Names are but breath," he notes—in a poem that resembles the brief contribution typical in a friendship album. At the same time, the central conceit of his piece—that a name is not a deed—is

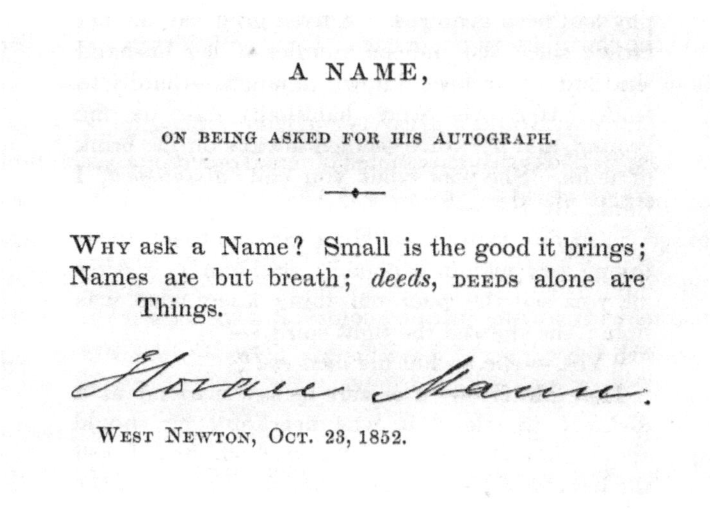

A NAME,

ON BEING ASKED FOR HIS AUTOGRAPH.

Why ask a Name? Small is the good it brings;
Names are but breath; *deeds*, DEEDS alone are
Things.

Horace Mann.

WEST NEWTON, OCT. 23, 1852.

FIGURE 2.4 Horace Mann, "A Name," in *Autographs for Freedom*, ed. Julia Griffiths (John P. Jewett, 1853), 18.
Source: Photo courtesy of Special Collections, Louisiana State University.

undercut by the fact that the contribution of his autograph to this volume is a political act. Here, Mann supplies his signature for copy—as a "deed"—even as he disavows it. An act of signature, like the Declaration of Independence; an act of "friendship," like an autograph album; and a trace of himself, a mark of active support. A politician, he contributes a couplet that encourages deeds—the next step.[59]

If the popularity of collecting author signatures rises with the idea of the author as an individual genius, these facsimile collections group those geniuses together in new ways. They range widely in register—from Poe's satire on contemporary writers to Putnam's hagiography of American authors to the petition-like structure of the contributors to *Autographs for Freedom*—and thus create networks among celebrity authors.[60] These books show transatlantic forms and names circulating—and how fluid literary forms and political work were. They show the centrality of editors and publishers in producing literary celebrity. And they show the different kinds of work that celebrity writers did. In their overview of early nineteenth-century American authorship, Lara Langer Cohen and Meredith McGill emphasize that novels were only a small slice of literary culture: "Of the sixty-eight authors Rufus Wilmot Griswold profiled in his 1847 *The Prose Writers of America*, only fifteen had ever written a novel (and several of those, including Henry Wadsworth Longfellow, Edgar Allan Poe, and Charles Fenno Hoffman, were more famous as poets, writers of tales, or editors)."[61] The antislavery gift book was a networked form that included many nonfictional contributions. In the next chapter, I focus on one key genre: the antislavery travelogue.

3

WHITE LADY AUTHORESSES CROSS THE ATLANTIC

Antislavery Gift Books and Travelogues

Books and periodicals that call attention to a set of authors as celebrated individuals also illuminate those figures as part of a set. Gift books traded on collections of many kinds of celebrity contributors. Lorraine Janzen Kooistra observes that "as a form of mass art, the gift book was conceived not as a creative expression by individual artists but rather as a commercial literary venture by entrepreneurs," one that "marshaled the talents of numerous workers—artists, poets, editors, engravers, printers, and binders, to create books that would sell."[1] In this form, the author-contributor appears to the gift book audience as only one of a number of cultural producers. As a material exemplar of miscellaneous forms of prose and poetry that characterized the broader literary landscape, the antislavery gift book shows off its authors working in different forms and different discourses. The gift book I focus on here is *The Liberty Bell*, an annual produced for the Christmas bazaar organized by the Boston Female Anti-Slavery Society "in conjunction" with William Lloyd Garrison's American Anti-Slavery Society almost every year from 1839 to 1858.[2] I argue that the very miscellaneousness of the antislavery-gift-book context makes it a good place to see an individual author emerge in multiple figurations.

I take up work by two white authoress-contributors to *The Liberty Bell*: Harriet Martineau and Fredrika Bremer. Martineau figures here as a poetess, an antislavery advocate, and a British protoimperialist whose contribution to the 1848 edition was not about travel to the United States but to North Africa; the Swedish novelist Fredrika Bremer's contribution in 1845 emphasizes her unfitness to intervene in antislavery debates, but she followed up that contribution with a three-volume travelogue in 1853 about her voyage to the United States and Cuba that participated in antislavery discourse in the form of a celebrity travel narrative (a collection of letters to her sister) that circulated in English in the context of U.S. imperialism.

The author in this context emerges in a kind of chaos of competing images—as public figure, as private figure, as lady, as advocate, as artist, as imperialist, as foreigner—that flash in and out of focus. At the same time, there is something straightforward about the way that Martineau's and Bremer's race, class, and gender combine to create a version of the authoress as not only a white woman but also a white lady—a part of the author's image that appears consistently across discussions of antislavery, imperialism, and women's literary work. Any work Martineau and Bremer published under their own names—fiction or nonfiction, didactic tales or collections of letters—would have been written by a white lady authoress. My thinking about this position is indebted to Tricia Lootens's work on the political poetess, which calls attention to the political elements within the very idea of the "privatized Poetess . . . quietly performing on behalf of separate spheres (and with them of racialized national sentimentality), even as controversies over feminism, literary theory, historiography, and philosophy have exploded around her." Lootens argues that "Victorian femininity, even in its most idealized, privatized form," used that position to engage with narratives about abolition and empire.[3] Like the poetesses in Lootens's book, whose political engagements have mostly been elided by critics, Martineau and Bremer foregrounded for contemporaries their own feminized, racialized perspectives on antislavery.

Scholarship attending to the figure of the author in antislavery gift books and travel narratives has called attention to nineteenth-century women's frankly public, frankly political writing across genres. Anne K. Mellor's *Mothers of the Nation* (2002) opens with "the historical fact of women's full participation in the very public sphere theorized by Habermas himself."[4] Special issues of *Nineteenth-Century Gender Studies* on campaign writing and of *European Romantic Review* on women and protest suggest a renewed interest in the ubiquity of topical writing by nineteenth-century women.[5] One contribution of this chapter is to consider topical writing as travel writing without losing sight of travel writing as a celebrity genre. The political deployment of literary celebrity is particularly clear in writing by British and European writers about their travels to the antebellum United States because these narratives were always explicitly or implicitly an engagement with American slavery.

Travel writing, "the narrative of an actual journey told by the person or persons who undertook it," was incontestably literature in the nineteenth century, although it is less clearly so now.[6] In taking up travel writing as a genre of literary celebrity, I respond to Nicola Watson's call to challenge a disciplinary tendency to prioritize "literary" texts at the expense of "competing contexts, intertexts, paratexts, and, especially, to the biographical evocation of the Author."[7] From a publishing perspective, a celebrity travelogue had a built-in market because it was both by and about a person of interest. And many literary celebrities wrote them. Charles Dickens wrote an account of his journey through antebellum America; William Wells Brown and Harriet Beecher Stowe wrote accounts of their time in Europe.[8] Such accounts offer very clear examples of Brenda R. Weber's argument that "cultural production and literary celebrity were recognized (and created) on both sides of the Atlantic."[9] The travelogue is a text "about" an author and part of the author's work. It integrates an author's public profile into their oeuvre. As nineteenth-century readers well knew—but as it is possible for twenty-first-century literary critics to forget—novelists did not write just novels.

THE LIBERTY BELL: AN ANTISLAVERY LITERARY ANNUAL, FEATURING CELEB CONTRIBUTORS

How did the cultural capital associated with being a celebrity writer change the way writers intervened in particular social and political debates of the nineteenth century? In gift books designed to raise money for a cause, editors solicited contributions by prominent individuals. In some cases, then, some authors' celebratedness was thus the occasion for their intervening in political debates. Although gift books and literary annuals featured both reprints and solicited contributions, *The Liberty Bell* tended to rely on solicited contributions, and contributors were only sometimes famous for their antislavery work. Meaghan Fritz and Frank Fee note the presence of both "celebrated writers" and "relatively unremembered writers and abolitionists" in the volumes.[10] Benjamin Quarles sketches out a broad rubric: in *The Liberty Bell* "no article was welcomed that did not have a direct bearing on antislavery."[11] In some cases, though, the writer's identity may have taken the place of explicitly abolitionist content. Marjorie Stone notes that "British writers like the ardent abolitionist, Mary Howitt, as well as American writers like Thomas Wentworth Higginson, sometimes contributed innocuous poems with no clear connection to slavery." Stone argues that the Martineau essay I discuss later, "Incidents of Travel," looks "relatively tame, despite [Martineau's] long history of abolitionist activism."[12] *The Liberty Bell*'s contents were miscellaneous. For example, the 1848 volume with Martineau's essay also included an essay by William L. Bowditch on the limits of Lysander Spooner's legal argument in *The Unconstitutionality of Slavery* (1845); Jane E. Hornblower's sonnet on West Indian emancipation; and Frederick Douglass's takedown of a movement to buy "Bibles for the slaves." The 1845 edition of *The Liberty Bell* included not only a sixteen-page letter by the major British antislavery advocate Thomas Clarkson but also a letter from Bremer, whom Poe called a "notable authoress" in the *Broadway Journal* of August 2, 1845.[13] Bremer stresses her unfitness to take a principal part in the "concerto" for abolition: "I shrink back, from the very natural feeling that my voice is not strong, not good enough for such a part, and that this effort is not needed, and cannot add an iota to the benefit of the cause." One scholar quotes this passage from a letter from Bremer to Maria Weston Chapman, *Liberty Bell*'s editor, dated August 25, 1844, as evidence of Bremer's refusal to contribute public support to the American Antislavery Society, which it clearly is—yet the letter was nevertheless also printed in *The Liberty Bell* in

1845. As Bremer acknowledges in a postscript, the refusal serves as her contribution: "If my letter seems to you good for publication, you may dispose of it as you like."[14] A letter written by "Fredrika Bremer" (though now no longer a household name among Anglophone readers) specifically for inclusion in *The Liberty Bell* would likely be worth printing, whatever it said. *The Liberty Bell* may not have included images of author signatures, but in some respects it worked like an autograph book.

Gift books monetized celebrity author brands in quite explicit ways. Some gift books paid celebrity authors very well for their contributions—from the author's perspective, a "handsome" reward for a "relatively small outlay," as Barbara Onslow puts it.[15] Contributions to *The Liberty Bell* were offered as gifts, part of the more diversified economic picture of the business of letters Leon Jackson describes in his account of the literary market.[16] Such books draw from celebrity authorship, but not just through the publication of their "greatest hits." Miranda Marraccini shows how Emily Faithfull, the founder of the woman-run Victoria Press, drew on her "coterie's connections to prominent men" to promote the feminist press. Marraccini's social network approach shows that, by contrast with the periodicals, pamphlets, and nonanthology books the press published, "men contributed most heavily to Victoria Press anthologies." For example, in the 1861 gift book *Victoria Regia*, a literary anthology designed to demonstrate "the high literary support" for the press, the editor Adelaide Procter emphasized the importance of high-profile contributors—or as Marraccini puts it, "maximum name recognition." For Procter, a contribution by Tennyson was valuable because it was a contribution by Tennyson—and, indeed, "The Sailor Boy" was singled out and quoted in full by the journal *Athenaeum* as a product of the poet-laureate.[17]

In this instance, the reputation of the contributor might matter more than the substance of their contribution. As Procter pointed out, too, Tennyson was of value in this context because his contribution was also a demonstration of support for the project of the press.

Per Marraccini's argument that we consider each contributor as part of a broader network outside and inside the literary anthology, let me return to how Bremer calls attention to the way she raises her voice in concert with others, aligning herself with other supporters of antislavery. As we have seen, John R. McKivigan and Rebecca A. Pattillo argue for the political alliances created by Julia Griffiths's selection of contributors to *Autographs for Freedom*; Marjorie Stone illuminates the political affiliations of *Liberty Bell* contributors in the late 1840s.[18] In the antislavery gift book, the table of contents manifested a network of supporters. The texts in the volume drew power from one another as well as from the contributors' reputations.

The celebrity contributors who raised the value of a collection also include the figure of the editor who put the collection together. Alexis Easley characterizes the pairing of high-profile contributors and editor as a celebrity collaboration that cross-promoted its central figures.[19] In their discussion of *The Liberty Bell*, Fritz and Fee note that even though Maria Weston Chapman did not name herself as editor (her name does not appear on the cover or title page), most of the volume's audience would have known she edited it.[20] Literary celebrity might thus illuminate works even without articulating a famous name.[21] In fact, both antislavery gift books I highlight were associated with even more celebrated names: *Autographs for Freedom*, edited by Griffiths, was associated with Frederick Douglass, and *The Liberty Bell*, edited by Chapman, was associated with Garrison.[22]

HARRIET MARTINEAU, POETESS

Unlike Bremer, Martineau was well known for her antislavery writing at the time of her contribution to *The Liberty Bell*. Following the success of *Illustrations of Political Economy* (1832–1834), Martineau was a major transatlantic celebrity. From her tour of the United States in 1834–1836 and the publications that followed it, in particular *Society in America* (1837), that celebrity was linked with America and antislavery. In Deborah Logan's overview, "From [Martineau's] earliest writing on slavery (pre-1834) to the books published as a result of her American tour (post-1836), to the many hundreds of newspaper leaders and political articles about America's 'Martyr Age' written over the next 30 years, Martineau's commitment to 'my dearly beloved Americans' is central to her identity as a writer and social reformist."[23] Amanda Claybaugh argues that Martineau is an exemplary figure for understanding transatlantic nineteenth-century social reform.[24] Martineau's gender was a critical part of her authorial identity. Logan shows how in Martineau's travels in the States she "sought the widest range of experiences, gratified that her professional fame and her gender facilitated access to parts of American society typically denied tourists. As a writer of political economy, her fame [*sic*] secured contacts with federal and state government officials and public figures; as a woman, she had access to the domestic interiors (nurseries, kitchens) unlikely to attract or be accessible to male travelers."[25] Martineau was careful in her deployment of gender across different prose genres. As Easley has shown, Martineau wrote anonymously about the woman question, which suggests how women writers might "influence the direction of debates over social and political issues without exhibiting themselves as high-profile political celebrities and to engage in professional careers without being labelled 'public women,'" but in *Society in America* Martineau wrote in an embodied first person and emphasized from the introduction how being a woman let her into "the nursery, the boudoir, the kitchen."[26] Martineau's writings in *The Liberty Bell* would also have been contextualized by the distribution of the gift book in the gendered context of the fundraising bazaar, to which Martineau contributed not only writing but also needlework.[27] Martineau's celebrity authorship encompassed handwork as well as political economy.

Martineau is "the quintessential Victorian woman of letters" in Linda H. Peterson's account, one who wrote "dozens of didactic tales, multiple volumes of biography, history, and travel writing, and seminal studies in political economy, sociology and British imperialism."[28] Martineau's contributions to *The Liberty Bell* reflect these genres and include both a letter to Elizabeth Pease that gave a history of factions in the American abolitionist scene that testified to her long-standing involvement with the American antislavery movement as well as the travel sketch I discuss later. But the context of a literary annual that invited one-offs from contributors reveals her use of a genre that literary history might not have led us to expect from her: in 1844, her contribution was a six-page poem called "Pity the Slave."

The inclusion of this poem demonstrates how the figure of a writer closely identified with prose would also for contemporaries have been shaped by the publication of a short poem in a gift book volume. The poem uses the first-person to underscore Martineau's relation to disability by contrasting enslavement with the speaker's invalidism: she is too ill to leave home but is nevertheless free "from every yoke that galls." This poem followed about five years of home confinement for Martineau, and it connects thematically with her *Life in the Sick Room*, which had been published anonymously that same year, 1844.

Martineau's poem draws on her reputation as a traveler and as an invalid and opens with a direct address to the reader, putting them in direct conversation with Martineau as speaker:

> You pity me, because
> My days and years are passed within the square
> Of these two rooms

The reader is thus invited into a personal relationship with Martineau, who reframes her position as one of relative freedom:

> never dare
> To spend your pity on the sick, the prisoner,
> Caged but by God's kind hand.[29]

Maria H. Frawley emphasizes Martineau's place in the development of a culture of invalidism, drawing on Alison Winter's argument that for Martineau the sickroom was "a place in which the invalid became *more* independent rather than less so."[30] The reflection on the limits to her mobility in this poem contrasts implicitly with what Amanda Adams has characterized as the freedom and "embodied mobility" that Martineau often depicts in discussions of American slavery not only in the travel writing published in *The Liberty Bell* but also in her account of traveling in the Lake District for *Sartain's Union Magazine of Literature and Art* in 1850.[31] From a twenty-first-century critical perspective, this poem lets us see the Martineau of disability studies in the context of the Martineau of antislavery. It also reveals how Martineau, as an historical figure working through the conventions of lyric, might emerge as a political poetess, at once sequestered and engaged.

HARRIET MARTINEAU'S "INCIDENTS OF TRAVEL": ORIENTALISM AND ANTISLAVERY IN *THE LIBERTY BELL* OF 1848

From the perspective of scholarship on Victorian women's travel writing, "Incidents of Travel" uses orientalist tropes characteristic of imperialist discourse to sharpen the contrast between Martineau's own liberty and the enslavement of others, in particular women. It is a very clear example of what Clare Midgley describes in her work on feminism and empire as the "triple discourse" of slavery, which "positioned the emancipation of women as the culmination of progress in western civilization, and presented the oppression of women, like the enslavement of Africans, as out of place and time in developed Western society."[32] As Deborah Logan has argued, Martineau also deployed an idea of "oriental slavery" to imagine liberty in her writings about travel in the United States.[33]

"Incidents of Travel" is at once a typical specimen of an imperial travelogue and a significant departure from other contributions to the gift book that focus on the United States and Britain. By appearing in an antislavery gift book, the essay integrates Martineau's global travel writing into her U.S.-oriented antislavery work. Logan argues that Martineau's "experiences travelling in America early established the ideological bases for a body of work driven by her desire to eradicate slavery in its various forms: racial slavery, seen in her abolition-themed writings; sexual slavery, demonstrated by her focus on the global oppression of women; and social slavery, demonstrated by her aim to educate the industrial working classes about the economic forces creating and perpetuating their exploitation."[34] Martineau's contribution is typical of the 1848 *Liberty Bell* volume in one important way: like about 70 percent of the volume, it is written in prose. This is a simple computational observation and surprising only because the volume's best-known contribution is a poem by Elizabeth Barrett Browning (EBB), "The Runaway Slave at Pilgrim's Point."[35]

A dramatic monologue written by a white English poet from the perspective of a self-liberated American woman of African descent, the poem speaks in implicit relation to EBB's international fame as a white poetess. As different as EBB's and Martineau's entries are, both trade on the position of the celebrity contributor. Lucy Sheehan has argued that EBB's poem simultaneously dares to imagine enslavement and asserts implicitly that it cannot do so. Thus, the poem subtly inscribes the limits of EBB's perspective into the text of the poem. If the poem elides the distance and privilege from slavery inscribed by the poet's name, it does so only partially, withholding, for example, the "song" the speaker sings.[36] Seen alongside EBB and her contribution, Martineau's British-inflected whiteness clearly signals her remoteness from the institution of U.S. slavery at the same time that it adds to her value as a contributor. Jennifer Sorensen argues that the transatlantic context is central to *The Liberty Bell*, which opens with a contribution by a "Southron," thus highlighting the Barrett Browning poem that follows it, signed from "England," as a contribution by "a Briton far removed from the sights of slavery's horror."[37] The famous white women writers from across the Atlantic make up a subcategory of contributors whose privilege and distance are unmissable. If Martineau's previous contributions emphasized that she wrote from England (as would EBB's "A Curse for a Nation," which opens the 1856 *Liberty Bell*), "Incidents of Travel" places her much farther away, a distance she uses to figure the impossibility of her understanding the experience of enslavement. Unlike

EBB's imaginative appropriation of the perspective of an enslaved woman, Martineau's essay, an imperialist account of her travels to North Africa, encounters slavery on American soil at multiple figural removes. At the end, she signs off from "England" and describes a scene even farther away: about twenty miles from Korosko in Egyptian Nubia, present-day Sudan. She uses orientalist tropes to argue that what is truly alien is the American South. Martineau's contribution to the 1848 volume of *The Liberty Bell*, "Incidents of Travel," makes more intuitive sense in the context of imperialism than in the context of abolitionism.[38] Martineau's little essay reveals her interest in economics and the global oppression of women within the antislavery context of its gift book publication and the protoimperialist context of its republication.

The principal incident of travel is that Martineau wanders into someone's home in Nubia and reflects on the threat of slavery hanging over the heads of the absent family. The account of her intrusion lays out the imaginative distance between herself and the experience of enslavement, between the autobiographical "I" and the family whose space she has temporarily usurped, between that family and the people they once knew, now enslaved, and, finally, between Martineau herself and those enslaved in America.

Martineau's home intrusion prompts an imaginative reflection focused on local agricultural practice. In the account, she and her companion see a home and are "not sorry to find it empty, that we might examine fully so fair a specimen of a Nubian dwelling. The family were absent—no doubt hoeing their plot of ground, their crop of lupins, or wheat, or beans, or castor oil . . . one or two might be working the sakia,—the wheel by which they raise the water of the Nile."[39] Martineau's "no doubt" suggests both certainty and near-certainty since she speculates with the force of empirical knowledge of local domestic economy. The second signal of uncertainty—that some of the family only "might be" drawing water—also serves to introduce the idea of the sakia. Of the actual people temporarily absent from home, she concludes, "Here is enough for their happiness, if what they may obtain were but secure" from the threat of enslavement. "Here are some, cheerful, sleek, and hopeful. Where are others who were born and reared by their side? the bastinado, or in prison, or carried off to the hated army, because they cannot pay their taxes. Others in the Slave-market, or placed in houses where it is an affair of chance whether they are happy or not; but where it is certain that they cannot be happy if they have any yearning towards that home from which they are forever exiled."[40]

Martineau's question here—"Where are others?"—invites answers that, like her observations on agriculture, come from what she already understands. The missing others she imagines are fully objectified, passively being tortured, imprisoned, impressed, enslaved, and exiled. Despite this willingness to objectify those others, she refrains from telling us what she thinks that objectification would feel like. Instead, she underlines the limits of her experience as a "mere passenger through the country": "Why, if I, a mere passenger through the country, look back with a sort of tender regret upon those free and quiet scenes which I shall see no more . . . what must the remembrance of these things be to the man doomed to be for life the spy and jailor of the hareem? or the girl imprisoned for life behind the curtains of the women's abode?"[41] Martineau asserts that her privileged position sets limits to what she can and cannot imagine. The turn here underscores the limits of her capacity to feel, pitting the "tender regret" she feels as a tourist against the yearning of a man "doomed" or a girl "imprisoned" for life. The "freedom" of the absent family in this essay is compromised by an implicit threat of slavery and contrasts sharply with Martineau's own freedom.

When Martineau shows herself imagining someone else's experience, she underscores the difference of that experience from her own by recoding it in an elaborately exoticized setting. Martineau's essay for *The Liberty Bell* meets an annual call to address transatlantic slavery with another strain of racist thought, using a received narrative about Eastern despotism to heighten the contrast between slavery and liberty so central to the American narrative. The white/Black binary gives way to a West/East binary or, more accurately, a West/East intersection in what Mia Bagneris characterizes as "the echoes between the exotic 'Orient' and the antebellum South in the Victorian cultural imagination." Bagneris uses the sculpture *The Octoroon*, John Bell's answer in 1868 to Hiram Powers's *The Greek Slave* of 1850, as evidence of a broader "association of both regions with the trafficking of pretty women as 'sex slaves.'"[42] As Logan points out, Martineau also uses the idea of a Middle Eastern harem to address sexual exploitation in the American South in writings set in the United States.[43] The *Liberty Bell* essay fits in both the broader context of transatlantic discourse about slavery and the narrower context of Martineau's work. Martineau refrains from speaking "on behalf" of the enslaved. Rather, she uses what she considers to be the knowable—that is, unexamined imperialist objectification—to lay out what she cannot imagine or feel. Her essay is not especially sympathetic. It seems content to connect, vaguely, her privileged position with the antislavery movement and, like Bremer's letter, works as a receipt acknowledging that the power of the writer's position makes anything she has to say a selling point for the volume.

If the power of Martineau's contribution depends on her reputation as a white lady authoress, it foregrounds her embodied perspective. In defining herself against the women she imagines, Martineau deploys the notion of oppressed women to construct a position of freedom for white British women. If "white feminism" is often characterized as a position that presumes to speak for others and then speaks only of itself, Martineau's travel writing—raced white and gendered feminine—indicates the imaginative limits of that embodied perspective. I have suggested that *The Liberty Bell* is an example of how the social Anglo-American reform network took shape through print, revealing how separate strands of thought intersected discursively, as in the language of imprisonment in "Pity the Slave." But Martineau's contributions to *The Liberty Bell* also demonstrate that the invalid and the traveling lady political economist *were* the same figure for readers. Though Martineau's contribution to the 1848 *Liberty Bell* came from farther afield than many other contributions, as a travelogue it would have chimed with what readers had come to expect from her. This contribution also indicates the broader availability and popularity of the travelogue as a commercial literary form.

TRAVELOGUES AS LIFE WRITING, TRAVELOGUES AS NOVEL ADJACENT

To understand travel writing, a form that has been central to postcolonial approaches, as life writing helps to clarify the political charge in *The Liberty Bell*'s particular performance of literary celebrity. Antislavery travelogs like Martineau's and Bremer's show how literary celebrity intersects with the structuring presence of a colonial perspective.

The same Fredrika Bremer who claimed to be reluctant to submit a formal contribution to *The Liberty Bell* in 1845 also published a travelogue extensively treating slavery in 1853. That both Martineau and Bremer contributed to *The Liberty Bell* as celebrated authoresses is both a coincidence and not a coincidence: both were part of the Anglo-American literary and social reform network.[44] Like Martineau, Bremer capitalizes on her distance from the American South to make her point, and, taken together, they demonstrate a more global perspective within an Anglo-American version of transatlantic writing.

To focus on literary celebrity as the connection between the travel writing of these two authors, however, means pulling together the very different contexts of those travelogues—hopscotching from Sudan to Cuba. This move runs counter to Susan Morgan's foundational principle of understanding travel writing: that "place matters."[45] Nineteenth-century travel writing responded to domestic and imperial contexts, and discourse varied from place to place. As Inderpal Grewal argues, even the roles women travelers might take up varied by locale.[46] If Bremer and Martineau wrote two major narratives of travel through the United States, both writers also traveled to different parts of the world from distinctive authorial positions and geopolitical investments. Moreover, to read Bremer's narrative in its English edition demands an account of its circulation in translation.

Bremer's travel narrative was absorbed into the U.S. context as part of its translation into English, as Judith Johnston argues. For Johnston, translation can take on "forms of appropriation in which the source language and author disappear altogether, and meanings and ideas become authorized as integral to the target culture's own sense of identity and nationhood."[47] Bremer's epistolary account of her visit to Cuba should be read among other early-to-midcentury accounts of the beauty of Cuba that circulated alongside discussions of Cuba as a potential new slave state, which offered what Ivonne M. García characterizes as "literary expressions of a colonial vision . . . [that] anticipated the discourses that later served to legitimize U.S. imperial ambitions."[48] Bremer's *Homes of the New World* (1853) has been of continued interest to scholars working on Cuba. Adriana Méndez Rodenas offers Bremer's representations of Afro-Cuban life, "particularly those dealing with African dances," as "an ethnographic approach to non-Western cultures." Aisha K. Finch uses Bremer's narrative "to think about the discursive terrain of gender and race that arguably became central to many Cuban slaveholding practices."[49] Thus, a Swede's "look outward" at slavery in the United States and then Cuba (under Spain) has political implications beyond what the text suggests. In the context of antislavery debates in the United States, as Susan P. Casteras notes, Bremer's contemporary Barbara Leigh Smith Bodichon pointed to Bremer as a person who in *Homes of the New World* "tolerated" arguments about the "'benevolence' of slavery and its economic 'necessity' to the functioning of the South."[50]

Homes of the New World takes the form of a series of letters by Bremer about her travels through the United States, down the Mississippi through New Orleans, and then onward to Cuba. It came out in English before it came out in Swedish. Because Bremer went to Cuba, the book trades on an exaggerated representation of differences between the Global North and the Global South. Bremer's feminism and her Swedishness were the hallmarks of her Anglophone celebrity, and her fame as a novelist at the time of her trip was comparable to that of Charles Dickens or Frances Trollope. Ezra Greenspan quotes her anecdote from *Homes of the New World*: "The Captain of a ship sailing for Charleston refused to take her on board when he found out her identity for fear that she might expose him in print as

Trollope and Dickens had done to various people in publishing travelogues of their American excursions."[51]

Cross-pollination between fictional and nonfictional forms is quite clear in books such as *Jane Eyre* (1847) and *David Copperfield* (1849–1850), but it is also evident in travel writing. Frances Trollope's *Domestic Manners of the Americans* (1832) may not have been the first account of a British writer's travel to the states, but it can seem so as we look back: it was a major commercial success that set a pattern for writers in the years to come. Trollope was relatively unknown at the time of the book's success, and the book of her travels launched her career as a novelist. As noted in the introduction, Elsie Michie's account of Trollope's first novels underscores their relation to *Domestic Manners*: Trollope "quickly sought to give that non-fictional material a fictional form, producing two American novels, *The Refugee in America* (1832) and *The Life and Adventures of Jonathan Jefferson Whitlaw; or Life on the Mississippi* (1836). The latter [was] a bestseller that went through three editions in its first year."[52] Bringing travel writing into conversation with novels in a writer's oeuvre makes it possible to recognize how that same writer might treat similar material in nonfictional and fictional modes. Bremer herself recognized a connection across fictional and nonfictional forms, and *Homes of the New World* concludes with a consideration of her own antislavery travelogue in relation to Stowe's *Uncle Tom's Cabin* (1852).

THE "MISS AUSTEN OF SWEDEN" IN CUBA

Bremer highlights her foreignness in a travel narrative that represents not "Swedish life," like her novels, but a Swedish perspective on the "new world." Later in *Homes of the New World*, however, this distance ultimately also functions to emphasize the reach of slavery beyond the transatlantic trade system, as when Bremer pauses to write: "This is the history of the sugar-cane before it comes into your coffee-cup."[53] Bremer calls the reader's attention from a distance as far as the North Star to the coffee she holds in her hand. Instead of signaling a place apart from and opposite to the sites of slavery, Sweden is materially entangled with it. In January 1854, Bremer described her account of slavery in America as "the chief work of my work."[54] As García argues, Cuba, one of the "new world" places Bremer visited, could function as a "gothic signifier" that stands in for the American South.[55] That is, though Cuba is clearly connected to the United States and U.S. imperial interests, it also offers a kind of global-scale version of the North/South binary in the United States, where Bremer originates from north of the North and visits Cuba, south of the South. Bremer dramatizes this in the text, describing to her sister one of the "solitary rambles of discovery" that mark an unusual degree of freedom for a single woman. She describes an encounter with a group of travelers in a visit to the Yumurí Valley in which her effort to describe Sweden in Italian-infused Spanish as *"un paeso sotto la estreja del Norte"* suggests to her interlocutors that she is trying to say she comes "from the north star." This episode is played for laughs ("they look at one another, and smile significantly, and wrinkle their brows; they now comprehend that *la signora* is somewhat wrong in the head, and, compassionately shaking their heads, they drive on their horses"), and the misunderstanding also resonates with what Bremer refers to elsewhere in the volume as "the way of the North Star," a journey to freedom that underscores a profound perspectival distance between Sweden and the Americas.[56] By this light, Bremer's work is repatriated into an American readership while retaining the "Swedishness" that sets her apart from other writers in English.

As Åsa Arping demonstrates in her discussion of Bremer as the "Miss Austen of Sweden," Bremer-in-English was part of the transatlantic feminist network, a figure both distinctively Swedish and central to emerging ideas about American literature in the 1840s.[57] Bremer emerged in relation to the person who introduced her to an Anglophone readership, Mary Howitt, her translator. Howitt is a great example of someone whose figure requires the multiple critical perspectives of literary celebrity, antislavery, and nineteenth-century print culture. Her literary reputation was such that her name as translator appeared in bigger font than Bremer's in both U.S. and British translations of Bremer's early novels.[58] As a writer and editor, Howitt was involved in a variety of writing and publishing projects, including literary annuals, and she supported younger women writers, including Elizabeth Gaskell.[59] She figures as an "ardent abolitionist" in Marjorie Stone's discussion of *The Liberty Bell*, as noted earlier. Both Bremer and Howitt are important figures in a U.S. history of authorship in translation, particularly in debates about copyright and collaborative literary creation.[60] Howitt addressed unauthorized reprintings of her translations with "a detailed attack on competing publishers and their cheap editions" in her preface to Bremer's *New Sketches of Every-Day Life* (1844).[61] She also translated *Homes of the New World*.

Bremer became a major figure among readers of English through the publication and reprinting of her novels of Swedish manners in the 1840s—a generic fad, like the Stieg Larrson thrillers of the early 2000s. In Arping's account, their popularity was due to the novels' genre (they met the expectations of a Victorian novel but also provided a glimpse of Scandinavian life), their translation (by Mary Howitt), and the moment in media history (their release in the explosion of cheap print and broad distribution, which meant that her first novel was printed in an American weekly within three weeks of its appearance in volume form in England).[62] Åsa Arping and Yvonne Leffler trace the resounding success of Bremer's novels in the Anglo-lexic market to their genre—stories of domestic life focused on a single heroine—and note that many of Bremer's titles were changed to a woman's name when translated.[63] In a review of Bremer's novel *Hertha* (1856), George Eliot characterizes the novels of the 1840s like this:

> No one quotes them, no one alludes to them: and grave people who have entered on their fourth decade, remember their enthusiasm for the Swedish novels among those intellectual "wild oats" to which their mature wisdom can afford to give a pitying smile. And yet, how is this? For Miss Bremer had not only the advantage of describing manners which were fresh to the English public, she also brought to the description unusual gifts—lively imagination, poetic feeling, wealth of language, a quick eye for details, and considerable humour, of that easy, domestic kind which throws a pleasant light on everyday things. . . . [One reason the novels have not kept] a high position among us is, that her luxuriant faculties are all overrun by a rank growth of sentimentality, which, like some faint-smelling creeper on the boughs of an American forest, oppresses us with the sense that the air is unhealthy.[64]

Eliot calls attention to Bremer's gifts—for language, for detail—that would clearly lend themselves to travel sketches. Her critique of a "rank growth of sentimentality," like a parasitic vine in an American forest, might also suggest American sentimental novels. This review, written only three years after *Homes of the New World* was published, gives a sense of what characteristics the book's author brought to her subject.

Julia Johnston uses periodical reviews of *Homes* to consider it as a contribution to transatlantic abolitionist discourse in conversation with *Uncle Tom's Cabin* and frames it as one of the antislavery "publications by women [written from the view of] the lens of the domestic." She cites a letter Bremer wrote to Elizabeth Gaskell, praising *Mary Barton* (1848) and letting her know to expect a complimentary copy of *Homes of the New World*. Gaskell's novels, Bremer told her, "have opened many an eye, many a mind in Sweden as well as in England."[65] This letter, in context with the connection to Stowe, is part of the well-documented discursive connection between novels about the working class in England and slavery in the states. For example, Maria DiBattista and Deborah Epstein Nord draw together novels by Gaskell, Harriet Jacobs, Martineau, and Stowe to trace the role of domesticity in politically engaged fictions, antislavery writings, and industrial novels. In their discussion, Martineau figures there "as a kind of lynchpin between women who wrote about slavery in the United States and those who wrote about industrial life in Britain."[66] In this context, the quality of the novelist's perception becomes a basis for political engagement. To recognize travel writing as a literary form is to recognize an even more straightforward connection between the person of the celebrated white lady writer and the political work of prose.

In the 1845 *Liberty Bell*, Bremer's role as a domestic novelist seemed to undercut her ability to speak to American politics. But the travelogue, as a literary form, seems to draw on the novelist's privileges outlined by Eliot—imagination, language, and eye for detail—that authorized women's sentimental political novels. At one point, Bremer's dreamy travel narrative turns, as her steamboat moves South on the Mississippi, into a highly mediated account of the horrors of slavery: "Two hours later I still sat aft on the piazza, and inhaled the same mild, delicious atmosphere, still beheld the same scene of southern beauty, but gazed upon it with a heart full of bitterness. Yes, for a dark picture had been unfolded before my gaze—a picture which I never shall forget; which perpetually, like a spectre of the abyss, will step between me and the memory of that enchanting veil which one moment captivated and darkened my vision." The narrative shifts dramatically in the pastoral scene she describes, which begins in a mood of believing the "best of all men" and looking "on the sunny side"—a "spirit of human love"—but turns out to be a lesson about failing to empathize or love the humans who form, for her, part of the prospect.[67]

Bremer frames her experience of revealed truth as an anecdote about a handsome stranger. She writes to her sister, "Yes, if I were younger, and if my life's purpose were less decided than it now is, I confess that there is here and there one of these American gentlemen, with their energy, their cordiality, and chivalric spirit who might be dangerous to my heart. . . . But now, as particularly regards this agreeable gentleman, he is already married, and traveling with his family to Cuba where, on account of the health of his wife, they will spend the winter, and after that to Europe." The agreeable gentleman is both a particular gentleman and an exemplary American one; she says, "I seek not for them, but when they come, I enjoy them as flowers given by the hand of the all-good Father." He is one part of the scenery as she cruises down the Mississippi, and he is responsible for replacing an "enchanting veil" with a "spectre of the abyss":

I sat and gazed upon that beautiful scene as one looks at the scene of a theatre. I enjoyed with childish delight the decorations. Then came my new friend, the planter, and seated himself in an arm-chair on the piazza. We spoke a few words about the deliciousness of the air, which he enjoyed as much as I did. Then we sat silently contemplating the scenery of the shores. We saw the caravans of slaves and their overseers proceeding over the fields. I said to my neighbor in that spirit of human love which I have mentioned,

"There is a great deal more happiness and comfort in this life (the slaves' life) than one commonly imagines."

The planter turned to me his beautiful head with a glance which I shall never forget; there was astonishment, almost reproach in it, and a profound melancholy.

"Oh!" said he, in a low voice, "you know nothing of that which occurs on these shores; if you did, you would not think so. Here is much violence and much suffering!"[68]

She writes: "I will not repeat those scenes which the planter related to me"—a promise of restraint that, as my colleague Hillary Eklund drily observed, she does not keep. Rather, she quotes three full pages of his testimony, then repeats key moments from them in the first person: *I beheld*; *I heard*; *I saw*.[69] Laurel Ann Lofsvold points out that this story, like most of the "tales of horror," are secondhand in this book, and it is important that the scene is staged to maximize the contrast between her tourist's gaze and his knowing one: the silent contemplation they share is not presided over by the spirit of human love but by her own inability to read what she is seeing.[70] She processes the deep South twice, once in hearing, once in "seeing" or paraphrasing. She records the gentleman's testimony and responds—twice. Her own foreignness appears in contrast to an exemplary American gentleman, offering an extranaive version of the naive convert to abolitionism as she goes from thoughtless thoughtfulness to the dark picture unfolded to her gaze—which is, presumably, a version of the outwardly identical scene.

Homes of the New World ends with a wish to write a novel like *Uncle Tom's Cabin*:

> Often when I have heard the adventures of fugitive slaves, their successful escape or their destruction, and have thought of the natural scenery of America, and of those scenes which naturally suggest themselves on "the way of the North Star," I have had a wish and a longing desire to write the history of a fugitive pair, so as it seems to me it ought to be written, and I have been inclined to collect materials for that purpose. And if I lived by this river and amid these scenes, I know for what object I should then live. But as it is, I am deficient in local knowledge. I am not sufficiently acquainted with the particular detail of circumstances, which would be indispensable for such a delineation, which ought to be true, and to take a strong hold upon the reader. That office belongs to others besides myself. I will hope for and expect—the *American mother*.[71]

In the appendix to *Homes*, Bremer waives the necessity of including details because Stowe has already written and published *Uncle Tom's Cabin*—and, crucially, her key to it.[72] Bremer argues here that the travelogue's blend of rhetoric and observation becomes redundant in light of the novel and the compendium. By participating in the same conversation and in a sentimental, domestic mode, Bremer's work stands as another entry in the broader genre of antislavery writing by celebrity white lady authoresses. Understanding the gift book contribution requires a sense of the volume, the contributor, and the intersecting genres they engage. There is more overlap between what novels are doing and what travelogs are doing than we tend to think. Bremer's travelogue engages with Stowe's novel, just as the re-release of Henson's life would. These nonfictional counterpoints to the novel—the material history of print books, the colonial histories of travel writing—are also deeply connected discursively to the history of the nineteenth-century novel at its most familiar.

4

BECOMING THE "REAL UNCLE TOM"

A Textual History of the Lives of Josiah Henson

According to the last chapter of *Uncle Tom's Cabin*, the question that correspondents all over the country asked Harriet Beecher Stowe as the novel was being serially published in 1852 was "whether this narrative is a true one."[1] The following year, Stowe answered by publishing *A Key to* Uncle Tom's Cabin (1853), a five-hundred-page compendium or "mosaic of facts" that mixed "gloss, evidence, and analysis."[2] The first part of the *Key* dedicates a chapter to sources for each character, and it says that one of the sources for Uncle Tom is "the published memoirs of the venerable Josiah Henson."[3] Henson was an important public figure well before the publication of *Uncle Tom's Cabin*. As a founder of the Dawn settlement for self-liberated people near what is now Dresden, Ontario, he "functioned as patriarch of Dawn and as a spokesman for Canada's growing black population," touring throughout the Midwest, New England, and New York between 1843 and 1847 and across England from 1849 to 1851 and 1851 to 1852.[4] Henson became even more famous after Stowe's *Key* was published in 1853, when he began to be identified as the "real Uncle Tom," and after he released a much-expanded version of his autobiography in 1858—and then another expanded edition in 1876. He was part of the star system of literary celebrity in the second half of the nineteenth century, but his star status has been occluded since then by his being inextricably linked to Uncle Tom, a character who circulates in our own time as a symbol of racial treason. According to Robin W. Winks, Stowe had likely not met Henson before writing her novel and may not even have read his narrative.[5] I argue that, in retrospect, the best-known "life of Henson" of all the versions published might be understood to be the novel itself.

As Francis Smith Foster has argued, the three major editions of Henson's autobiography that appeared in his lifetime emerged in such very different contexts and took such distinctly different forms that they ought to be understood as "completely new works."[6] What united these divergent accounts in the nineteenth century was Henson himself, the author. As Martin R. Delany framed the relation between Henson and Stowe in the pages of *Frederick Douglass' Paper* in 1853, Henson's "*living testimony*" was critical to the reception of Stowe's novel.[7] I refer to the three published autobiographies as Henson's *lives*, a term that captures the sense of lived experience and published autobiography. Rather than understanding Henson's lives as either fundamentally self-expressive or as peripheral to the *Uncle Tom's Cabin* text network, I argue that Henson's books—or these books about Henson—should be read as a commercial enterprise that worked in tandem with his public role as a preacher and lecturer.[8]

The first edition of Henson's life, *The Life of Josiah Henson, Formerly a Slave* (1849), was a 76-page pamphlet that sold six thousand copies in its first three years; the second was *Truth Stranger Than Fiction: Father Henson's Story of His Own Life, Now an Inhabitant of Canada, as Narrated by Himself* (1858); and the last major edition, *Uncle Tom's Story of His Life: An Autobiography of the Rev. Josiah Henson (Mrs. Harriet Beecher Stowe's "Uncle Tom"), from 1789 to 1876*, published in London in 1876, was a 257-page book that by 1907 had sold a quarter of a million copies.[9] The history of the texts is interwoven with the public persona Henson developed in the years following the Civil War. When Henson announced to the crowds who had gathered to see the "original Uncle Tom" that "my name is not Tom," he was drawing on both the novel's cultural power and his own higher claim to the story.[10] Adena Spingarn argues that Henson "took Stowe's endorsement and ran with it, revising his previously published autobiography to follow the novel more closely (the new title was *Truth Stranger Than Fiction*) and making tours of the United States and England as 'the real Uncle Tom' and 'the original Uncle Tom' for the rest of his life."[11]

The history of the major editions of Henson's life illuminates an array of nonfictional genres that circulated around the novel as Henson's life increasingly came to read like Stowe's novel.[12] Winks characterizes *Truth Stranger Than Fiction* as "an almost classic opportunity" to study how a "text might be altered to serve a cause."[13] The 1858 edition that followed Stowe's novel and *Key* is more sharply polemical in its denunciation of slavery than the earlier editions but also incorporates minstrel tropes from the novel. In the third edition, Henson doubles down on his relation to the novel; he claims to have met with Stowe shortly before the novel was published and to be "particular friends" with the originals of George Harris and Eliza in the novel. Henson reappropriates his story from Stowe but does so in a way that brings it closer to the famous and fame-giving text of *Uncle Tom's Cabin*.

From the publication of his first life, Henson was always a public speaker as well as an author, and the *Life* (or lives) of Henson would continue to complement his fame as a lecturer and preacher in the United States and England. He was one of the "scores of Black activists" who "traveled to England, Ireland, Scotland and even parts of rural Wales during the nineteenth century to educate the British public on slavery."[14] This education could involve connecting with the audience in a number of ways; Stephanie J. Richmond argues, for example, that Sarah Parker Remond "used her own status as a member of the black middle class in America and as a woman who had experienced oppression" to "connect to both middle- and working-class audiences during her speaking tour."[15] In an account of literary authors on lecture tours, Amanda Adams argues that "authors stood on stage authoring their own selves, [and] lecture tours fed the celebrity culture that was, more and more, replacing the published work with the author; this meant that in the public marketplace, an author's persona was beginning to be consumed as a commodity." For Adams, the lecture could also afford someone with a marginalized identity, such as Frederick Douglass, "the chance to author one's own public selfhood."[16] It is nevertheless important to recognize the limits of the "authorship" available to such speakers. Daphne A. Brooks uses feminist performance theory to read the staging of escape in the work of "formerly enslaved Black abolitionist speakers as international figures called on to exemplify the essential humanity of African Americans and to body forth the atrocities of the slave trade on a global stage."[17] Hannah-Rose Murray studies modes of "adaptive resistance" such speakers used to advocate for freedom within white public spaces through performance but also through the mobilization of abolitionist networks and print coverage of those performances.[18] In comparison to Douglass—who was neither more nor less than the author of his own life—Henson was the author of Stowe's novel *and* the person on whose experience Stowe claimed to draw. When Henson addressed a crowd, he stood adjacent to this doubled claim, the source of text and of experience whose life was bound with Stowe's novel and her choice to use his narrative as evidence.

Beyond the account of composition offered by the lives themselves (i.e., that the first edition was "dictated" and the third "edited"), we have no evidence of the extent of Henson's authorial control over these editions. Critical histories of the slave narrative demand that we account for the circumstances of its production and circulation, which are often murky. The form often frames a firsthand account of enslavement with supplemental documentation and white-authored endorsement. Even the most "authentically" authored narratives are further complicated by the element of the racialized politics of literary critics who treat the authors of this form as only the original experiencers of events rather than literary authors, a phenomenon that Lewis R. Gordon argues continued through late twentieth-century readings of Black autobiography.[19] Henson's "I" is the center of all three major editions. Stowe's *Key* refers specifically to his 1849 memoir or written account and quotes it at length. I therefore include her *Key* among the lives of Henson I discuss in the final two-thirds of this chapter.

In the next section, I offer an account of Henson's lives through textual history that prioritizes the shape of the texts that circulated rather than the circumstances of their production. Teresa A. Goddu argues that authorial agency in the case of slave narratives looks different in the absence of textual histories of them and calls for us to appreciate "the complex discursive and cultural negotiation of a corporate authorship." Lara Langer Cohen and Jordan Alexander Stein argue that Black writers played important roles in print culture "both on the page (as writing subjects as well as subjects of writing) and off (as readers, editors, printers, engravers, compositors, papermakers, librarians, and so on)."[20] Henson's story shows how closely authorship and print culture were imbricated with public performance. My approach here emphasizes Henson's centrality as an author figure within the text and as part of its circulation but creates space to recognize other potential figures in its creation. In *Textual Scholarship* (1992), David C. Greetham points out that the Modern Language Association (MLA) guidelines for scholarly editions take Foucault's description of the author's "work" ("everything that he [*sic*] wrote, said, or left behind") one step farther by "[raising] the question of 'second-party' textual materials."[21] Current MLA guidelines on scholarly editions formulate the question as "How many other people are involved in producing the object being edited, and what are their roles?"[22] The idea of a collaboratively produced "social text" creates a way of reading Henson's lives as asynchronous collaborative work that emerged across his lifetime.

Rather than trying to prize apart the contributions by different authors, I isolated differences across texts of the lives using two software programs designed for textual analysis at the volume level. This approach reduces the changing roster of cultural producers to the results of the textual changes they made. To understand how these "editions" of Henson's life emerged and changed, I pair textual changes by volume with a careful analysis of the editions' circulation. Though the editions differ significantly from one another, they were bound to one another by Henson's name and his public appearances. Henson is an ideal case study for a book about figures of the author because of the interplay between the fictional and factual accounts of his life. The complex contest over the authorship of his life as Uncle Tom and Henson's own active role in shaping a public persona shows how the author emerges from fact, fiction, text, and public performance.

THE LIFE OF JOSIAH HENSON, FORMERLY A SLAVE, NOW AN INHABITANT OF CANADA, AS NARRATED BY HIMSELF

The 1849 edition of Henson's lives, *The Life of Josiah Henson*, is the text that was misidentified as a novel by the algorithm in Ted Underwood's Digital Humanities project "Understanding Genre in a Collection of a Million Volumes" (see chapter 1), and it is the version of Henson's life untouched by the novel Stowe had not yet written. By its own account, this text was narrated by Henson, recorded by Samuel A. Eliot, and then read back to Henson for approval. William Andrews's seminal bibliography of 1986 (which became the basis of the online North American Slave Narratives archive) thus identifies this text as an autobiography.[23] *The Life of Josiah Henson* appears in retrospect as part of the aftermath of Douglass's famous *Narrative* of 1845, but, like many other narratives of the 1840s, it was not published by the American Anti-Slavery Society.[24] Eliot paid for it to be printed in order to raise money for the British-American Institute in the Dawn Settlement in Canada. More than 20 percent of the events described in the first pamphlet are set in Canada, and it directed attention and money toward the development of a Black-led community in Canada rather than toward the antislavery movement in the United States.[25] Printed in Boston, *The Life of Josiah Henson* receives significant attention in "Narratives of Fugitive Slaves," Ephraim Peabody's review of the form in the *Christian Examiner and Religious Miscellany* in July 1849, the same year of its publication. Peabody briefly addresses the narratives of Henry Watson, Lewis and Milton Clarke, William Wells Brown, and Douglass but dismisses them as possessing "no especial interest beyond what must belong to the life of almost any fugitive slave." He singles out Henson's as "the best picture of the evils incident to slave life on the plantations which can be found," dedicating nearly half the review's length (fifteen of thirty-three pages) to discussion and lengthy quotation of Henson's narrative.[26]

Peabody's review of major slave narratives argues that conciliating slaveholders and strengthening antislavery sentiment in the South are critical to achieving emancipation, and it connects the published narratives with political positions within the antislavery movement. Samuel A. Eliot, the amanuensis and editor of Henson's life as well as a member of the U.S. House of Representatives, had ties to the *Christian Examiner* and would ultimately "[earn] the ire of abolitionists for his vote in Congress for the Fugitive Slave Act of 1850."[27] A letter from the *Essex Country Freemen* (reprinted in *The Liberator*) in 1850 provided this bio for Eliot: "In 1849 I wrote and printed for cheap distribution the life of Josiah Henson, a fugitive slave. In 1850 I went to Congress for a month, and was one of the three northern Whigs who voted for Mason's Fugitive Slave Bill."[28] This early association between Henson and a conciliatory politics sets the stage for William Andrews's twentieth-century critical political analogy between Henson and Booker T. Washington, comparing the *Christian Examiner*'s positive response to Henson to the response from "white readers of *Up from Slavery* fifty years later." He argues that Henson created a narrative that applied "the traditional American work ethic to racial uplift."[29]

Peabody's review frames Henson politically in opposition to Douglass. Both men appear in the periodicals not only as authors and "fugitive slaves" but also as active public figures. Thus, though the review notes that Douglass's narrative contains the life of a "superior man," it criticizes his "violent and unqualified statements." Henson appears as an orator by implicit contrast to

Douglass: "Though an effective speaker, he is not one of the popular declaimers; he is a large-hearted, large-minded man, tolerant, calm, benevolent, and wise." This review, ostensibly about Henson's book, becomes an argument about his fitness as a leader. Peabody praises Henson for having the "wisdom to conceive, and the practical talent and energy to carry out, large and far-reaching schemes for the improvement of his brethren."[30]

If Henson's narrative was read in relation to his life—and to the narrative and life of Douglass—another important intellectual, social, and commercial context for his lives is his identity as a preacher, evident in the use of "Father Henson" in the 1858 book's title and the flash of white at his collar in the 1877 Sunday-school edition of his life, a third-person account closely based on the 1876 autobiography that significantly expands on Henson's original scene of conversion to Christianity in the 1849 edition. Peabody's review of the 1849 edition classified it as a "fugitive slave narrative," but it also dwelled on Henson's description of his religious experiences, which suggests a connection between that form and spiritual autobiographies like those of Black "female preachers active in the antebellum North," such as Sojourner Truth, Zilpha Elaw, Nancy Prince, and Jarena Lee, for whom the printed autobiography functioned as merch.[31] Lee, a preacher and free woman of color, describes how the first edition of her spiritual autobiography "went off as by a wind" when she preached in Cincinnati in 1839.[32] Sojourner Truth, according to Nell Irvin Painter, attended the women's rights convention in Akron in 1851—the occasion of the speech that would later circulate as the "Ar'n't I a Woman?" speech—"primarily to sell her book, and Frances Dana Gage reports that indeed she did a brisk business on the first day."[33] Henson's written lives worked in parallel with oration throughout his life.

After the publication of the first autobiography in 1849, Henson took his first trip to Britain.[34] As Vanessa D. Dickerson argues in *Dark Victorians* (2008), "England was ultimately much more than a sanctuary. It was the land of appeals or better yet the amplifier of publicity." R. J. M. Blackett's book on Black American abolitionists in England states that Henson raised $7,500 in his two trips to England.[35] Delany argued in 1853 that the "person of Father Henson will increase the valuation of Mrs. Stowe's work very much in England, as he is highly known and respected there."[36] Delany paints the figure of Henson as a leader of international repute and as the author of *The Life of Josiah Henson*.

A KEY TO UNCLE TOM'S CABIN; *PRESENTING THE ORIGINAL FACTS AND DOCUMENTS UPON WHICH THE STORY IS FOUNDED, TOGETHER WITH CORROBORATIVE STATEMENTS VERIFYING THE TRUTH OF THE WORK. BY HARRIET BEECHER STOWE*

Uncle Tom's Cabin is known as an overnight bestseller, but after its initial success, no further copies were printed in the United States for the next nine years. Stowe's key, however, is reported to have sold ninety thousand copies. Claire Parfait suggests that demand for copies of *Uncle Tom's Cabin* declined because the market was "saturated" by 1854 and observes that readers may also have "turned to Stowe's new book, *Key* . . . and to the many pro- and antislavery works which came out in the wake of the success of Stowe's novel."[37] Through Parfait's lens of publishing history, we can see that theme or subject outweighs genre:

Stowe's novel owed a significant part of its impact to the antislavery movement. The *Key*'s genre is an example of another common form of antislavery "work," the compendium. In *Selling Antislavery* (2020), Goddu argues that the nineteenth-century slave narrative should be understood as a compendium. In Goddu's reading of antislavery forms, the emphasis on "individuality and self-expression" that characterizes Douglass's narrative is unusual in a landscape of compendia that emphasized likeness across stories and "subordinated formerly enslaved people's narratives to the imperatives of facticity." In this reading, the compendia developed by the American Anti-Slavery Society worked to "solve the problem of veracity posed by the slave narrative" by "[regulating] slave testimony through white empiricism." Goddu points to a range of texts that, like Henson's, directly responded to Stowe's novel and "were produced to capitalize on the success of *Uncle Tom's Cabin* or validate its fiction as fact: such as [Wilson] Armistead's *Five Hundred Thousand Strokes for Freedom*, Stowe's *A Key to* Uncle Tom's Cabin (1853), John Passmore Edwards's *Uncle Tom's Companions; Or, Facts Stranger Than Fiction, A Supplement to Uncle Tom's Cabin: Being Startling Incidents in the Lives of Celebrated Fugitive Slaves* (1852), and *Uncle Tom's Cabin Almanack or Abolitionist Memento* (1853)."[38] Thomas Koenigs argues that Stowe makes a specific claim about the quality of fiction in her text: "By authenticating her fiction's 'reality,' Stowe suggests the legitimacy of *Uncle Tom's Cabin* as public sphere discourse, but she simultaneously figures this process of authentication as first and foremost ratifying its sentimental impact."[39]

Delany's contemporaneous critique of Stowe's *Key* in a series of letters to *Frederick Douglass' Paper* offers an alternative reading of the compendium as a testament to the limits of white expertise about Black experience. Delany argues that Stowe's gesture to documentary testimony in the *Key* underscores the limits of her subject position: "In all due respect and deference to Mrs. Stowe, I beg leave to say, that she *knows nothing about us.*" *Uncle Tom's Cabin* draws "largely from the best fugitive slave narratives as well as the living Household of old Father Henson," so Henson therefore deserves a portion of the profits of the novel. Although Stowe gestures to "the published memoirs of the venerable Josiah Henson," Delany emphasizes that what supports *Uncle Tom's Cabin* is actually the "living testimony" of Father Henson.[40]

Delany also implicitly argues that Stowe's novel should be read as a second telling of Henson's life story—and not a good one. In the printed correspondence, Delany appeals to Douglass's personal knowledge of Henson, a man "well known to both you and I," and criticizes the novel for misrepresenting Henson: "The 'negro language,' attributed to Uncle Tom by the authoress, makes the character more natural for a slave; but I would barely state, that Father Josiah Henson makes use of as good language, as any one in a thousand Americans."[41] Delany's criticism of *Uncle Tom's Cabin* through the *Key* reveals how Henson's life and his *Life*—that is, both his experiences and his published narrative—could be understood as the basis of Stowe's novel for subsequent readers, almost as if he were the true author of her novel.

TRUTH STRANGER THAN FICTION: FATHER HENSON'S STORY OF HIS OWN LIFE

Henson's pamphlet-turned-book *Truth Stranger Than Fiction* (1858) opens with a preface by Stowe acknowledging Henson's fame: "The numerous friends of the author of this little work will need no greater recommendation than his name to make it welcome."[42] Stowe's preface is an acknowledgment of her intervention in Henson's public reputation, but the text does not directly address her novel, and the name "Stowe" does not appear in Henson's narrative. The publisher John P. Jewett would later assert that he had published—and also partially written—the first edition of Henson's narrative.[43] Claire Parfait suggests that this "self-aggrandizing description [by] Jewett . . . makes the publisher an integral part of the mythology surrounding the novel." Augusta Rohrbach points out that the subtitle, *Father Henson's Story of His Own Life*, competes with Stowe and "lays claim to [Henson's] life as *his* to commodify through publication." For Mary Ellen Doyle, the second edition is important precisely because it "has creative elaborations proper to the genre of fiction" and thus exemplifies the "slave narrative as a developing genre and as forerunner of Black fiction." John Ernest argues that the substantial introduction of fictionlike material makes Henson "the most striking example of an African American life virtually lost to Stowe's novel."[44] If Henson's first narrative should be read in the context of other Black life narratives published in the 1840s, the second should be read as one of several re-released narratives in the 1850s. As many who regularly assign Douglass's lives with an eye to page counts well know, the *Narrative* of 1845 is a pamphlet, and *My Bondage and My Freedom* of 1855 is a book. Frances Smith Foster argues that autobiographical "series" like Henson's were "revised in so many ways that many of them should be considered as completely new works."[45]

Lucy Sheehan points out that the blurring of fiction and nonfiction as well as the republication of material in different contexts formed a strategy for writing about slavery and Black history for Black writers in this era, as when William Wells

Brown used his own autobiography as an "introduction" to his novel *Clotel or, The President's Daughter: A Narrative of Slave Life in the United States* (1853), which he republished in multiple versions.[46] The second edition of Henson's life, *Truth Stranger Than Fiction*, is a longer, bound book with more dialogue—and reads more like a novel in the style of *Uncle Tom's Cabin*. It was part of a trend in the 1850s that grew out of the success of *Uncle Tom's Cabin*, which, as Rohrbach argues, offered a kind of proof of concept for the market for antislavery books that highlighted each book's "literariness as well as its historical and social accuracy."[47] Goddu describes Jewett's company as a "commercial anti-slavery press." Michael Winship notes that Jewett was "an established publisher of many religious works representing the evangelical wing of Congregationalism" and had "likely met the Beecher family during his brief stint as a publisher in Cincinnati in 1844, since when he had published works by Stowe's brother, Henry Ward Beecher, and husband, Calvin Stowe, and would soon go on to begin publication of the collected *Works* of [Harriet's] father, Lyman Beecher."[48] The commercial element of publishing in the period was clarified for me by Jewett's subsequent careers as "in turn a purveyor of 'Peruvian Syrup,' an agent for a safety match company, and a negotiator of patents" before 1866, when "he left Boston for New York City, where he eventually relinquished his work in patents to return to bookselling in a quiet way."[49] Jewett's is a story about the intersection of enterprise and literary history.

According to Rohrbach, the slave narrative was popular not only because of its subject matter but also because of its dedication to realism: a *Liberator* ad for a Jewett book in 1856 promised that "no anti-slavery novels" were "needed when the truth is so much stronger and stranger than fiction."[50] Contemporary reviews of *Truth Stranger Than Fiction* also register a shift toward sentiment in the reception of Henson's narrative. Whereas in 1849 Peabody characterizes Henson's version of his life as "simple, straightforward, and to the point," a reviewer describes the 1858 version as not only "simple" but also as written in a "style of pure simplicity and genial piety" that "touches the 'sympathetic source of tears' by its unstudied pathos."[51] The quote "unstudied pathos" from Thomas Gray underscores the textual construction of natural feelings at work in *Truth Stranger Than Fiction*.

UNCLE TOM'S STORY OF HIS LIFE: AN AUTOBIOGRAPHY OF THE REV. JOSIAH HENSON (MRS. HARRIET BEECHER STOWE'S "UNCLE TOM"), FROM 1789 TO 1876

Uncle Tom's Story of His Life (1876) is the final major edition of Henson's autobiography and—as is clear from its title—the most embroiled with Stowe's novel. It includes a full chapter titled "Mrs. Stowe's Characters" in which Henson makes a claim that does not appear in the *Key* or his previous autobiographies: George and Eliza Harris "were my particular friends."[52] Henson returned to England late in life, and it was there that this book was printed.[53] As the story goes, most of his friends from the tours in the 1850s were dead, but he fell in with the newspaper publisher John Lobb of the *Christian Age*, who organized the major final lecture tour in Britain and produced a very much expanded account of Henson's later life. According to this edition, the terms of publication were that Henson would keep the money raised at the engagements and Lobb would keep the copyright to the autobiography. Lobb subsequently produced *The Young People's Illustrated Edition of "Uncle Tom's" Story of His Life (from 1789 to 1877)*, a Sunday school book closely based on the autobiography but related in the third person.⁵⁴ The title page advertises a preface by the earl of Shaftesbury and "an address to the young people of Great Britain by 'Uncle Tom,'" and the portrait of Henson is accompanied by a somewhat ghostly image of Lobb, floating as if he had been photoshopped in. According to Winks,

> Lobb had been a religious journalist who knew how to attract an audience: when he took over the faltering *Age* in 1872, its circulation was five thousand, and in four years he raised the figure to eighty thousand. Morley and Sturge asked him to help solicit money for Henson, still in need of assistance at debt ridden Dawn, and in seven months Lobb attracted 3,000 [pounds]. . . . Adding an index and drawing from Henson the promise that Lobb's would be the "only authorized edition" of his life, the editor soon had sales moving up to ninety-six thousand. Lobb's narratives sold a quarter of a million copies and became a Sunday School favourite; but Henson seems to have received very little money from the enterprise and his estate certainly received none.⁵⁵

Uncle Tom's Story of His Life includes a significant amount of new material, such as new chapters about Henson's relation to the novel and his later life. Although Lobb more or less rebranded Henson's story, he would later publish the English edition of *The Life and Times of Frederick Douglass* with only minor changes, "[imposing] British spellings and [deleting] names of persons who would be unknown in England."⁵⁶ Lobb's new edition of Henson's (auto)biography is also a compilation that appends many short pieces by others. In this way, too, it is a collaborative enterprise. In addition to Stowe's introduction, the book contains an advertised introductory note by George Sturge and

S. Morley, Esq., MP; a phrenological "sketch" by Lorenzo Niles Fowler complimentary to Henson's powers; and an appendix on contemporaneous "slavery in the East" from Joseph Cooper's *The Lost Continent* (1857). It also features half-a-dozen testimonials.

TRACKING CHANGES TO THE LIVES

Although changes to key scenes across different editions of Henson's autobiography are obvious in reading by eye, the full scope of these changes emerges more clearly with digital comparison tools. I compared three editions of Henson's autobiography (1849, 1858, 1876), edited and selected by the archivists of the University of North Carolina's Documenting the American South, which according to the website's homepage is "a digital publishing initiative that provides Internet access to texts, images, and audio files related to southern history, literature, and culture."[57] I used two computational tools to compare variants across texts. For line-by-line comparison of variant texts, I used Juxta, developed by a team led by Jerome McGann. Juxta works best with the kind of clean, marked-up texts available at Documenting the American South. For large-scale concordance work, I used Voyant, the flagship suite of distant-reading tools developed by Stéfan Sinclair and Geoffrey Rockwell, to create an overview of the three texts based largely on word frequency.[58] These tools create a new body of textual evidence consisting only of editorial changes—the revisions and expansions that reshaped Henson's story.

The bird's-eye view of the three editions offered by Voyant reveals changes to the autobiography that suggests it was "novelized" in several simple ways.[59] For one thing, the narrative gets longer. As it does, vocabulary density gets progressively lower, and sentence length gets shorter, characteristics often related to an increase in reported speech (dialogue) and associated more closely with fiction than with nonfiction. The most distinctive words (a method for measuring relative word frequency across texts) suggest that the 1858 edition introduces stereotyped depictions of plantation life of the kind that became widely associated with Stowe's novel.

The most distinctive words reflect the introduction of terms that signal plantation dialect as it would come to circulate in minstrel shows: among the words that distinguish the 1858 edition from both the 1849 and the 1876 editions—even when *Uncle Tom's Cabin* is included among the texts—is the word *massa*.[60] In a study of African diasporic literary dialect, David West Brown finds that term to be "particularly indexical": "Used to signal the subordinate position of African diasporic characters, it indicates an imagined consciousness that cheerfully accepts its own subservience."[61] In the 1858 edition, the word appears in Henson's own first-person descriptions of his life under enslavement, writing this imagined consciousness into the narrative even alongside more explicit denunciations of slavery.

The line-by-line comparison of the texts using Juxta revealed many changes that render the 1858 edition not only more sharply antislavery but also more in line with a "comic" minstrel mode, as if it had passed through a filter. For example, in *The Life of Josiah Henson* in 1849 Henson illustrates his early ambition by writing that at fifteen "I was competent to all the work that was done upon the farm, and could run faster and farther, wrestle longer, and jump higher, than anybody about me." The 1858 edition omits the emphasis on work and adds a "shakedown": "I could run faster, wrestle better, and jump higher than anybody about me, and at an evening shakedown in our own or a neighbor's kitchen, my feet became absolutely invisible from the rate at which they moved."[62] The introduction of this fun sits uneasily in the context of a passage in which Henson reflects on his complicity with the violence of slavery. In the 1849 edition, Henson acknowledges that in his efforts to "[improve his] condition," he not only participated in extracting labor by persuading others to work extra hours but also used his position to supply his "fellow sufferers" with meat by "taking from [Riley] some things that he did not give, in part payment of my extra labor."[63] The narrative simply describes both roles, allowing any contradiction to emerge by juxtaposition. The 1858 edition disrupts this uneasy characterization of Henson's position by cutting the reference to "[inducing] others to toil" and adding the following paragraph:

> I have no desire to represent the life of slavery as an experience of nothing but misery. God be praised, that however hedged in by circumstances, the joyful exuberance of youth will bound at times over them all. Ours is a light-hearted race. The sternest and most covetous master cannot frighten or whip the fun out of us; certainly old Riley never did out of me. In those days I had many a merry time, and would have had, had I lived with nothing but moccasins and rattle-snakes in Okafenoke swamp. Slavery did its best to make me wretched; I feel no particular obligation to it; but nature, or the blessed God of youth and joy, was mightier than slavery. Along with memories of miry cabins, frosted feet, weary toil under the blazing sun, curses and blows, there flock in others, of jolly Christmas times, dances before old massa's door for the first drink of egg-nog, extra meat at holiday times, midnight visits to apple orchards, broiling stray chickens, and first-rate tricks to dodge work.[64]

These "jolly," "merry" times have no counterpart in the 1849 narrative. Their closest counterpart might rather be found in minstrelsy and other idealized images of plantation life circulating in the same period.

One helpful feature of the line-to-line comparisons offered by Juxta is that it calls attention to "hot spots," shorter passages where extensive changes have been made. Two of these hot spots align with two of the incidents quoted extensively in Stowe's *Key* and with treatments of Henson ever since—including Clint Smith's article about Henson in *The Atlantic* in September 2023. For Stowe, the incidents are examples of Christian rectitude; for Smith, they force us to confront the "insidious implications" of Henson's fidelity to an "understanding of God's will that had been manipulated by enslavers."[65] The first is a crisis in which Henson could have liberated himself, his family, and eighteen other people from slavery but instead "resists" the opportunity. In *Key*, Stowe characterizes it as a "sublime act of self-renunciation": "He was exceedingly tempted and tried, but his Christian principle was invulnerable. No inducements could lead him to feel that it was right for a Christian to violate a pledge solemnly given, and his influence over the whole band was so great that he took them all with him into Kentucky."[66]

David S. Reynolds describes this incident as Henson's "most self-abnegating moment—when he refuses to claim freedom in Ohio due to Christian honor." Reynolds points out that this refusal is "presented as a sign of strength, not weakness," to argue that "Henson's story casts light on a perennial question about Uncle Tom: Does Christianity produce sheepish passivity? In Henson's narrative and Stowe's response to it, the answer is no."[67] In *The Life of Josiah Henson*, Henson expresses "painful doubts" about his decision but notes simply that "I acted as I thought at the time was best."⁶⁸ In *Truth Stranger Than Fiction*, he elaborates:

> Often since that day has my soul been pierced with bitter anguish at the thought of having been thus instrumental in consigning to the infernal bondage of slavery so many of my fellow-beings. I have wrestled in prayer with God for forgiveness. Having experienced myself the sweetness of liberty, and knowing too well the after misery of numbers of many of them, my infatuation has seemed to me the unpardonable sin. But I console myself with the thought that I acted according to my best light, though the light that was in me was darkness. Those were my days of ignorance. I knew not the glory of free manhood. I knew not that the title-deed of the slave-owner is robbery and outrage.⁶⁹

Here, what Stowe called a "sublime act" in 1853 is recast as "infatuation," a false belief. The passage concludes by suggesting that one must carry out one's personal responsibility against the "darkness" of slavery: "He that is faithful over a little, will alone be faithful over much. Before God, I tried to do my best, and the error of judgment lies at the door of the degrading system under which I had been nurtured."⁷⁰ *Truth Stranger Than Fiction* promotes an ideal of Christian rectitude *and* criticizes a Christianity that would prioritize the false rights of an enslaver.⁷¹

The 1858 edition also makes substantial changes to Stowe's second example of Henson's "disinterestedness" by transforming not the moment itself but its context.⁷² Henson describes a kind of divine intervention at a moment he had planned to commit murder to win freedom. In *The Life of Josiah Henson*, Henson—trapped on a steamboat on the way to the slave market in New Orleans—makes a plan to kill his four captors with an axe and escape. At the last minute, "suddenly the thought came to me, 'What! commit murder! and you a Christian?' I had not called it murder before. It was self-defence,—it was preventing others from murdering me,—it was justifiable, it was even praiseworthy. But now, all at once, the truth burst upon me that it was a crime."[73]

In both editions, Henson further reflects "that it was better to die with a Christian's hope, and a quiet conscience, than to live with the incessant recollection of a crime that would destroy the value of life."[74] The changes that Juxta identifies are not actually in the scene itself but in the material that precedes it. In *The Life of Josiah Henson*, Henson's plan to escape is prompted by an encounter with his former companions—the people he allowed to be kept enslaved on the previous journey: "I had met, on the passage, with some of my Maryland acquaintance who had been sold off to this region; and their haggard and wasted appearance told a piteous story of excessive labor and insufficient food. I said to myself, 'If this is to be my lot, I cannot survive it long. I am not so young as these men, and if it has brought them to such a condition, it will soon kill me.'"[75]

In *Truth Stranger Than Fiction*, this reunion with the people he had allowed to be kept in bondage prompts only remorse:

> Four years in an unhealthy climate and under a hard master had done the ordinary work of twenty. Their cheeks were literally caved in with starvation and disease, and their bodies infested with vermin. No hell could equal the misery they described as their daily portion. Toiling half naked in malarious marshes, under a burning, maddening sun, and poisoned by swarms of musquitoes [sic] and black gnats, they looked forward to death as their only deliverance. Some of them fairly cried at seeing me there, and at thought of the fate which they felt awaited me.

Their worst fears of being sold down South had been more than realized. I went away sick at heart, and to this day the sight of that wretched group haunts me.[76]

This passage collects the tropes about the South and concludes by turning people into ghosts. Their condition leaves Henson "sick at heart" instead of clear-eyed about the danger he is in. It thus shifts the narrative focus from Henson's conclusion that to be "sold down South" will kill him to a depiction of a group of suffering victims of slavery. In *The Life of Josiah Henson*, Henson's recognition that his life is at stake links the moment of his greatest complicity (his decision to keep his companions enslaved) with his decision to become a revolutionist (in creating a plan to break free). In *Truth Stranger Than Fiction*, this self-determination is broken into two episodes, removing the analytical link between them. If, as Winks argues, Henson "became a tool to be used in a propaganda campaign" in the 1858 edition, it happens through the transformation of the framework around the original material as well as through changes to the original account.[77]

A line-by-line comparison of different editions of a book not only lets you track more subtle changes at the book level but also reveals which parts did not change and which parts changed the most. In the case of Henson's autobiography, this comparison shows that the bulk of the changes comprised new material incorporated into the text rather than rewritings of the original text. A text published after Stowe's novel might well have meant heightening key tropes (Henson on the auction block as a child; his scene of conversion), but there are actually very few changes to the prose of Henson's 1849 account; the narration of his life in Canada is reprinted almost verbatim.[78]

One substantial addition establishes a key element of Henson's story: two new chapters describe his involvement in the

Underground Railroad, "Conducting Slaves to Canada" and "Second Journey on the Underground Railroad" (twenty pages, or about 10 percent of the total material in the second edition). *Truth Stranger Than Fiction*, then, is both the volume in which Henson is first identified as Stowe's "original of Uncle Tom" but also his first appearance as the man W. E. B. Du Bois would call a "black revolutionist" in *Black Reconstruction* (1935). The important retrospective re-creation of Stowe's Uncle Tom as a living man and active leader is captured in the title of H. A. Tanser's article on Henson: "Josiah Henson, the Moses of His People" (1943). The transformation of Uncle Tom the character "back" into Josiah Henson the man is also evident in the title of Jessie Beattie's book *Black Moses: The Real Uncle Tom* (1957).[79]

The second major addition is four new chapters about Henson's work to raise money for the Dawn Settlement through his trips to England (about 18 percent of the 1858 edition). Henson's description of his work in Dawn is greatly expanded in this edition. The latter part of the story traces Henson's transformation into a community patriarch and his visit to exhibit timber at the World's Fair in 1851 as the only Black exhibitor, where he first met Queen Victoria. One review of *Truth Stranger Than Fiction* in 1858 notes that "on the shores of the dividing river a friendly guide points him to 'free soil;' not under the canopy of our boasted democratic cap of liberty, but beneath the shadow of the British scepter!"[80]

The edits to previously published material throughout the 1876 edition, *Uncle Tom's Story of His Life*, are light but very suggestive. Per Voyant, the most distinctive words in the 1876 edition are *colour* and *labour*, marking an Anglicization that underscores how Henson's narrative was reshaped from the outside. As dull as these changes might seem, they open up two interesting topics that merit future investigation: first, Henson's status in the colonial context of Canada in the late nineteenth century (as one reviewer put it in 1870, Uncle Tom "is not in heaven, but in Canada") and, second, the effect of his celebrity on the postbellum London "Tom" shows of the later 1870s.[81] Hannah-Rose Murray argues that Henson both benefited from and sparked a renewed interest in minstrelsy. [82] His late-century celebrity is from one angle a mark of British investment in the idea of the South.[83] Winks argues that Henson's story continues to serve histories of British imperialism more broadly and Canadian disavowals of anti-Blackness in particular "as Canadians came increasingly to assign Henson's role to Tom and as the myth of the North Star, the Underground Railroad, and the Fugitives' haven 'under the lion's paw' . . . grew in the post–Civil War years."[84]

When Stowe identified Henson as the "original" of Uncle Tom, his story seemed to become at once the novel's origin and its product, an instance of the *Uncle Tom* mania characterized by Sarah Meer as the commercialization of antislavery politics. Stowe's narrative had a complex effect on Black antislavery speakers, as Meer notes: "Like slave narrators in the United States, black fugitives and antislavery lecturers received more public attention in Britain as a result of Stowe's book, but their new recognition also came with the risk of seeing their lives conflated with her fiction." Meer points out that both Solomon Northrup and Frederick Douglass corrected *A Key to* Uncle Tom's Cabin in their narratives issued after its publication.[85] Stowe wrote the article "Sojourner Truth, the Libyan Sibyl" for the *Atlantic Monthly* in 1863, an essay in which she claimed that the statue of that name was inspired by her anecdote about meeting with Truth in 1852. For Truth biographer Margaret Washington, the essay's work is clear: "Stowe's literary Truth was an oddity, speaking in a droll, thick, almost incomprehensible dialect, uttering queer homilies and phrases, and expressing herself with gullibility and foolish reciprocity. Stowe also saturated her 'Sibyl' with naïve religious faith.... Stowe's 'Libyan Sibyl' was not only a fiction; it was Sojourner Truth in blackface."[86] In response to Stowe's inaccurate anecdotal account of their meeting, Truth wrote a letter clarifying that (1) she'd never say "honey," (2) her parents weren't from Africa, and (3) what *was* true was that she had an autobiography and that people would soon be able to buy her picture. Truth made Stowe's essay the occasion of announcing to the press that she would be selling *cartes de visites*.[87] If Stowe wrote about Black celebrities to increase her own notoriety, the print record shows how Douglass, Northup, Truth, and Henson countered Stowe's appropriative tactic with a "truer" story.

Henson did and did not displace Stowe as the literary celebrity most closely associated with *Uncle Tom's Cabin*. Stowe pointed outward to document her fiction, acknowledging her own distance from the material she describes. In citing Henson, she opened a space to recognize a better authority, and he became the "real Uncle Tom." For Delany, Henson the man demonstrated the fundamentally derivative quality of Stowe's knowledge and ultimately of her unwillingness to support anything like equality. When Stowe pointed to Henson as documentary source, Henson owned it, even as he claimed *not* to be Uncle Tom. You could think that Henson was a spin-off of Uncle Tom, and people have, but the critical nineteenth-century perspective emphasizes, simply, that he was the *original*.

Henson's fame was amplified and distorted not only by its relation to Stowe's novel but also by the cultural stereotypes the novel draws on. Here and in the following chapter, I consider how nonfiction and novels that purport to share an historical source create a kind of mutual heightening between both texts—and the figure of the author that unites them. Henson's identification with Uncle Tom makes one element of this "mutual heightening" deadly obvious: his fame was animated not only by Stowe's claim that he was the source of the novel but also by the broader cultural narratives about race and Christianity that gave that novel currency. In *Uncle Tom: From Martyr to Traitor* (2018), Spingarn argues that the figure of "Uncle Tom" that circulates now as "a widely recognized epithet for a black person deemed so subservient to whites that he betrays his race" is "as much a product of black discourse as of the white imagination, a figure drawn upon and shaped by fundamental debates within the black community over who should represent the race and how it should be represented."[88] The traitor that Uncle Tom became has its novelistic origins in a figure who was a martyr. Henson represented an alternative history in his own time and outlived the novel. In Du Bois's *Black Reconstruction*, Henson briefly appears with Harriet Tubman as a Black revolutionist. For Smith's essay "The Man Who Became Uncle Tom" in late 2023, Henson is human, among the "generations of people . . . forced to make a series of impossible decisions within [the institution of slavery]." If Henson's identity in his own lifetime was shaped by his connection with Uncle Tom—as articulated through life writing and public speaking—his legacy has continued to develop in histories and biographical accounts.

5

A TRUE HISTORY OF *JANE EYRE*

The Collaborative Posthumous Creation

of Charlotte Brontë

In 1858, when the life of Josiah Henson was being promoted as a kind of corrective to *Uncle Tom's Cabin*, reviewers of Elizabeth Gaskell's *The Life of Charlotte Brontë* (1857) were widely reading the biography as a narrative key to *Jane Eyre* (1847). The stakes of both texts could not have been more different: Henson's life spoke to a direct experience of enslavement and his perspective as a Christian leader, whereas Gaskell's biography spoke to Brontë's roles as a woman and author—and to the question of who might be the original of Mr. Rochester. Despite the stark contrast in the political stakes of these texts, both books reveal how the figure of the author emerges though disparate but related genres. Turning to Charlotte Brontë (1816–1855) shows the forces of literary celebrity at work in an iconic example of literary mythmaking about authorship outside of explicit antislavery discourse.

One straightforward connection between the figures of Henson and Brontë is that they emerged not only in relation to Uncle Tom and Jane Eyre but also in relation to Stowe and Gaskell—who knew each other as literary celebrity women writers of social reform and who corresponded for years. Gaskell and Stowe first met during Stowe's lecture tour in 1853 following the success of *Uncle Tom's Cabin*.[1] Amanda Shaw traces their letters to reveal how "public-facing concerns were cultivated through private relations" among professional women writers. Shaw analyzes Stowe's letter of introduction to Gaskell that she wrote for Mary Webb in 1856, a free woman of color known for her literary readings and for whom Stowe developed a version of *Uncle Tom* expressly designed for public reading, *The Christian Slave* (1855).[2] This letter illustrates the intersections among public lectures, print forms, and personal relationships. As Shaw observes, "As a well-connected public figure in England, Gaskell would have been in an ideal position not only to do this 'personal favor' for Stowe but also to lend a visible hand to the anti-slavery cause."[3] In the focus on the relationship between two outsize figures, a third celebrity emerges, an antislavery speaker whose work demonstrates the intersection of drama and literature in the lecture circuit.

Brontë was connected to these more personal professional networks through Gaskell and Martineau, and because of the reach of transatlantic antislavery networks she also wrote in the context of social reform literature in general and antislavery discourse in particular.[4] Julia Sun-Joo Lee traces how language and tropes from the slave narrative illuminate *Jane Eyre*, calling attention to Brontë's "emphasis on literacy and freedom, dispossession and exile, in conjunction with its potent combination of autobiography, history, and gothic fiction."[5] In a letter to her publisher in 1848 following the publication of *Jane Eyre*, Brontë rejected the idea of writing about social problems or "Situations," as Frances Trollope did in *The Life and Adventures of Michael Armstrong, the Factory Boy* (1840), but she did go on to publish a factory novel of her own, *Shirley*, in 1849.[6] In 1852, she wrote a letter to her publisher, George Smith, praising *Uncle*

Tom's Cabin.[7] To the history of relationships among individuals and the circulation of shaping forms, I add a consideration of how the figure of the author emerged from the coincidence of competing accounts of their lives.

Elizabeth Gaskell's *The Life of Charlotte Brontë*, like the later lives of Henson, is predicated on the assumptions that fact becomes more interesting when you can show that it inspired fiction and that fiction becomes more interesting when you can show that it was based on fact. Literary characters such as Uncle Tom and Jane Eyre came to be constituted by autobiographical and biographical accounts of individuals as well as by eponymous novels because the novels were understood to draw freely from real life. Literary celebrity emerged from an amalgamation of fictional and nonfictional forms. Seeing these texts and their authors in relation highlights something evident: that celebrity is shaped and powered by familiar cultural narratives. Nonfictional and fictional accounts might amplify the figure of an author in part because of the cultural narratives—or stereotypes—that the stories promulgate.

The Rise of Celebrity Authorship asks what it means to bring broad perspectives on dispersed literary culture to bear on stellar figures and their most famous works, and its final turn is to one of the most familiar celebrity/novel pairs of the period: Charlotte Brontë and *Jane Eyre*. Using the framework established in this book, I decentralize the figure/text dyad to illuminate the many people and texts just adjacent to them. This chapter shifts away from antislavery to show the broader payoff of the method of studying celebrity authorship as it was refracted through fiction-adjacent texts: Gaskell's *Life of Brontë* but also the implicit claims to nonfiction in Brontë's novel, which, after all, was titled *Jane Eyre: An Autobiography*.

In an essay on Charlotte Brontë in 1897, Margaret Oliphant refers to work on Brontë as "a little literature of its own," observing that "scarcely Scott has called forth more continual droppings of elucidation, explanation, remark." Oliphant's essay, "The Sisters Brontë," leads a volume of essays on women novelists by women novelists, *Women Novelists of Queen Victoria's Reign*, and it leads with Charlotte: "The effect produced upon the general mind by the appearance of Charlotte Brontë in literature, and afterwards by the record of her life when that was over, is one which it is nowadays somewhat difficult to understand."[8] In underscoring that the Brontë effect was produced through texts by her *and* by the "record of her life when that was over," Oliphant shows how the effect was created by the resonance between life and work. Lucasta Miller's investigation of the "Brontë myth" is in part an analysis of how consistently the lives of the Brontës have overshadowed their work. Miller describes the relationship among lives, works, and readers like this: "If the distinction between history and fiction was not always clearly marked, this also reflected the fact that Charlotte had used personal experience as the raw material for creative writing. Once this became widely recognized, the consequent attempts of enthusiasts to trace real life models for every character and place in the Brontë oeuvre were frequently naively literal, and could have some odd results: Clement Shorter even met an old man in America who claimed to be the younger brother of Mr. Rochester."[9]

Such naively literal readings were not limited to enthusiasts in the period. According to most accounts, fictionality—stories that do not purport to be true—was firmly in place as a norm of realist fiction by the middle of the nineteenth century. Yet literary reviews and biographical accounts of Brontë reveal a widespread theoretical assumption that tracing real-life models was a valid reading practice. The categories "autobiography," "memoir," "autobiographical fiction," and "literary biography" remain clear examples of how easily truth and fiction collapse into each other. In the nineteenth century, fictional and nonfictional accounts of life stories were so closely woven together that the difference between them was hardly discernible. In one recent account, Alison Booth notes that in the later nineteenth century "autobiography frequently masquerades as fiction," and she uses *Jane Eyre* to show how Victorian novels can "take the form of first person life-writing."[10] Linda H. Peterson includes discussions of Brontë's novel and Elizabeth Barrett Browning's *Aurora Leigh* (1856) in her book *Traditions of Victorian Women's Autobiography* (2001). She suggests that Brontë herself understood her text to circulate as autobiography, citing Harriet Martineau's account in the *Autobiography* (1877) that Brontë described the circumstances of her childhood as "told or not told" in *Jane Eyre*.[11] The distinction between fact and fiction, author and narrator, was (much) less clear in the nineteenth century than we sometimes think, and my central contention here is that in the case of *Jane Eyre* and *The Life of Charlotte Brontë*, what Catherine Gallagher frames as the imaginative possibility of telling "nobody's story" is overshadowed by a readerly obsession with whose story is being told.[12]

In turning to Gaskell's account of Charlotte Brontë as Jane Eyre, I turn to a well-established feminist critical tradition for reading the biography as primarily one novelist's account of another. Linda K. Hughes and Michael Lund restore Gaskell's biography to its discursive context to demonstrate how Gaskell's "representation of Brontë is . . . self-defense as well as defense, self-advertising as well as rescue of a beloved friend and sister novelist." Gabriele Helms frames Gaskell's *Life* as a "coincidence of biography and autobiography."[13] Gaskell, like Brontë, was implicated in the gendered narratives about authorship that she details in the biography. In the context of my work here, it is also clear that the biography is kin to the celebrity collaborations in the gift books described in chapter 3 insofar as it traded on Brontë's fame as well as on Gaskell's. Gaskell presents herself explicitly as a friend and implicitly—Deirdre d'Albertis argues—as a rival to Brontë, and her *Life* has been an important document in Victorian ideas about women of letters.[14] In *A Literature of Their Own* ([1978] 1998), Elaine Showalter argues that "Gaskell helped create the myth of the novelist as tragic heroine, a myth for which readers had been prepared by *Jane Eyre*."[15] The jacket copy of Juliet R. V. Barker's carefully documented account of the Brontës claims that it sets out to "demolish" the myths established in part through Gaskell's biography.[16] Brenda R. Weber argues that Gaskell's biography is part of a broader pattern of studies of famous women writers that depended on "familiar intimacy fostered in both media accounts and fictional representations." Weber shows how Gaskell deployed the "representation of celebrity to destabilize Anglo-American prescriptive norms about gender in the last half of the nineteenth century." In this first work published under her own name, Gaskell "forms a model of literary celebrity that occupies the same (female) body as the genius writer, thus serving as an important legitimation of the 'public woman.'"[17] The role of literary tourism in Gaskell's text and the afterlife of Haworth Parsonage as a pilgrimage site that it helped to inaugurate have been important touchstones for studies in literary tourism and understanding the "homes and haunts" books I discuss in chapter 2.[18] Deborah Wynne gathers and analyzes a "body of writing" by Victorian "Charlotte cult" visitors to Haworth from Gaskell to Woolf—whose first publication was her essay "Haworth, November 1904."[19]

In the next section, I offer a study of the buzz about Charlotte Brontë as Jane Eyre as it appeared in retrospect and after Brontë's death through reviews of Gaskell's biography that used scandals to theorize the relation between truth and fiction in Brontë's novels. One of these reviews deploys Brontë's and Gaskell's treatment of "Lowood school" to make a broader argument about the admissibility of fiction as evidence in the court of public opinion about an institution. At the end of the chapter, I move out to the broader array of biographies and edited compilations that succeeded the flurry of responses to Gaskell's biography, including Margaret Oliphant's essay in 1897. Like Brontë and Gaskell, Oliphant was a novelist, but she was also known in the period for writing biographies and literary criticism. In their analysis of the professional context of Oliphant's essay on "the sisters Brontë," Alison Booth, Isabel Bielat, Lloyd Sy, and Valerie Voight note that Oliphant framed her decision to contribute to *Women Novelists of Queen Victoria's Reign* as weighed against a "less prestigious but more certain competing offer."[20] Although critics have persuasively argued for the professional context of the most apparently "personal" elements of Gaskell's *Life*, Oliphant's essay better illuminates the professional woman author in a literary marketplace rather than against ideals of femininity or creativity. In framing Brontë as a retiring, tragic figure, Gaskell followed Brontë's lead in her presentation of her sisters' work, so I also consider Brontë's own biographical and editorial work done in connection with her sisters' novels. This is a chapter about the Brontë industry as it emerged in and around her novels before and after her death—it's not really about Brontë and maybe not even really about Gaskell. Rather, it picks up on the writings of other people working in the little literature around Brontë.

The singly authored, one-figure biography, such as *The Life of Charlotte Brontë*, recognizable now as "literature" because of its author and subject, was exceptional in its time, as Booth's work has made clear. In her tally of the number of times specific figures appear in Victorian collective biographies of women, Charlotte Brontë is the top literary figure from 1850 to 1870 (eight biographies) and from 1880 to 1900 (fifteen biographies).[21] In the spirit of Booth's work, I must point out that the statistics she cites here demonstrate not only Brontë's centrality but also the many biographical sketches that circulated in general.

The storytellers of the Brontë myth emerge as the people who wrote or adapted or reprinted the twenty-three versions of her life printed before 1900. Biography—particularly of the magpielike, lives-and-letters kind—bears the traces of its collaborative production more clearly than the novel. Such literary mythmaking, as Weber argues, has much to tell us about individual women thinking about individual women in order to create new possible narratives for women writers.

"WHO *COULD* HAVE WRITTEN THIS QUEER BOOK?" A RETROSPECT

Initial reviews of *Jane Eyre* were notoriously preoccupied with the relation between the heroine and the gender—and life experience—of the author. Gaskell's biography promises the kind of intimate author portraiture that gave currency to collections of author autographs and sketches of their homes, but it also responds to widespread interest in Charlotte Brontë's sex life. The most notorious formulation of this curiosity is the review of *Jane Eyre* from 1848 that Algernon Swinburne would characterize as "fork-tongued" almost thirty years later in *A Note on Charlotte Brontë* (1877).[22] Charlotte Brontë responded to this review in her unpublished preface to *Shirley* the same year the review was published and, as others have argued, implicitly in her biographical sketches of Emily and Anne in her collection of their works in 1850. Gaskell responded to it in the biography. "Without entering into the question whether the power of the writing be above [a woman author], or the vulgarity below her," this review by Elizabeth Rigby (later Lady Eastlake) argues the novel can have been written only by a man but concludes that "if we ascribe [*Jane Eyre*] to a woman at all, we have no alternative but to ascribe it to one who has, for some sufficient reason, long forfeited the society of her own sex."[23] The review disavows a rumor that ensued after Brontë's dedication of the second edition to William Makepeace Thackeray: that *Jane Eyre* was "Becky Sharpe's" revenge. In this gossipy narrative—which, as Brontë pointed out in her response, the review both denies and propagates—the character of Jane Eyre is not only as real as Becky Sharpe but as real as Thackeray.[24] By the time of Brontë's death, the strong suggestion among the novel's contemporaries was that it told all too much about the meaning of the life in its focus on the heroine's desire. If Elizabeth Gaskell wrote a biography to set the record straight about Charlotte Brontë the woman, the primary narrative she challenged was the set of extratextual rumors and assumptions about Brontë based on the "autobiography" that circulated as *Jane Eyre* and later *Villette* (1853).[25] Because *Jane Eyre* turned out to have been written by a woman, the relation between the facts of her life and the narratives of novels was an especially interesting question for readers of her work and Gaskell's biography.

What was the relation between the person who wrote the stories and the available stories of what women could be?

At the time of Brontë's death in 1855, her identity as the author of *Jane Eyre* was known. Several reviews of Gaskell's *Life* begin by recalling public curiosity about the identity of Currer Bell, identified on the book as its author when *Jane Eyre* came out in 1847. A review of Gaskell's *Life* for *National Magazine* reflects back on what it had been like not to know: "Who *could* have written this queer book? Man or woman, old or young; a masculine mind gifted with unusually subtle perceptions; or a 'strong-minded' woman, whom life had embittered, whom experience had hardened,—who *could* be the author?"[26] By offering itself as the definitive answer to this question, the *Life* is a snapshot of the roman à clef—and of the formal and legal problems this genre posed—in the nineteenth century. Sean Latham's account of the roman à clef opposes it to the realist novel, arguing that the roman à clef "trades, after all, on the inability to distinguish fact from fiction and thereby disrupts the aesthetic autonomy through which the realist novel develops."[27]

In a way, then, the *Life* of a controversial and popular authoress promises to work like one of those "keys" to potentially libelous political allegory that figure in Gallagher's account of fictionality in *Nobody's Story* (1994). There, the indices that point fictional names to historical counterparts attest to "the excess of representation in relation to reference" in political allegory, while the very "routineness of their production testifies to the period's desire to open every book to some extra-textual reality, to read everything double."[28] The eager reception of Gaskell's *Life* demonstrates the durability of this desire. Despite the separation of a novel like *Jane Eyre* from historical events, readers continued to seek not only verisimilitude in novels but also verifiable facts about their events. With Henson, readers wanted the extratextual reality of his life, and they wanted him to be a double of the fictional Uncle Tom.[29]

The Victorian twist to the story is that as a key to Brontë's works (Maria Brontë is Helen Burns, Emily Brontë is Shirley Keeldar, etc.), Gaskell's *Life* is notably deficient: Gaskell suppressed Brontë's letters to Constantin Héger, her teacher in Brussels from 1842 to 1844, whom, in the spirit of this discussion, I might name M. Paul of *Villette*. The effect of Gaskell's choice to distance Brontë's heroes from this man was to draw a clear line between life and art. The only positively identified "original" of M. Paul in the *Life* turns out to be Thackeray, who once asked Brontë's opinion of a lecture, which, Gaskell writes, "she mentioned to me not many days afterwards, adding remarks almost identical with those which I subsequently read in 'Villette,' where a similar action on the part of M. Paul Emanuel is related."[30]

In order to baffle the double-seeking public, the *Life* creates a myth around the family life of Charlotte Brontë to shroud and soften the myth of Charlotte Brontë as Jane Eyre or Lucy Snowe. The *Life* seeks to contextualize—even to apologize for—for the fictional life of Charlotte Brontë that began with *Jane Eyre* by offering an account of Brontë's imaginative development in which the things that didn't happen are as important as the things that did. Gaskell's *Life* and its reviews foreground the moral and aesthetic questions of how best to represent a true story: by imaginative representation or by extensive documentation. That question pertains to both literary biography and fictional practice.

In the biography, Gaskell's suppression of Héger becomes implicit evidence for the triumph of imaginative representation.

Gaskell acknowledges the Rochester figure only in connection with "one or two" men Brontë had known "since early girlhood," while reviewers of the *Life* celebrated Brontë's creative genius in creating that hero with no real-life prototype.[31] Hughes and Lund argue, "Not only did Gaskell clear Brontë from the charges of coarseness or impropriety, but in doing so she also expanded the claims for genius in Brontë, who could create out of sheer brilliance rather than personal experience."[32] They quote a *Saturday Review* article on Gaskell's *Life* that defends the reviewer's right to have read the book in order to discover the original of *Jane Eyre*'s hero, claiming that the desire to know is not owing to the "vulgar curiosity which likes to hear the story of every woman's heart" but to "that anxiety which men in all ages have felt, and will feel, to ascertain the mystery of genius. . . . It was an inquiry as legitimate as it was interesting, how Charlotte Bronte [sic] came to draw the character of Mr. Rochester."[33] Here, the yearning to learn about Brontë's love life is both "natural" and "legitimate": curiosity about the woman is transmuted into "anxiety . . . to ascertain the mystery of genius." Twenty years after that review, Algernon Swinburne would write in *A Note on Charlotte Brontë* (1877) that Brontë "doubtless" had models for Madame Beck and Miss Fanshawe in *Villette* and "must have had some kind of model" for M. Paul, "but how she came to conceive and finally to fashion [Rochester] that perfect study of noble and faultful and suffering manhood remains one of the most insoluble riddles ever set by genius as a snare or planned as a maze for the judgment of any lesser intelligence than her own."[34] The discussion of a hero drawn from nothing slides quickly into a discussion of the material that was drawn from life.

The *Saturday Review* essay makes a clear case in favor of imaginative representation, noting that Brontë drew on her genius for Rochester and on her environment for more general inspiration, but also that when we "descend still lower, and seek merely for the origin of particular incidents in her fictions," we can see Brontë use the "facts of experience." The "creative" genius exists in a dialectic with the responsibilities of writers living in the same world as their neighbors: "We must acknowledge that the right of novelists to draw such very accurate and unfavourable pictures of individuals with whom the intimacies of private life have brought them in contact, is more than questionable."[35] For the reviewer, the lowest and most ethically problematic form of fiction is that which is most closely based on life.

If the reviewer argues that Brontë is a genius insofar as the novels are not drawn from life, Gaskell argues that Brontë is a genius insofar as they are. Gaskell exhaustively documents life at the real-life original of the boarding school attended by the Brontës as a way to authorize Brontë's fictionalized treatment of it and to create through the biography a truer story about what happened there. Gaskell's book is not just next to Brontë's novel—it is inside the novel. If Henson brought Stowe's novel to life by presenting himself as the original that preceded and exceeded it, Gaskell's text reanimates *Jane Eyre* with the life history of its posthumous author.

The biography implicitly asks what constituted the "true" story of *Jane Eyre*: the truth of its fictional narrative or the truth of that narrative's historical antecedents? The *Life* neither straightforwardly defends the factual accuracy of Brontë's *Jane Eyre* by adducing biographical evidence nor argues for the irrelevance of biographical evidence to a reading of the novel. Rather, it finds in the biography of Brontë a justification for the transformation of historical fact into novelistic fiction through biographically determined but idiosyncratic perspective.[36]

THE LICENSE OF MODERN NOVELISTS: COWAN BRIDGE SCHOOL, PUBLIC INSTITUTIONS, AND PUBLIC ABUSES

In Gaskell's account of Cowan Bridge, the school that the Brontë siblings attended, extensive documentation of the "true facts" behind *Jane Eyre* coexists with an aesthetic commitment to the legitimacy of individual perception. Gaskell uses the types of evidence that signaled credibility in early forms of the novel—letters, dates, and anecdotes—to retell the story of Jane Eyre's childhood but then uses strategies integral to realist fiction—an opposition between interior experience and external circumstance—to set the historical record straight. She portrays Brontë's interiority through the written record of Brontë's letters as against a set of facts described with an ethnographer's distance. Here, factual testimony works according to the conventions of realism by privileging the story of Brontë's psychological development over the "particular incidents" recorded in the fictions.

While contemporary readers of *Jane Eyre* were extremely interested in the story behind its authorship and its heroine, it bears reiterating that *Jane Eyre* comes to us as an intimate depiction of a living, suffering mind (what Terry Castle, in a review of Juliet Barker's biography of the Brontës, calls "a fiercely intimate, self-dramatizing feel"[37]). George Henry Lewes's praise of the novel in *Fraser's* in 1847 is about a more familiar notion of realism as faithful to a higher reality: "[*Jane Eyre*] is an autobiography,—not, perhaps, in the naked facts and circumstances, but in the actual suffering and experience."[38] Against Lewes's dismissal of "naked facts," what does it mean for Gaskell to document the "naked facts" so extensively? The *Life* is a literary biography in an oddly literal sense when it serves to supplement or document the materials in Brontë's novels: when it illustrates the truth behind the fiction. Gaskell develops Brontë's institutional suffering at her school in comparison to Jane Eyre's experience at Lowood School. Gaskell's account of what really happened at "Cowan's [sic] Bridge (Lowood) School," as a chapter subhead in the *Life* had it, is one way in which the *Life* presents itself as a return to fact from Brontë's fictions.[39] Brontë believed that her two eldest sisters died young because weakened by the terrible conditions of the school all four girls attended. Jane Eyre is sent to just such a school, where her friend Helen Burns dies. Gaskell writes, "I need hardly say, that Helen Burns is as exact a transcript of Maria Brontë as Charlotte's wonderful power of reproducing character could give," and classmates thought they recognized by the scathing portrait of the teacher Miss Scatcherd in *Jane Eyre* "an unconsciously avenging sister of the sufferer."[40] To understand Jane Eyre as the avatar of Charlotte Brontë means recognizing the blood tie that "really" bound her to Helen Burns. The *Life* can flow from fiction to fact because of the way *Jane Eyre* flowed from fact to fiction.

The conflation of person and character and the identification of Jane Eyre with Charlotte Brontë drove many then, as now, to Gaskell's biography—there to discover that it was all really that way, or if it wasn't quite that way, it must have felt that way to Brontë. The narrative form of Gaskell's non-novel based on facts is ultimately the story of how Brontë came to see the world the way she did. The notion of fictionality that emerges is based not only on a much more integrated notion of author and narrator but also on a set of surprisingly consistent expectations that readers brought to fictional and nonfictional forms. David Amigoni argues against a tendency to characterize a "one-dimensional literary 'tradition' for writing about biography and autobiography," when "complex, overlapping contested constituencies such as class, gender, familial and domestic relations ... contest 'literature' as a source of identification."[41] Readers weren't reading only a nonfictional account of Brontë—an argument about women writers as daughters, sisters, and wives and a complement to *Jane Eyre*; they were also reading travel writing and an institutional analysis of a private boarding school.

Gaskell's documentation of objective facts about Cowan Bridge at the time Brontë attended the school suggests that things were even worse there than at Lowood—legitimizing Jane Eyre's experience—even as it offers an alternative analysis of the institution's failings, attributing them to the poor management rather than to the cruel and despotic tendencies of its founder. Gaskell emphasizes the childishness of Brontë's impressions of Cowan Bridge that underwrote her later portrait of the school: "The pictures, ideas, and conceptions of character received into the mind of the child of eight years old, were destined to be reproduced in fiery words a quarter of a century afterwards."[42] This statement might equally apply to Charlotte Brontë and Jane Eyre except that Charlotte was even younger and sicklier than Jane when at Cowan Bridge. Here as elsewhere in the section on Cowan Bridge, Gaskell documents the account that appears in *Jane Eyre*—and then tops it. Gaskell includes an eyewitness account of the "Miss Scatcherd" figure treating Maria Brontë perhaps even more cruelly than Helen Burns was treated in the novel and asserts that the food at Cowan Bridge was even worse than at its fictional counterpart.[43] In *Jane Eyre*, Jane tucks into the porridge only to find that, "the first edge of hunger blunted, I perceived I had got in hand a nauseous mess: burnt porridge is almost as bad as rotten potatoes: famine itself soon sickens over it"; in the *Life*, the porridge was "too often sent up, not merely burnt, but with offensive fragments of other substances discernable in it."[44] The burnt porridge features in both accounts, but the evidence signifies very differently in each: rather than supporting a firsthand account of being hungry yet unable to eat, Gaskell's porridge is evidence of a bad cook, who is in turn evidence of Rev. Carus Wilson's poor management of the school. Gaskell's focus is institutional: she attests that the ingredients were decent and that, having seen the "dietary," she knew it was "neither bad, nor unwholesome; nor, on the whole, was it wanting in variety."[45] Evaluated by her competent eye, the problem was in the execution, not in the plan.

The case has been made that Gaskell, in covering the same ground as Brontë, would necessarily have to offer a competing account of the events. Reviews of Gaskell's treatment, however, emphasize its continuity with Brontë's representation. If Gaskell erred in her corrective treatment of Cowan Bridge, Charlotte's artistic "genius"—in Gaskell's own phrase—had done worse by it. The *Christian Observer*, in responding to Gaskell's biography, took the opportunity to argue that "one of the great evils, as well as crimes" of *Jane Eyre* is its treatment of the Rev. Carus Wilson. The review argues that, despite the fact that *Shirley* was condemned for being based on invention instead of experience, "all Miss Brontë's stories have the same mixture of fact and fiction. The various incidents are founded upon facts of which the author had heard, or refer to scenes which she herself had witnessed; but which are so enlarged, coloured, modified, exaggerated by the hand of the artist, as to make it impossible to distinguish truth from falsehood."[46] In the question of painting from life, the problem was not that Brontë worked from facts of scenes but that her depiction of them was larger, more vibrant, altered, and altogether stronger than what was. A "great evil" of her novels was the persistence of fact into fiction, unconstrained by the norms of factual narrative.

Another review by James Fitzjames Stephen (jurist, brother to Leslie) connected Gaskell's defense of Brontë with fictions that sought to engage with real-world problems: novels founded on fact. In July 1857, he included a discussion of the exposé of "Lowood" in Gaskell's biography *and* Brontë's novel in a review that also included novels by Charles Reade (*It Is Never Too Late to Mend* [1856]) and Charles Dickens (*Little Dorrit* [1855–1857]). Stephen understands Brontë's "crime," like that of the novelists of purpose, to be the drawing of material from life without giving it fair treatment. The novel by Brontë and the biography by Gaskell—like novels by Reade and Dickens—unfairly pilloried "the institutions which give method and order to free government."[47] Lisa Rodensky argues that Stephen's objections to "fictional" treatments of history cluster around the representation of the unknowable inner lives of historical actors.[48] He criticizes how Brontë's novel and Gaskell's ostensibly nonfictional *Life* bring "public institutions and public abuses" into "the domain of private charity and the recesses of private life." Stephen quotes, with added emphasis, Gaskell's account of a half-apology from Brontë for the "vivid picture" of Cowan Bridge/Lowood:

> Miss Bronte more than once said to me, that she should not have written what she did of Lowood in "Jane Eyre," if she had thought the place would have been so immediately identified with Cowan Bridge, although there was not a word in her account of the institution but what was true at the time when she knew it; she also said that *she had not considered it necessary, in a work of fiction, to state every particular with the impartiality* that might be required in a court of justice, nor to seek out motives, and make allowance for human feelings, as she might have done,

if dispassionately analysing the conduct of those who had the superintendence of the institution.[49]

For Stephen, the idea that fiction doesn't have to play fair is a perfect expression of how novelists justify the representation of persons and institutions without benefit of "dispassionate analysis": "there is a very wide distinction between creations wrought up to the true ideal, and attempts to copy life by throwing a false and distorted light on real incidents."[50] What begins in the *Life* as an apology for a "partial" account—that Brontë would not have "written what she did" about Cowan Bridge had she known how quickly it would be recognized—gives way to the best defense against libel: there was "not a word in her account of the institution *but what was true at the time when she knew it.*"[51]

The second part of the defense creates a paradox: the representation was justified (1) because it was fictionalized and (2) because it was true. The names are made up, but the problems are real. Stephen's account shifts quite easily between Gaskell's novelization of Brontë's personal history and Brontë's novelization of her own personal history: her novels are good, "yet it must be said that in drawing from her own experiences the materials of her novels . . . she greatly abused the license of her art."[52] Brontë's abuse of fiction consists in subjectively representing real-world persons and events without an appropriate dose of impartiality and dispassionate analysis and in exposing real people to what Gaskell calls, with respect to "Miss Scatcherd," "opprobrium."[53] Gaskell's defense is that Brontë told the truth not merely as it happened but as she experienced it—thus emphasizing Brontë's psychological development and the essential truth of her account rather than the artistry that might have "enlarged, coloured, modified, exaggerated" those events. In the *Life*, biography—just like the novel—demands careful attention to the relationship between individual perception and external fact.

When Gaskell revises her discussion of the school following public controversy about it, she maintains in the face of conflicting evidence that Brontë, "suffering her whole life long, both in heart and body, from the consequences of what happened there, might have been apt, to the last, to take her deep belief in facts for the facts themselves—her conception of truth for the absolute truth."[54] Such an aesthetic commitment to a "partial" or subjective truth in defiance of an "absolute truth" is reminiscent of the narrator's vow in George Eliot's novel *Adam Bede* (1859) to speak "as if I were in the witness-box, narrating my experience on oath," even though the testimony is that of a mirror "doubtless defective."[55] Gaskell's acknowledgment of Brontë's commitment to her vision of the truth is, finally, the strongest argument she makes in favor of the novels: the purpose of Gaskell's narration is to show how the events of Brontë's life shaped her *perception* of those events; circumstances being what they were, the "fiery words" were destined to come.

Stephen's charges against Brontë and against Gaskell are strikingly similar in their focus on the treatment of individuals; he credits Gaskell with presenting a more balanced picture of Cowan Bridge, but he criticizes her "arrangement of lights and shades and colours" in the "biography that opens exactly like a novel"—above all, in the treatment of Branwell Brontë.[56] In "The Relation of Novels to Life" (1855), he compares Gaskell's novels *Ruth* (1853) and *Mary Barton* (1848) unfavorably to Daniel Defoe's *Robinson Crusoe* (1719), a novel "which adds to the information and excites the feelings of its readers in a manner almost as natural and complete as if it were a real history of real facts."[57] By contrast, Gaskell's novels improperly heighten details and distort reality in order to make good reading. To condemn fiction for representing reality "unfairly"—and to use the same terms for nonfiction—is to assert the fundamental connection that both forms share with objective evidence.

Likewise, Gaskell's defense of Brontë's account of Cowan Bridge moves between anecdotal accounts of conversation and external facts in a way that avoids direct representation of Brontë's consciousness—leaving that to the novels, outside Gaskell's project, and the letters, which are at the heart of it. In the larger biography, she extensively uses Brontë's letters as a first-person counterpoint to her own third-person presentation of events. The use of letters to make a mind transparent is, perhaps, a clue to Richard Altick's puzzle about the dominance of letters in nineteenth-century biography: "By the early nineteenth century the epistolary novel was passé. Ironically, however, its relative, the epistolary biography, flourished for another hundred years." Altick attributes this shift to an ideal of the biographer as a "compiler": "it was axiomatic that the letters of a man *contained* his life; that, indeed his life could be narrated most effectively and authentically by reproducing large portions of his correspondence and other personal papers."[58] Such compendium-style works connect clearly with nonfictional miscellaneousness, but Gaskell's biography shows how closely they continue to connect with the novel.

But correspondence also creates the effect of intimacy with the subject. In contrast to Stephen's argument that art is the enemy of historical truth, Gaskell implicitly claims a fictional mode of reading as most appropriate to nonfiction: an interplay between subjective individual experience—rendered primarily through letters rather than through direct portrayal of mind—and lived external detail. The key to reading reality turns out also to be a perspective of imaginative sympathy. Gaskell restores the "historical truth" behind Brontë's art not only to emphasize that the novel was true in many of the naked facts and circumstances as well as in the actual suffering and experience—but also simultaneously to present a more authentic version of the novel. If a premise of fiction is to engage the reader's sympathy through engagement in a world adjacent to and separate from everyday life, Gaskell's biography invokes that mode as a way of reading the facts of real life. After producing evidence that would seem to justify a strictly biographical interpretation of *Jane Eyre*, Gaskell rejects that evidence as less important than the reader's imaginative engagement with Brontë's experience of those facts.

Gaskell reintroduces documentary evidence to *Jane Eyre* to create a text of letters threaded together by narrative prose. Nineteenth-century life writing depends so much on the collation of materials that it is always implicitly a collective form. Following Stephen, one might judge any book—a novel, autobiography, or biography—by its treatment of facts. Though the account of Brontë's love life was designed to disappoint the inquisitive, Gaskell produces factual evidence from Brontë's experience at school that coincides with Brontë's fictional representations and cites passages from Brontë's novels to illustrate the grief she experienced in life. Gaskell's liberal deployment of evidence from Brontë's life and from Brontë's fiction depend on the reader's willingness to read double—to read, in the tautological spirit Ian Duncan's describes for the biographers of Scott, the work in the life and the life in the works.[59]

"HAD SHE BUT LIVED": BIOGRAPHICAL SKETCHES OF WHAT MIGHT HAVE BEEN

This chapter concludes by considering posthumous figurations of the author from two perspectives: first, the tradition of feminist literary history that creates a figure of an author from the texts that author left behind (a contemporary writer fills in the sketch through an act of imagination); second, the market for information about a famous author, where an author's death becomes an opportunity for working writers.

Deirdre d'Albertis titles and opens her essay about Gaskell's *Life* with a line from a letter in 1857 from John Blackwood to G. H. Lewes on Gaskell's project: "I detest this bookmaking out of the remains of the dead."[60] Gaskell's book is, indeed, both a meditation on Brontë's life as well as a bestseller that profited by Brontë's death.

In summing up Brontë, Gaskell brings up all the extenuating circumstances that she has dwelled on in the biography. "I do not deny for myself the existence of coarseness here and there in her works, otherwise so entirely noble. I only ask those who read them to consider her life,—which has been openly laid bare before them,—and to say how it could be otherwise."[61] Critics of the biography have long noted Gaskell's unwillingness to fully defend the novels: William Caldwell Roscoe remarked in July 1857 that, with a concession like this, "we wonder the writer had the heart to accuse the *Quarterly* reviewer of injustice or pharisaism."[62] Gaskell's passage continues: readers should "do her [Brontë] justice for all that she was, and all that she would have been (if God had spared her). . . . Every change in her life was purifying her; it could hardly raise her. Again I cry, 'If she had but lived!'"[63] The first time Gaskell cried "If she had but lived!," she was quoting Charlotte Brontë.

In his biography *Elizabeth Gaskell* (1979), Angus Easson points out that "Gaskell had one model for a possible memoir in Charlotte's 'Biographical Notice of Ellis and Acton Bell' (Emily and Anne) prefixed to the Literary Remains edition (1850), a brief sketch of about two thousand words," though it was soon clear that Gaskell's project would be much more extensive.[64] Charlotte Brontë's "Biographical Notice," signed "Currer Bell," lays the groundwork for the myth of her life that Gaskell also circulates and shows Brontë's writing as biographer and editor. In appending "Currer Bell" to the names "Ellis and Acton Bell," she uses her own fame to sell the works of her sisters—a practice reminiscent of Stowe's preface to the first expanded edition of Henson's life in 1858.

In Brontë's preface to *Wuthering Heights* in 1850, she writes of Emily: "Had she but lived, her mind would of itself have grown like a strong tree, loftier, straighter, wider-spreading."[65] In both instances, the sentiment "had she but lived!" is offered in partial apology for the novels. Gaskell, in her novel-length representation of Charlotte Brontë's life, makes a different choice from Charlotte's re-presentation of Emily as Shirley in the novel of that name. Gaskell notes that she prefers Shirley to Emily because what she has learned about Emily "has not tended to give either me, or my readers, a pleasant impression of her. But we must remember how little we are acquainted with her, compared to that sister, who, out of her more intimate knowledge, says that [Emily] 'was genuinely good, and truly great,' and who tried to depict her character in Shirley Keeldar, as what Emily Brontë would have been, *had she* been placed in health and prosperity."[66] Here, Brontë, like Gaskell, works to immortalize Emily's better qualities and illustrates one meaningful difference between a novel and a life: Brontë creates an Emily in ideal circumstances; Gaskell creates an ideal Brontë as an unrealized possibility.

Both Brontë's biography of Emily and Gaskell's biography of Charlotte ask the reader to read the fiction against an excusing backdrop of biography. Both accounts work by contrast with the idealized portrait of Emily in the character of Shirley Keeldar: Shirley is a distinctly counterfactual double. To understand her, one need not look outside the novel. Because circumstances have been created to suit her in the novel, Emily Brontë is seen as she only could have been had she been placed in health and prosperity. One of the simpler "clef" structures in Gaskell's *Life*—Shirley = Emily—becomes relevant to Brontë's life only at its end, when Gaskell presents through Brontë's marriage the unfulfilled glimpse of a happier circumstances. Meghan Burke Hattaway argues that Gaskell's depiction of Brontë's suffering is ultimately an argument for fewer restrictions on women so that readers might, "by viewing the thankless pains that accompany [Brontë's] struggle, concede that such standards might be detrimental, or even impossible, to meet."[67] Charlotte's fictional portrait of her sister Emily imagines what might have been different—a set of fictional circumstances suited to a real character—while the biographical preface, like the bulk of Gaskell's biography, laments the real character as understood through a double lens of life and fiction.

Brontë's biographical preface, paired with Gaskell's biography, reveals the two women connected as writers of biography rather than of fiction—also a popular genre. Gaskell's biography was not only a labor of love, memorialization, or even feminist self-definition but also a marketable commodity; it went through a second printing before she could get to the revisions demanded by those who read the first edition.

Writing a life to defend the work might seem like a step away from meaningful aesthetic engagement with the work, but it offers the biographer a chance to imagine alternative life histories for a woman novelist, a practice that has taken very different forms. In documenting a life for the author of *Jane Eyre*, Gaskell's *Life* seems to imagine a history around that character that would protect her from the accusations of vulgarity, impiety, and rebellion that her story invites. In combining an idealized counterhistory with details from Brontë's life to explain—or at times to explain away—the works, Gaskell's biography claims to reveal the truth that lies within the fiction.

The shape of this argument also animates Virginia Woolf's argument about Brontë in *A Room of One's Own* (1929). Woolf also indulges in a counterfactual narrative based not on what happened but on what might have happened. Her reading is based on a conflation of Brontë and Jane Eyre beginning from Jane Eyre's line "Anybody may blame me who likes," from which Woolf concludes that Brontë "is at war with her lot. How could she help but die young, cramped and thwarted? . . . She knew, no one better, how enormously her genius would have profited if it had not spent itself in solitary visions over distant fields; if experience and intercourse and travel had been granted her."[68] Like Brontë and Gaskell before her, Woolf frames her criticism of the fiction in terms of the limits of a writer's life to imagine what might have happened had *"experience and intercourse and travel been granted"* Brontë. And what might have happened had "experience and intercourse and travel been granted" to women writers is, in Woolf's argument, better literature.

I have traced a line from Brontë to Gaskell to Woolf. "Let me imagine," writes Woolf, "since facts are so hard to come by, what would have happened had Shakespeare had a wonderfully gifted sister called Judith."⁶⁹ If Woolf's lament for the constraints on Brontë imagined what might have been possible in another world, her lament for the constraints on Judith Shakespeare—who dies by suicide without writing a word—is rooted in an historical reality that altogether forecloses the possibility of creating art. In her essay "In Search of Our Mothers' Gardens" (1972), Alice Walker rewrites what Woolf calls the "story [she] had made about Shakespeare's sister" by transforming Judith into the poet Phillis Wheatley. In Walker's version, it is not the fictional "Judith" but the real Wheatley who exemplifies the certainty that, as Woolf wrote, with bracketed changes by Walker, "a highly gifted girl who had tried to use her gift for poetry would have been so thwarted and hindered by contrary instincts [add: 'chains, guns, the lash, the ownership of one's body by someone else, submission to an alien religion'] that she must have lost her health and her sanity to a certainty." Walker inscribes the conditions of slavery into Woolf's imagined history, then turns to address Wheatley: "You kept alive, in so many of our ancestors, *the notion of song*."⁷⁰ Walker opens an alternative to imagining a different past by suggesting one might look differently at the past as it was, but to do so for places that have been conventionally overlooked or not counted. Walker's engagement with Woolf's story turns Woolf's attempt to imagine the kind of thing that might have happened into an ethical project of understanding a real person. In seeking to redress an irrecoverable past through imagination, Walker anticipates theories of temporality in Black feminist thought, such as Saidiya Hartman's speculative treatment of the archive in *Wayward Lives* (2019). Hartman's method creates a way of understanding the past: it "elaborates, augments, transposes, and breaks open archival documents so they might yield a richer picture of the social upheaval that transformed black life in the twentieth century."⁷¹

Her work figures a trajectory for speculative history that represents an urgent engagement with the past. If Bronte's and Gaskell's intellectual projects prefigure Woolf's discussion, then Walker's, and then Hartman's, they also prefigure a mode of speculation with no investment in recovering an unknowable past or in how the past relates to the present and the future. I now turn to a form of "what might have been" that is not at all invested in what really happened. Rather, it is fantasy—the kind of fantasy that sells books.

When Brontë died a celebrity, her death served as a hook for other people to publish on her and her work. Louisa Yates offers a perspective on bookmaking from the remains of the dead that is quite different from the biographical sketch and yet, Yates argues, clearly connected to it: a BDSM version of *Jane Eyre* in the Clandestine Classics series by Totally Bound Publishing that introduces explicit sex scenes, even while the novel essentially "remains untouched." Yates explains that these works should not be understood primarily in the context of a neo-Victorian trend but in the commercial context of E. L. James's novel *Fifty Shades of Grey* (2011) and the awareness that "Brontë's celebrity is as much a commodity as her text." Yates points out that the reinvention of Brontë as what one journalist called a "filthy bitch" is but a reimagining of Sandra Gilbert's portrayal of Brontë as "hungry, angry, and rebellious. . . . Clandestine Classics require that readers fail to see any of the sex, sensuality and sadomasochism that some readers see in Brontë's novel." Yates uses the press materials for the series to show that *Jane Eyre* erotic fiction is always also about *Brontë's* desire: "Charlotte's sexual nature was repressed by Victorian society, ergo her Jane Eyre must be in need of an explicit reimagining."[72] Such a portrait shows Brontë (to paraphrase Christina Rossetti) not as she was, but as she fills our dream. The expansion of *Jane Eyre* can be seen as a kind of restoration or fleshing-out of Charlotte Brontë developed for Kindle erotica, an emerging genre in the twenty-first-century book market. Charlotte Brontë and *Jane Eyre* have long been in dialogue—as novel and as life writing—and Brontë's authorship continues to develop through emerging forms of print.

CODA
Refiguring Authorship

In the travel narratives and biographical sketches and occasional contributions I have written about, the literary creators of the texts emerge again and again as people whose lived identities shaped the reception of the texts they wrote and the texts written about them. Elements of the many cultural discourses that saturated nineteenth-century print culture crystallize in textual form around the figure of the author.

Sharon Marcus emphasizes the link between the nineteenth-century celebrity culture and our own: "The decline of the film studios in the 1960s, the breakdown of broadcast television that began in the 1980s, and the rise of the Internet since the 1990s have returned celebrity culture to its anarchic nineteenth-century roots."[1] By tracing those roots through antislavery discourse, I suggest another historical throughline: individual celebrity figures brought the cultural power of their racialized and gendered identities to bear on political issues.[2]

While antislavery groups and individuals used popular literary forms and organized endorsements by literary celebrities to amplify their messages, literary celebrities such as Fredrika Bremer engaged with the political cause of antislavery in disorganized, unpredictable ways. Rather than offering an account of how authors used the power of literary celebrity to effect political change or, conversely, how authors seized on a movement for political change to further their public careers, my look at the texts covered in this book reveal figures of the author emerging from the intersection of culture, commerce, and politics. These texts and the various points of intersection created and continue to create a composite portrait of the author that looks very different depending on the constellation of texts that readers have access to.

Contemporary disciplinary perspectives on the past often generate relevant constellations of texts by filtering out irrelevant and apparently unconnected ones—that is to say, by creating a lens on literary history. A focus on the figure of the author shows miscellaneous discursive strands intersecting and reveals texts that are nonliterary in the most straightforward sense: informational and self-promotional. Computational perspectives, in particular those focused on the sociology of literature, restore the commercial context from which celebrity authors emerged. This makes it possible to recognize, for example, the different Harriet Martineaus—the celebrity contributor, the protoimperialist, the abolitionist, the political economist, the sage, the invalid, the lady with the ear trumpet—pulled together under one name. Literary celebrity offers a filter through which to view print culture that makes it possible to recover the different aspects of the nineteenth-century Harriet Martineau that would have been obvious to her contemporaries as properties of a single figure.

A key dynamic that emerges from the perspective of the sociology of literature is how major author names are produced in collaboration with minor and unknown figures, a dynamic that is also evident in the contemporary literary celebrity system. As author brands become an entrenched commercial category, more and more people are involved in producing and distributing the branded author's work. When Karl Berglund and I compared Swedish editions of Stieg Larsson's novel *The Girl with the Dragon Tattoo* (2005) and its sequels with the editions designed for the U.S. market, we found thoroughgoing changes to the books through a production process that involved the author, the translator, and a team of uncredited editors and proofreaders.[3] Though the Millennium series was published in the United States under the name "Larsson," it was the product of a collective effort. Dan Sinykin offers another account of conglomeration in American publishing that shows how "big fiction" has increasingly instrumentalized writers to create major brands.[4]

The converse trend in twenty-first-century publishing—a growing expectation that aspiring authors manage their own brands—also speaks to this book's historical perspective on self-promotion, publicity, and content production/curation. Transatlantic print culture makes sense as the casualized cultural marketplace that we know now, in which the creator bears the risks and responsibilities of self-promotion. I close here with some reflections on how contemporary authorship can refigure how we think about authorship in the nineteenth century.

One hallmark of the new media landscape is platforms that allow writers to publish directly to readers, such as AO3 and Wattpad.[5] If the collective creation of literary works is easily obscured in studies of the author, these sites are helpful because they make the collectivity explicit. Aarthi Vadde explores how the rise of amateur creativity shifts the discourse of authorship, citing Wattpad star novelists who, writing in constant engagement with their readers, "see writing as fundamentally social and supportive."[6] Another hallmark is that although it might seem as if the author's identity might be less relevant in the more communal context of these platforms, that is not the case.

Kristina Busse argues that fan authorship is marked by the way the "often close-knit community of fans allows readers and writers to interact, creating an environment of often shared ideas and collective creation, but also one in which writers are accessible and can be held accountable for their words and ideas." That is, "authors must always be actual people whose experiences and identities shape their works."[7] Nineteenth-century texts reveal the same explicit consciousness of an actual person behind and within them. The authenticity effect is an important part of Simone Murray's argument that today's authors play a growing role in the design and development of their brands through online engagement with readers.[8]

Murray's work clarifies an important element of how literary celebrity emerged through texts and performance in the nineteenth century. The lecture circuit offered readers the chance to see authors onstage—not necessarily to interact with them, as in a Reddit "Ask Me Anything," but to stand near them while they brought a text to life. Josiah Henson's authorship emerged, like that of other literary and antislavery celebrity authors, in tandem with public presentations. Henson outshone Harriet Beecher Stowe's novel not only with the "lives" he wrote but also with a series of lectures that put his history in dialogue with her fiction, allowing listeners to complement or supplant a literary experience with interpersonal proximity, if only in a large hall so full it was standing-room only.

In the online community of fan fiction, new writing is grounded on an existing cultural work, but the world of fan fiction is not limited to fictional universes. One thread of fan fiction is "real-person fiction," in which fans "write about a version of the private lives of their favorite public figures" that expands on that parasocial relationship.[9] If the Clandestine Classics list is built on creative engagement not only with *Jane*

Eyre but also with Charlotte Brontë, fan fiction about historical authors puts the imaginative connection with the author at the heart of a new literary enterprise. Platforms that empower fan readers to become fan authors clarify the relevance of biographical reading to conceptions of literary celebrity that emerge from authors and the texts about them.

The digital literary sphere Murray describes promises an even less-mediated version of the intimacy promised by Putnam's *Homes of American Authors* in its descriptions of the interiors of authors' homes or the re-creation of an author's (William Prescott's) act of writing. Poe's second "Autography" series used his own celebrity as a writer to demonstrate his professional connection with other authors, foregrounding his role (by contrast with the original British "Miller Correspondence") as a correspondent with authors in a range of genres.

A twenty-first-century perspective on *Homes of American Authors* and *Autographs for Freedom* also reveals the power of an influencer collab at work: brands intersect. The gift book reveals authors working together as writers with a host of other producers. The idea of a collab pulls together aims that do not necessarily go together: to create, to achieve, to sell. By working together, parties gain access to a platform they would not have had individually. Nineteenth-century gift books reveal how professional literary networks could operate in a political sphere. Writers moving between roles as editors and celebrity contributors created commodities that were also a physical record of support. Antislavery gift books that pulled together focused advocates and casual supporters, essays by celebrities and essays by anonymous correspondents, reflected an intersection of strategic aims—literary and political, interpersonal and accidental—to create a bouquet of genres and figures in volume form.

The notion of the author that emerges through such competing, complementary portraits is a composite, but it is not a composite of all the texts written by and about that author. It is a composite of the constellation of texts that a reader has encountered or has access to. And it's this engagement—personal, partial, and emerging out of a connection with the reader's own experiences—that creates so many figures out of one writer. This was as true in nineteenth-century print culture as it is in digital media now. The ideal of intimacy with a producer through their content in digital celebrity culture echoes the nineteenth-century fascination with—or even hunger for—a real author.

ACKNOWLEDGMENTS

This book is dedicated to my friend and writing partner Elsie B. Michie. Elsie's work—published and in progress—and her questions, advice, and responses to drafts made this project possible to write.

In the notes, I have acknowledged where formulations are traceable to others' ideas and words. As the consistent attributions to my friend and work wife, the art historian Mia L. Bagneris, make clear, our ongoing conversations have shaped this project from its foundation.

This book is centrally interested in the way people produce ideas together. Kate Adams has been an indispensable strategist on questions large and small. Rachel Sagner Buurma's curiosity and commitment to the idea that intellectual life is wide enough to accommodate all the forms of work we do—even teaching, even service—have been inspiring throughout the process. I'm grateful to Rachel Feder for her correspondence, for inviting me to think through the implications of the gift book as nineteenth-century collaboration, and for suggesting "figures of authorship" as a guiding conceit. Casie LeGette's wry, unerring wisdom on intellectual and practical questions has been critical—although only a few of her aphorisms are present here, she is a sage for our time. Jana Lipman, historian of labor and U.S. empire, has been talking with me throughout the writing of the book and helpfully reminds us all that an academic argument is not a mystery novel. My thanks to Mary Mullen, who recognizes the highest stakes of an argument and sees them in the context of major theoretical and social questions; she is a transformative force for good. Chris Rovee's responses to my work throughout this project have been on point and characteristically lovely. Megan Ward combines an openness to how an argument might turn with a commitment to having it make sense.

This is, in part, a book about the importance of building on the work of others and the collective creation of ideas. Special thanks to the following: Annie Barva, Karl Berglund, Alison Booth, Karen Bourrier, Lara Langer Cohen, MJ Devaney, Alexis Easley, Danny Hack, Melanie Hucklebridge, Lucy Sheehan, Amanda Shubert, Richard Jean So, Jenny Sorensen, Johan Svedjedal, Ajania Thaxton, Ted Underwood, and Alex Woloch.

I'd also like to thank the groups who workshopped this material with me: Loyola's English Literary Forum; the Philadelphia literature and culture seminar P19; the Stanford Literary Lab; and the participants in Priti Joshi's 2022 NAVSA Seminar "Materiality | Ephemera | Periodicals." The book benefited from ongoing discussion with colleagues at the University of Uppsala's Section for the Sociology of Literature and Computational Literary Studies Group.

Thanks also to my students for working through some of the big questions about celebrity and authorship.

At Loyola University New Orleans, I wrote with the support of the William and Audrey Hutchinson Distinguished Professorship. I am grateful to my wonderful colleagues there and owe special thanks to Heidi Braden, Chloe Evans, Curry O'Day, and Jessica Perry. My thanks to Special Collections at Louisiana

State University, the University of Minnesota Libraries, and the Harry Ransom Center at the University of Texas at Austin. Glen Layne-Worthey helped me connect with the sources I needed during a hurricane.

I thank Philip Leventhal of Columbia University Press for an inspiring commitment to intellectual inquiry and for working with me throughout the project. I thank the readers for the press; the book is stronger for their insightful, generous responses.

Thanks also to those who worked with me on earlier forms of this book. Material from chapter 3 appeared as "Elizabeth Barrett Browning and Harriet Martineau: On the Limits of White Ladyism" in Lucy Sheehan, Jennifer Sorensen, and Sarah Allison, "Miscellany as Method: A Trio of Approaches to 'The Runaway Slave at Pilgrim's Point' and the 1848 Liberty Bell Gift Book," *Victorian Poetry* 59, no. 3 (2021): 261–308. A version of the discussion of Elizabeth Gaskell's *Life of Charlotte Brontë* in chapter 5 appeared as "Narrative Form and Facts, Facts, Facts: Elizabeth Gaskell's *The Life of Charlotte Brontë*," *Genre* 50, no. 1 (April 1, 2017): 97–116. Parts of chapter 1 grew out of the essay "Authorship After AI," *Public Books*, June 25, 2019, and the essay "Literature" for the special issue "Keywords" of *Victorian Literature and Culture* 46, nos. 3–4 (2018): 745–49. Thanks to my people in New Orleans: Erin Crowley and the Seals, Hillary Eklund and Greg Larsen, Laura Jayne, Jen Myhre and the Legshes, Mia and Zora Bagneris, Isaiah Epstein-Bagneris, Heather Marinaro, Jonny Morton, Amanda McFillen, Elizabeth Pearce, Tina Boudreaux, Kelly Juneau Rookard, Lindsay Weidman, and Tim Welsh. The Horstreiffer family, the Dublin Fingers, the DeSoto Fingers, and the Adelmans have been making this place home for years. So glad to be in community together.

For their friendship and support, my thanks to Aileen Arrieta, Inger Bergom, Aby Behner, Andrea Caulfield, Kate Dyson,

Angela Fauth, Emily Harrington, Amanda Hill, Elizabeth Johansen, Sara Beth Levavy, Kenny Ligda, Anna Moseley, and Molly Sandomire.

Meri-Jane Rochelson belongs up with the interlocutors for bringing her insight, precision, and curiosity to reading the manuscript, and she here leads the paragraph on family. My love and thanks go to her and to Joel Mintz, Serafima Mintz, and Emily Colley. I wrote key parts of this book in Sweden at the home of Björn Holm and Katarina Andreasson. Åsa and Hugo Henriz, Susanne Holm, and Gunnar Olsson also made it possible to write from Sweden. My parents, Eva and Brian Allison, are the best. My sister, Theresa Allison, is also the best, as are Chris, Madeline, and William Hess. I'm so grateful for these people! My husband, Danny Mintz, has been supportive and scintillatingly brilliant. It has been a privilege to write this book as our childen, Sam and Karl, have been growing: love you two.

NOTES

INTRODUCTION: ANTISLAVERY CELEBRITY AND THE LITERARY AUTHOR

1. Meredith L. McGill, *American Literature and the Culture of Reprinting, 1834–1853* (University of Pennsylvania Press, 2007), 252.
2. Joe Moran, *Star Authors: Literary Celebrity in America* (Pluto, 2000), 17. Susan S. Williams gives 1840–1880 as a period that "witnessed a shift in literary publicity from an emphasis on the author's relation to his or her work to an emphasis on what we might term a 'cult of personality': an interest in the private as well as the literary lives of authors." Williams, "Authors and Literary Authorship," in *A History of the Book in America*, vol. 3: *The Industrial Book, 1840–1880*, ed. Scott E. Casper, (American Antiquarian Society, University of North Carolina Press, 2007), 105.
3. McGill, *American Literature*, 252. In the history of copyright, Stowe is famous not for stealing the "life" of Josiah Henson, as she was also accused of doing, but for suing the German translator of *Uncle Tom's Cabin*. McGill, *American Literature*, 272–74. This legal case is featured in both Melissa J. Homestead, *American Women Authors and Literary Property, 1822–1869* (Cambridge University Press, 2005), 105–49; and Mark Rose, *Authors in Court: Scenes from the Theater of Copyright* (Harvard University Press, 2018), 36–63.
4. My thanks to Rachel Feder for the idea that antislavery discourse creates a visible shape within the diffuse atmosphere of

nineteenth-century literature: "If you throw a cloth over a figure, the shape emerges."

5. Meredith L. McGill, "Copyright," in *The Industrial Book, 1840–1880*, ed. Casper, 158–78. See also Mark Rose, *Authors and Owners: The Invention of Copyright* (Harvard University Press, 1993); and Paul K. Saint-Amour, *The Copywrights: Intellectual Property and the Literary Imagination* (Cornell University Press, 2003).
6. McGill, *American Literature.*
7. Saint-Amour, *The Copywrights*, 8.
8. Peter Lindenbaum, "Milton's Contract," in *The Construction of Authorship: Textual Appropriation in Law and Literature*, ed. Martha Woodmansee and Peter Jaszi, Post-contemporary Interventions (Duke University Press, 1994), 185.
9. Catherine Fisk, "The Modern Author at Work on Madison Avenue," in *Modernism and Copyright*, ed. Paul K. Saint-Amour, Modernist Literature and Culture (Oxford University Press, 2010), 190. Oliver Gerland characterizes the right to publicity as a neighbor to copyright. Gerland, "Modernism and the Emergence of the Right of Publicity: From *Hedda Gabler* to Lucy, Lady Duff-Gordon," in *Modernism and Copyright*, ed. Saint-Amour, 195.
10. Fisk, "The Modern Author at Work," 190.
11. Martha Woodmansee, "On the Author Effect: Recovering Collectivity," in *The Construction of Authorship*, ed. Woodmansee and Jaszi, 15–28. See also Andrea A. Lunsford and Lisa Ede, "Collaborative Authorship and the Teaching of Writing," in *The Construction of Authorship*, ed. Woodmansee and Jaszi, 417–38.
12. Patricia Okker, *Our Sister Editors: Sarah J. Hale and the Tradition of Nineteenth-Century American Women Editors* (University of Georgia Press, 1995); Jewon Woo, "The Colored Citizen: Collaborative Editorship in Progress," *American Periodicals: A Journal of History and Criticism* 30, no. 2 (2020): 110–13.
13. Fionnuala Dillane, *Before George Eliot: Marian Evans and the Periodical Press*, illus. ed. (Cambridge University Press, 2013); Lauren F. Klein, "Dimensions of Scale: Invisible Labor, Editorial Work, and the Future of Quantitative Literary Studies," *PMLA* 135, no. 1 (January 2020): 23–39.

14. Harriet Beecher Stowe to Susan F. Porter, June 20, 1852, Porter Family Papers, Rare Books, Special Collections and Preservation, Rush Rhees Library, University of Rochester, Rochester, NY, quoted in John R. McKivigan and Rebecca A. Pattillo, *"Autographs for Freedom* and Reaching a New Abolitionist Audience," *Journal of African American History* 102, no. 1 (Winter 2017): 39.
15. Sarah Meer, *Uncle Tom Mania: Slavery, Minstrelsy, and Transatlantic Culture in the 1850s* (University of Georgia Press, 2005).
16. Sharon Marcus, *The Drama of Celebrity* (Princeton University Press, 2019), 192, 17.
17. Manisha Sinha, *The Slave's Cause: A History of Abolition* (Yale University Press, 2016), 421.
18. Samantha Pinto, *Infamous Bodies: Early Black Women's Celebrity and the Afterlives of Rights* (Duke University Press, 2020).
19. Amanda Claybaugh, *The Novel of Purpose: Literature and Social Reform in the Anglo-American World* (Cornell University Press, 2007). For historical perspectives on social reform across Europe and North America, see Kathryn Kish Sklar and James Stewart, eds., *Women's Rights and Transatlantic Anti-slavery in the Era of Emancipation* (Yale University Press, 2007). For perspectives on the intersection of reform movements through print in Sklar and Stewart's volume, see especially Claire Midgley, "British Abolition and Feminism in Transatlantic Perspective," 121–40; and Jane Rhodes, "At the Boundaries of Abolitionism, Feminism, and Black Nationalism: The Activism of Mary Ann Shadd Cary," 346–66. For a perspective on the trajectory of transatlantic reform fiction and on the aesthetics of reform in the late nineteenth and early twentieth centuries, see Arielle Zibrak, *Writing Against Reform: Aesthetic Realism in the Progressive Era* (University of Massachusetts Press, 2024).
20. Margaret McFadden, *Golden Cables of Sympathy: The Transatlantic Sources of Nineteenth-Century Feminism* (University Press of Kentucky, 1999), 73.
21. Amanda Adams, *Performing Authorship in the Nineteenth-Century Transatlantic Lecture Tour*, Ashgate Series in Nineteenth-Century Transatlantic Studies (Ashgate, 2014).
22. Tricia Lootens, *The Political Poetess: Victorian Femininity, Race, and the Legacy of Separate Spheres* (Princeton University Press, 2016), 39.

23. Harriet Beecher Stowe, *A Key to Uncle Tom's Cabin: Presenting the Original Facts and Documents Upon Which the Story Is Founded, Together with Corroborative Statements Verifying the Truth of the Work* (Jewett, Proctor & Worthington, 1853), 26.
24. Clint Smith, "The Man Who Became Uncle Tom," *The Atlantic*, September 8, 2023.
25. Marcus, *The Drama of Celebrity*.
26. Ann R. Hawkins and Maura C. Ives, eds., *Women Writers and the Artifacts of Celebrity in the Long Nineteenth Century* (Ashgate, 2012).
27. Alexis Easley, *Literary Celebrity, Gender, and Victorian Authors, 1850–1914* (University of Delaware Press, 2011), 13.
28. Nicola J. Watson, *The Author's Effects: On Writer's House Museums* (Oxford University Press, 2020).
29. For the way writers' houses work as narrative constructs, see Alison Booth, *Homes and Haunts: Touring Writers' Shrines and Countries* (Oxford University Press, 2016).
30. Ann Wierda Rowland and Paul Westover, "Introduction: Reading, Reception, and the Rise of Transatlantic 'English,'" in *Transatlantic Literature and Author Love in the Nineteenth Century*, ed. Paul Westover and Ann Wierda Rowland (Palgrave Macmillan, 2016), 8.
31. Miranda Marraccini, "Feminist Types: Reading the Victoria Press," PhD diss., Princeton University, 2019.
32. Tom Mole, *Byron's Romantic Celebrity: Industrial Culture and the Hermeneutic of Intimacy*, Palgrave Studies in the Enlightenment, Romanticism, and Cultures of Print (Palgrave Macmillan, 2007).
33. Simone Murray, *The Digital Literary Sphere: Reading, Writing, and Selling Books in the Internet Era* (Johns Hopkins University Press, 2018).
34. Elsie B. Michie, "Reassessing the Cleverness of Frances Trollope's Social Fictions," review of *The Social Problem Novels of Frances Trollope*, 4 vols., by Frances Milton Trollope, ed. Brenda Ayres, *Nineteenth-Century Gender Studies* 5, no. 3 (2009), https://www.ncgsjournal.com/issue53/michie.html.
35. Hannah-Rose Murray argues that this wax "model of Henson indicated not only that he joined an illustrious roster of people but also that he was famous enough for his statue to last at least three years"

in an exhibition that was regularly updated. Murray, *Advocates of Freedom: African American Transatlantic Abolitionism in the British Isles*, Slaveries Since Emancipation (Cambridge University Press, 2020), 279–80.

36. Moran, *Star Authors*, 63.
37. Joanne Shattock, "Women Journalists and Periodical Spaces," in *Women, Periodicals, and Print Culture in Britain, 1830s–1900s*, ed. Alexis Easley, Clare Gill, and Beth Rodgers (Edinburgh University Press, 2022), 309–10.
38. For a theoretical perspective on seeing writers and texts in relation to one another in this period, see the exploration of "relational poetics" as a method in Jennifer Putzi, *Fair Copy: Relational Poetics and Antebellum American Women's Poetry* (University of Pennsylvania Press, 2021).
39. Troy J. Bassett's study of the three-decker novel reveals that the form was not typical of most novels—it was typical only of productions by established, well-known authors. See Bassett, *The Rise and Fall of the Victorian Three-Volume Novel* (Palgrave Macmillan, 2020).

1. CARDS ON THE TABLE: HOW DATA-DRIVEN APPROACHES TO LITERARY HISTORY SHAPED THIS ARCHIVE

1. Sarah Allison, *Reductive Reading: A Syntax of Victorian Moralizing* (Johns Hopkins University Press, 2018).
2. Deidre Lynch, *Loving Literature: A Cultural History* (University of Chicago Press, 2015), 248.
3. Richard D. Altick, *Lives and Letters: A History of Literary Biography in England and America* (Knopf, 1965), 205.
4. Catherine Gallagher, "The Rise of Fictionality," in *The Novel*, vol. 1: *History, Geography, and Culture*, ed. Franco Moretti (Princeton University Press, 2006), 337. Monica Fludernik, however, challenges the idea that the novel and the fictional are synonymous. "I take Lavocat's narrow definition of *fictionality* as my starting point and define *fictionality* as the invention of fictive worlds which are presented in textual, dramatic (i.e., performative) or visual (and audiovisual) form for

the entertainment, diversion, intellectual stimulation, and (moral) instruction of recipients. These recipients, in their turn, recognize that the truth claims proffered by these texts or artifacts are predominantly universal, moral, and philosophical rather than historical or factual." Fludernik, "The Fiction of the Rise of Fictionality," *Poetics Today* 39, no. 1 (2018): 78.
5. Daniel Defoe, *Robinson Crusoe* (1719), ed. John Richetti (Penguin Classics, 2003), title page, 4, capitalization edited.
6. Gallagher, "The Rise of Fictionality," 339–40.
7. Ian Watt, *The Rise of the Novel: Studies in Defoe, Richardson, and Fielding* (University of California Press, 1960), 32–34.
8. Srinivas Aravamudan, *Enlightenment Orientalism: Resisting the Rise of the Novel* (University of Chicago Press, 2011), 30.
9. Lynch, *Loving Literature*, 23.
10. Fludernik, "The Fiction of the Rise of Fictionality."
11. Ted Underwood, *Distant Horizons: Digital Evidence and Literary Change* (University of Chicago Press, 2019), 24–25, 26.
12. Ted Underwood, "Understanding Genre in a Collection of a Million Volumes," Digital Humanities Start-Up Grant Interim Performance Report, University of Illinois, Urbana-Champaign, December 29, 2014, 2, https://s3-eu-west-1.amazonaws.com/pfigshare-u-files/1857045/UnderstandingGenreInterimReport.pdf.
13. Ted Underwood, "Distant Reading and the Blurry Edges of Genre," *The Stone and the Shell* (blog), October 2014, https://tedunderwood.com/2014/10/.
14. James Fitzjames Stephen, "The License of Modern Novelists" (July 1857), in *Selected Writings of James Fitzjames Stephen: On the Novel and Journalism*, ed. Christopher Ricks (Oxford University Press, 2023), 131; Ted Underwood et al., "Mapping Mutable Genres in Structurally Complex Volumes," paper presented at the IEEE International Conference, Santa Clara, CA, October 6–9, 2013, https://arxiv.org/pdf/1309.3323v2.
15. Underwood et al., "Mapping Mutable Genres," 7.
16. Underwood, "Distant Reading and the Blurry Edges of Genre."
17. Ted Underwood, personal correspondence to the author, April 4, 2019, Underwood's emphasis. My thanks to Ted Underwood for his

commitment to making his work publicly accessible and easy to review—and for his generosity in rerunning an earlier model.
18. David S. Reynolds, *Mightier Than the Sword: Uncle Tom's Cabin and the Battle for America* (Norton, 2011), 104.
19. Thomas Keymer and Peter Sabor, *"Pamela" in the Marketplace: Literary Controversy and Print Culture in Eighteenth-Century Britain and Ireland* (Cambridge University Press, 2005), 50.
20. Elizabeth A. Harris et al., "A Trial Put Publishing's Inner Workings on Display. What Did We Learn?," *New York Times*, August 19, 2022. The authors quote a statement by Penguin Random House executives suggesting that about 4 percent of the publisher's list accounts for 60 percent of the profits. Laura B. McGrath argues that the practice of "comping" is an important factor in the publishing industry's continued exclusion of new writers of color. See McGrath, "Comping White," *Los Angeles Review of Books*, January 21, 2019.
21. Jordan Alexander Stein, *When Novels Were Books* (Harvard University Press, 2020), 11.
22. Claire Parfait, *The Publishing History of Uncle Tom's Cabin, 1852–2002* (Ashgate, 2007).
23. Alexis Easley, "Chance Encounters, Rediscovery, and Loss: Researching Victorian Women Journalists in the Digital Age," *Victorian Periodicals Review* 49, no. 4 (2016): 694–717. In *New Media and the Rise of the Popular Woman Writer, 1832–1860* (Edinburgh University Press, 2021), Easley organizes the discussion by case studies of authors, which allows her to treat the full breadth of genres and publishing venues across the career of each popular woman writer.
24. Monika Fludernik and Marie-Laure Ryan, "Factual Narrative: An Introduction," in *Narrative Factuality: A Handbook*, ed. Monika Fludernik and Marie-Laure Ryan (De Gruyter, 2019), 1.
25. On the limits of an idea of fictionality as a respected or even literary mode, see Lara Langer Cohen, *The Fabrication of American Literature: Fraudulence and Antebellum Print Culture* (University of Pennsylvania Press, 2011). Thomas Koenigs argues that "many early American uses of fiction . . . lie beyond our modern conceptions of literariness." Koenigs, *Founded in Fiction: The Uses of Fiction in the Early United States* (Princeton University Press, 2021), 6.

26. A few studies connect writing across forms with the author's gender; see especially Linda H. Peterson, *Traditions of Victorian Women's Autobiography: The Poetics and Politics of Life Writing*, Victorian Literature and Culture Series (University Press of Virginia, 1999); and Easley, *New Media and the Rise of the Popular Woman Writer*. Meri-Jane Rochelson considers the way Israel Zangwill worked across forms in light of his marginalization as a Jewish writer. See Rochelson, *A Jew in the Public Arena: The Career of Israel Zangwill* (Wayne State University Press, 2008).
27. Simon Eliot, *Some Patterns and Trends in British Publishing, 1800–1919*, Occasional Papers of the Bibliographical Society, no. 8 (Bibliographical Society, 1994).
28. Simon Eliot, "Some Patterns and Trends in British Book Production" (1994), in *Literature in the Marketplace: Nineteenth-Century British Publishing and Reading Practices*, ed. John O. Jordan and Robert L. Patten (Cambridge University Press, 2003), 38.
29. Alison Booth, "Life Writing," in *The Cambridge Companion to English Literature, 1830–1914*, ed. Joanne Shattock (Cambridge University Press, 2010), 56.
30. Eliot, "Some Patterns and Trends in British Book Production," 25. In a later essay, Eliot reflects on working with these data: "To cover production in the 1850s, I used no fewer than nine separate sets of data. Corroboration is not certain proof, but when two or more sets of data collected by different groups for different purposes indicate similar things, then one has a right, I think, to feel somewhat more confident in one's conclusions." Eliot, "Very Necessary but Not Quite Sufficient: A Personal View of Quantitative Analysis in Book History," *Book History* 5 (2002): 287.
31. Eliot, "Some Patterns and Trends in British Book Production,", 25.
32. Raymond Williams, *Keywords: A Vocabulary of Culture and Society*, rev. ed. (Oxford University Press, 1985), 152, my emphasis.
33. *Oxford Historical Thesaurus*, s.v. "specific types of literature," https://www.oed.com/thesaurus/?classId=232906.
34. Koenigs, *Founded in Fiction*, 5.
35. Mark Algee-Hewitt et al., "Around the Word 'Littérature': The English Case," paper presentation, May 2016, Stanford University, quote

from my notes. This presentation was one stage of a larger collaborative project called "'Literature/Littérature': History of a Word," which involved researchers from the Stanford Literary Lab; the Sorbonne, Paris; Loyola University, New Orleans; and the Max Planck Institute, Frankfurt.

36. "Daniel Webster" and "William Cullen Bryant," in *Homes of American Authors; Comprising Anecdotical, Personal, and Descriptive Sketches, by Various Writers*, ed. George Palmer Putnam (Putnam, 1853), 333, 70, 71, 76, 75, 76.
37. Linda K. Hughes, "*SIDEWAYS!* Navigating the Material(ity) of Print Culture," *Victorian Periodicals Review* 47, no. 1 (2014): 1.
38. Anne DeWitt, "Advances in the Visualization of Data: The Network of Genre in the Victorian Periodical Press," *Victorian Periodicals Review* 48, no. 2 (2015): 162.
39. Oscar Maurer, "Anonymity vs. Signature in Victorian Reviewing," *Studies in English* 27 (1948): 2.
40. Alexis Easley, *First-Person Anonymous: Women Writers and Victorian Print Media, 1830–70*, Nineteenth Century (Ashgate, 2004).
41. Derrick R. Spires, "Aliened Americans: Pseudonymity and Gender Politics in Early Black Social Media," *African American Review* 55, no. 1 (March 2022): 33, 36.
42. Roland Barthes, "The Death of the Author" (1967) in *Image, Music, Text*, trans. Stephen Heath (Hill and Wang, 1977), 143.
43. Maurer, "Anonymity vs. Signature in Victorian Reviewing," 1.
44. Frederick Oakeley [unsigned], "Cardinal Wiseman's Essays—Periodical Literature," *Dublin Review* 34, no. June (1853): 541–66, quoted in Laurel Brake, *Subjugated Knowledges: Journalism, Gender, and Literature in the Nineteenth Century* (New York University Press, 1994), 21–22.
45. Wordsworth quoted in Michael Gamer and Dahlia Porter, introduction to Samuel Taylor Coleridge and William Wordsworth, *Lyrical Ballads 1798 and 1800*, ed. Michael Gamer and Dahlia Porter (Broadview Press, 2008), 26.
46. Francesca Benatti and Justin Tonra, "English Bards and Unknown Reviewers: A Stylometric Analysis of Thomas Moore and the *Christabel Review*," *Breac: A Digital Journal of Irish Studies*, October 7, 2015,

https://breac.nd.edu/articles/english-bards-and-unknown-reviewers-a-stylometric-analysis-of-thomas-moore-and-the-christabel-review/.
47. Benatti and Tonra, "English Bards and Unknown Reviewers."
48. Susanna Ashton, *Collaborators in Literary America, 1870–1920* (Springer, 2003), 4.
49. Gerard Genette, *Paratexts: Thresholds of Interpretation*, trans. Jane E. Lewin (Cambridge University Press, 1997), 346. As Genette draws the boundary, "something is not a paratext unless the author or one of his associates accepts responsibility for it, although the degree of responsibility may vary" (9). Genette's work on paratexts orients itself around a central text, and he acknowledges that "the author's viewpoint is part of the paratextual performance, sustains it, inspires it, anchors it" (408). My thanks to Danny Hack for suggesting Genette's concept to frame the material in my study.

2. THE COLLECTIBLE AUTHOR: AUTOGRAPHS, HOMES AND HAUNTS, AND ANTISLAVERY GIFT BOOKS

1. Julia Griffiths, ed., *Autographs for Freedom* (John P. Jewett, 1854); McKivigan and Pattillo, *"Autographs for Freedom* and Reaching a New Abolitionist Audience."
2. Robert A. Gross, "Introduction: An Extensive Republic," in *A History of the Book in America*, vol. 2: *An Extensive Republic: Print, Culture, and Society in the New Nation, 1790–1840*, ed. Robert A. Gross and Mary Kelley (American Antiquarian Society, University of North Carolina Press, 2010), 28.
3. Rowland and Westover, "Introduction," in *Transatlantic Literature and Author Love*, ed. Westover and Rowland, 8.
4. Daniel Hack, *Reaping Something New: African American Transformations of Victorian Literature* (Princeton University Press, 2017), 21.
5. Thomas Starr, "Separated at Birth: Text and Context of the Declaration of Independence," *Proceedings of the American Antiquarian Society* 110, no. 2 (2000): 161, 166, 164.

6. John Bidwell, "American History in Image and Text," *Proceedings of the American Antiquarian Society* 98, no. 2 (1989): 264. This was around the same time that the first gift books appeared; Ralph Thompson dates the first English gift book to 1822 and the first U.S. one to 1825. Ralph Thompson, *American Literary Annuals & Gift Books, 1825–1865* (H. W. Wilson, 1936), 3, 4.
7. Darcy Grimaldo Grigsby, *Enduring Truths: Sojourner's Shadows and Substance* (University of Chicago Press, 2015), 15. My thanks to Mia Bagneris for the formulation that the signature replaces what could be a discursive account of a meeting with an artifact.
8. Tamara Plakins Thornton, "Handwriting in an Age of Industrial Print," in *The Industrial Book, 1840–1880*, ed. Casper, 406.
9. Isaac Disraeli, "Autographs," in Disraeli, *Curiosities of Literature: A New Edition, Edited, with Memoir and Notes, by His Son, the Earl of Beaconsfield, in Three Volumes*, vol. 3 (Frederick Warne, 1881), 163–66. Disraeli also mentions several volumes, including John Gough Nichols, *Autographs of Royal, Noble, Learned, and Remarkable Personages Conspicuous in English History* (Nichols and Son, 1829).
10. The text of *Historical and Literary Curiosities* consists only of a list of captions of plates of houses followed by facsimile reproductions of eighteenth-century letters, with no transcriptions.
11. Gerard Curtis, *Visual Words: Art and the Material Book in Victorian England* (Ashgate, 2002), 174, 2.
12. Tamara Plakins Thornton, "The Romance and Science of Individuality," chap. 3 in *Handwriting in America: A Cultural History* (Yale University Press, 1996), 72–107.
13. Thanks to Mia L. Bagneris for this illuminating counterexample.
14. Cohen, *The Fabrication of American Literature*, 16, quoting Walter Benjamin, "The Work of Art in the Age of Mechanical Reproduction," in *Illuminations: Essays and Reflections*, ed. Hannah Arendt, trans. Harry Zohn (1985; reprint, Schocken, 2007), 221.
15. While McGill describes a "system of reprinting" that author-centered literary histories can elide, I use literary celebrity to understand author-centered literary culture in the context of a system of reprinting. See McGill, *American Literature and the Culture of Reprinting*, 2.

16. Edgar Allan Poe, "Chapter on Autography," part 1, *Graham's Magazine* 19, no. 5 (November 1841): 225.
17. McGill, *American Literature and the Culture of Reprinting*, 183. According to McGill's history of reprinting and national identity, the "Autography" series show how Poe "uses handwriting of a doubtful authenticity to negotiate a position between British original and American copy, and between the twin risks of antebellum publishing: the subjection of authors to a propertyless dissemination, and the invisibility of editorial ownership" (177).
18. Edgar Allan Poe, "Chapter on Autography," part 3: "Appendix of Autographs," *Graham's Magazine* 20, no. 1 (January 1842): 44.
19. Edgar Allan Poe, "Chapter on Autography," part 2, *Graham's Magazine* 19, no. 6 (December 1841): 275, 276.
20. "The Miller Correspondence," *Fraser's Magazine for Town and Country* 47, no. 8 (November 1833): 624, 635.
21. Clayton Carlyle Tarr connects Poe's series to the threat of reprinted letters in Maria Edgeworth's novel *Helen*. Tarr, "Purloined Letters: Edgar Allan Poe, Maria Edgeworth, and the Study of Chirography," *Edgar Allan Poe Review* 14, no. 2 (2013): 178–98.
22. Edgar Allen Poe, "Autography," part 1, *Southern Literary Messenger*, February 1836, 205.
23. For an account of the contemporary reception of the series, see Kent P. Ljungquist, "Poe's 'Autography': A New Exchange of Reviews," *American Periodicals* 2 (1992): 51–63.
24. Poe, "Chapter on Autography," part 1, 225.
25. Poe, "Chapter on Autography," part 1, 225, 231.
26. Kevin J. Hayes, "Poe, the Daguerrotype, and the Autobiographical Act," *Biography* 25, no. 3 (2002): 479. Hayes reads "Autography" in the context of a discussion of Poe's later plans to include the daguerreotypes of authors in *Stylus*, the magazine he hoped to design.
27. Poe, "Chapter on Autography," part 1, 226; Thornton, "The Romance and Science of Individuality," 80.
28. Poe, "Chapter on Autography," part 1, 226.
29. Poe, "Chapter on Autography," part 1, 225.
30. Thornton, "The Romance and Science of Individuality," 79, 80.
31. Poe, "Chapter on Autography," part 2, 274, 276, 276, 275, 276, 286.

32. Poe, "Chapter on Autography," part 1, 230.
33. Ezra Greenspan, *George Palmer Putnam: Representative American Publisher*, Penn State Series in the History of the Book (Pennsylvania State University Press, 2000), 269.
34. Watson, *The Author's Effects*, 9.
35. Alison Booth, *How to Make It as a Woman: Collective Biographical History from Victoria to the Present*, Women in Culture and Society (University of Chicago Press, 2004), 19.
36. Ezra Greenspan suggests that the most likely explanation for the lack of a second edition is that Putnam "had lost faith in the work's financial viability." Greenspan, *George Palmer Putnam*, 272.
37. Scott E. Casper, "Biography," in *An Extensive Republic*, ed. Gross and Kelley, 459–60.
38. Michael Winship, "Manufacturing and Book Production," in *The Industrial Book, 1840–1880*, ed. Casper, 66.
39. Greenspan, *George Palmer Putnam*, 240.
40. Preface to *Homes of American Authors*, ed. Putnam, iv.
41. Paul Westover, "The Transatlantic Home Network: Discovering Sir Walter Scott," in *Transatlantic Literature and Author Love in the Nineteenth Century*, ed. Westover and Rowland, 159.
42. Booth, *Homes and Haunts*, 70, quoting "Washington Irving," in *Homes of American Authors*, ed. Putnam, 35, 48. For an account of how Irving's "writer's home" evoked Scott's, see chapter 8 in Watson, *The Author's Effects*.
43. Greenspan, *George Palmer Putnam*, 248.
44. Cohen, *The Fabrication of American Literature*, 44.
45. McGill, "Copyright," 166.
46. "George Bancroft," in *Homes of American Authors*, ed. Putnam, 91.
47. "William H. Prescott," in *Homes of American Authors*, ed. Putnam, 155.
48. Booth, *Homes and Haunts*, 17.
49. Prescott died between the composition and the printing of the sketch of him in *Homes of American Authors*, and, indeed, it was common for these collections to reprint autographs of the dead. Samantha Matthews suggests that for mid-Victorians the "characteristic autograph was tantamount to a piece of the person, the textual corpus analogous to the material corpse." Matthews, "Reading the

'Sign Manual': Dickens and Signature," *Dickens Quarterly* 9, no. 4 (2002): 237. Matthews quotes Charles Dickens speaking out against the cult value of the autograph in response to advertisements selling Lord Chamberlain's autographs after his death in 1852: "The sanctity of a seal, or the confidence of a letter, is a meaningless phrase that has no place in the vocabulary of Traders in Death. Stop, trumpets, in the Dead March, and blow to the world how characteristic we autographs are!" (236).

50. Leon Jackson, *The Business of Letters: Authorial Economies in Antebellum America* (Stanford University Press, 2007), 15, 17, and 126–38 (an extended discussion of the *Southern Literary Messenger*).
51. Meaghan M. Fritz and Frank E. Fee Jr., "To Give the Gift of Freedom: Gift Books and the War on Slavery," *American Periodicals* 23, no. 1 (2013): 64.
52. McKivigan and Pattillo, "*Autographs for Freedom* and Reaching a New Abolitionist Audience," 35. See also Thompson, *American Literary Annuals & Gift Books*.
53. Fritz and Fee, "To Give the Gift of Freedom," 71.
54. Michael C. Cohen, *The Social Lives of Poems in Nineteenth-Century America*, Material Texts (University of Pennsylvania Press, 2015), 77.
55. Jasmine Nichole Cobb, "'Forget Me Not': Free Black Women and Sentimentality," *Melus* 40, no. 3 (2015): 32; Jasmine Nichole Cobb, *Picture Freedom: Remaking Black Visuality in the Early Nineteenth Century*, America and the Long 19th Century, vol. 20 (New York University Press, 2015), 70.
56. Thompson, *American Literary Annuals & Gift Books*, 16, 18.
57. McKivigan and Pattillo, "*Autographs for Freedom* and Reaching a New Abolitionist Audience," 39. John P. Jewett published *Uncle Tom's Cabin* in 1852, *A Key to* Uncle Tom's Cabin in 1853, and *Truth Stranger Than Fiction*, the second version of Josiah Henson's life, in 1858, and he is an important figure in the discussion of Josiah Henson's lives in chapter 4.
58. Fritz and Fee, "To Give the Gift of Freedom," 72.
59. My thanks to Meri-Jane Rochelson for this observation.
60. My thanks to Lara Langer Cohen for calling my attention to the affective flexibility of this material form.

61. Lara Langer Cohen and Meredith McGill, "The Perils of Authorship," in *The Oxford History of the Novel in English*, vol. 5: *The American Novel to 1870*, ed. J. Gerald Kennedy and Leland S. Person (Oxford University Press, 2014), 195–96.

3. WHITE LADY AUTHORESSES CROSS THE ATLANTIC: ANTISLAVERY GIFT BOOKS AND TRAVELOGUES

1. Lorraine Janzen Kooistra, *Poetry, Pictures, and Popular Publishing: The Illustrated Gift Book and Victorian Visual Culture, 1855–1875* (Ohio University Press, 2011), 30.
2. Marjorie Stone, "Elizabeth Barrett Browning and the Garrisonians: 'The Runaway Slave at Pilgrim's Point,' the Boston Female Anti-Slavery Society, and Abolitionist Discourse in *The Liberty Bell*," in *Victorian Women Poets*, ed. Alison Chapman, Essays and Studies, no. 56 (D. S. Brewer, 2003), 34. *The Liberty Bell by Friends of Freedom* was published by the Boston National Anti-Slavery Bazaar in 1839, 1841–1849, 1851–1854, 1856, 1858.
3. Lootens, *The Political Poetess*, 8, 39.
4. Anne Kostelanetz Mellor, *Mothers of the Nation: Women's Political Writing in England, 1780–1830*, Women of Letters (Indiana University Press, 2002), 3.
5. See Flore Janssen and Lisa C. Robertson, eds., "Nineteenth-Century Women's Campaign Writing: Broadening the Realm of Women's Civic Engagement," special issue, *Nineteenth-Century Gender Studies* 17, no. 2 (2021); Elizabeth Kraft, ed., "Women and Protest," special issue, *European Romantic Review* 32, no. 3 (2021).
6. Alasdair Pettinger and Tim Youngs, introduction to *The Routledge Research Companion to Travel Writing*, ed. Alasdair Pettinger and Tim Youngs (Routledge, 2020), 4.
7. Nicola J. Watson, introduction to *Literary Tourism and Nineteenth-Century Culture*, ed. Nicola J. Watson (Palgrave Macmillan, 2009), 5.
8. Charles Dickens, *American Notes for General Circulation* (Harper & Brothers, 1842); William Wells Brown, *Three Years in Europe: Or,*

Places I Have Seen and People I Have Met (C. Gilpin, 1852); Harriet Beecher Stowe, *Sunny Memories of Foreign Lands* (Phillips, Sampson, 1854). For the connection between European travel writing and antislavery, see Charles Baraw, "William Wells Brown, 'Three Years in Europe,' and Fugitive Tourism," *African American Review* 44, no. 3 (2011): 453–70; and Denise Kohn et al., eds., *Transatlantic Stowe: Harriet Beecher Stowe and European Culture* (University of Iowa Press, 2006).

9. Brenda R. Weber, *Women and Literary Celebrity in the Nineteenth Century: The Transatlantic Production of Fame and Gender*, Ashgate Series in Nineteenth-Century Transatlantic Studies (Ashgate, 2012), 25.
10. Fritz and Fee, "To Give the Gift of Freedom," 68.
11. Benjamin Quarles, "Sources of Abolitionist Income," in *Black Mosaic: Essays in Afro-American History and Historiography* (University of Massachusetts Press, 1988), 76.
12. Stone, "Elizabeth Barrett Browning and the Garrisonians," 48.
13. Poe quoted in Åsa Arping, "'The Miss Austen of Sweden.' Om Fredrika Bremer i 1840-talets USA och litteraturhistorisk omvärdering," *Tidskrift för litteraturvetenskap* 48, nos. 1–2 (2018): 25.
14. Fredrika Bremer, "Letter," in *The Liberty Bell by Friends of Freedom* (National Anti-Slavery Bazaar, 1845), 73, 72, 76. Bremer's letter is quoted in Laurel Ann Lofsvold, *Fredrika Bremer and the Writing of America* (Lund University Press, 1999), 197. Although I use this passage to show Bremer's glancing engagement with abolitionism in the context of the volume, Lofsvold cites Bremer's exchange with Chapman in the context of Bremer's long-term positioning within American abolitionism, including her literary connections with Stowe and her two-page translation of a passage from Frederick Douglass's narrative in *Hemmen i den Nya Verlden* (*Homes of the New World*, 1853).
15. Barbara Onslow, "Gendered Productions: Annuals and Gift Books," in *Journalism and the Periodical Press in Nineteenth-Century Britain*, ed. Joanne Shattock (Cambridge University Press, 2017), 67–68. Onslow also points out that even less well-paid contributions meant money and exposure (76).
16. Jackson, *The Business of Letters*.
17. Marraccini, "Feminist Types," 34.

18. McKivigan and Pattillo, *"Autographs for Freedom* and Reaching a New Abolitionist Audience"; Stone, "Elizabeth Barrett Browning and the Garrisonians."
19. Alexis Easley, interviewed by the author, Zoom, October 24, 2022.
20. Fritz and Fee, "To Give the Gift of Freedom," 70.
21. Sometimes an editor's name was their chief contribution: Fionnuala Dillane observes that "Dickens, Trollope, Mary Elizabeth Braddon, and Thackeray in his last editorial role at the *Cornhill Magazine*, all used their names as editors or, even more overtly, were used *for* their names." Dillane, "'The Character of Editress': Marian Evans at the *Westminster Review*, 1851–54," *Tulsa Studies in Women's Literature* 30, no. 2 (2011): 285, Dillane's emphasis.
22. Fritz and Fee point out that whereas Chapman contributed a few pieces to *The Liberty Bell* under her own name over the years but didn't claim editorship, Griffiths claimed editorship but wrote only the introductions to *Autographs for Freedom*. Fritz and Fee, "To Give the Gift of Freedom," 68. As Barbara Onslow points out, gift books give us good purchase on the hybrid roles of editor/writer and editor/publisher. Onslow, "Gendered Productions," 83.
23. Deborah Anna Logan, "'My Dearly-Beloved Americans': Harriet Martineau's Transatlantic Abolitionism," in *Nineteenth-Century British Travelers in the New World*, ed. Christine DeVine (Ashgate, 2013), 203–4.
24. Claybaugh uses Martineau as a model figure in her preface to *The Novel of Purpose*, 2–3.
25. Logan, "'My Dearly-Beloved Americans,'" 207. On the breadth of Martineau's periodical work and depth of her engagement with U.S. politics, see Lesa Scholl, "Brewing Storms of War, Slavery, and Imperialism: Harriet Martineau's Engagement with the Periodical Press," in *Women, Periodicals, and Print Culture in Britain*, ed. Easley et al., 489–501.
26. Easley, *First-Person Anonymous*, 45, 132; Harriet Martineau, *Society in America* (Saunders and Otley, 1837), 12.
27. Logan, "'My Dearly-Beloved Americans,'" 209; Leslee Thorne-Murphy, "Women, Free Trade, and Harriet Martineau's 'Dawn Island' at the 1845 Anti–Corn Law League Bazaar," in *Economic Women: Essays*

on *Desire and Dispossession in Nineteenth-Century British Culture*, ed. Lana Dalley and Jill Rappaport (Ohio State University Press, 2013), 41–59. Thorne-Murphy argues that Martineau's tale "Dawn Island," which was a contribution to an anti–Corn Law bazaar, should be understood as a reflection on women's work (45).
28. Linda H. Peterson, *Becoming a Woman of Letters: Myths of Authorship and Facts of the Victorian Market* (Princeton University Press, 2009), 15.
29. Harriet Martineau, "Pity the Slave," in *The Liberty Bell by Friends of Freedom* (National Anti-Slavery Bazaar, 1844), 182–83, 186.
30. Maria H. Frawley, introduction to Harriet Martineau, *Life in the Sick-Room: Essays* (1844) (Broadview Press, 2003), 19; Alison Winter, "Harriet Martineau and the Reform of the Invalid in Victorian England," *Historical Journal* 38, no. 3 (September 1995): 603.
31. Amanda Adams, "'Here, I Could Rove at Will': Harriet Martineau, *Sartain's Union Magazine*, and Freedom in the Transatlantic Periodical Press," *Victorian Periodicals Review* 51, no. 1 (2018): 121–37.
32. Midgley, "British Abolition and Feminism in Transatlantic Perspective," 129. See also Clare Midgley, *Feminism and Empire: Women Activists in Imperial Britain, 1790–1865* (Routledge, 2007).
33. Deborah A. Logan, "Harem Life, West and East," *Women's Studies* 26, no. 5 (1997): 449–74.
34. Logan, "'My Dearly-Beloved Americans,'" 203.
35. Elizabeth Barrett Browning, "The Runaway Slave at Pilgrim's Point," in *The Liberty Bell by Friends of Freedom* (National Anti-Slavery Bazaar, 1848), 29–44.
36. Sheehan's contribution to Lucy Sheehan et al., "Miscellany as Method: A Trio of Approaches to 'The Runaway Slave at Pilgrim's Point' and the 1848 *Liberty Bell* Gift Book," *Victorian Poetry* 59, no. 3 (2021): 272.
37. Sorensen's contribution to Sheehan et al., "Miscellany as Method," 277.
38. To understand Martineau's "Incidents of Travel" in the context of the book in which it was soon reprinted, *Eastern Life, Present and Past* (1848), see Deborah A. Logan, *Harriet Martineau, Victorian Imperialism, and the Civilizing Mission* (Routledge, 2016). For a more comprehensive perspective of colonial women's travelogues, see Inderpal Grewal, *Home and Harem: Nation, Gender, Empire, and the Cultures of Travel*, Post-contemporary Interventions (Duke University Press,

1996); Sara Mills, *Discourses of Difference: An Analysis of Women's Travel Writing and Colonialism* (Routledge, 2003); and Mary Louise Pratt, *Imperial Eyes: Travel Writing and Transculturation* (Routledge, 2007).

39. Harriet Martineau, "Incidents of Travel," in *The Liberty Bell by Friends of Freedom* (1848), 83.
40. Martineau, "Incidents of Travel," 86. Jill Matus uses Martineau's treatment of the harem to open up the question of how British women contributed to orientalist discourse, noting that the "sympathetic observation" Martineau advocated elsewhere in her travel writing gives way to "disgust, anxiety, and horror." Matus, "The 'Eastern-Woman Question': Martineau and Nightingale Visit the Harem," *Nineteenth-Century Contexts* 21, no. 1 (1999): 68.
41. Martineau, "Incidents of Travel," 86–87.
42. Mia L. Bagneris, "Miscegenation in Marble: John Bell's *Octoroon*," *Art Bulletin* 102, no. 2 (2020): 69, 80.
43. Logan, "Harem Life," 455.
44. For more on this context, see Margaret McFadden's discussion of Bremer's critique of Martineau's *Society in America* (1837) and Martineau's critique of Bremer in *Autobiography* (1877). McFadden, *Golden Cables of Sympathy*, 159. McFadden also notes that Bremer met Stowe on her visit to the United States in 1849–1851 (154).
45. Susan Morgan, *Place Matters: Gendered Geography in Victorian Women's Travel Books About Southeast Asia* (Rutgers University Press, 1996).
46. Grewal, *Home and Harem*.
47. Judith Johnston, *Victorian Women and the Economies of Travel, Translation, and Culture, 1830–1870*, Nineteenth Century (Ashgate, 2013), 21.
48. Ivonne M. García, "Anticipating Colonialism: U.S. Letters on Puerto Rico and Cuba, 1831–1835," in *Letters and Cultural Transformations in the United States, 1760–1860*, ed. Theresa Strouth Gaul and Sharon M. Harris (Ashgate, 2009), 58.
49. Adriana Méndez Rodenas, *Transatlantic Travels in Nineteenth-Century Latin America: European Women Pilgrims*, Bucknell Studies in Latin American Literature and Theory (Bucknell University Press, 2014), 21; Aisha K. Finch, "Scandalous Scarcities: Black Slave Women, Plantation Domesticity, and Travel Writing in Nineteenth-Century Cuba," *Journal of Historical Sociology* 23, no. 1 (2010): 102. Lofsvold

notes that Eugene D. Genovese "quotes extensively" from Bremer in *Roll Jordan Roll: The World the Slaves Made* (1972). See Lofsvold, *Fredrika Bremer and the Writing of America*, 197.

50. Susan P. Casteras, "'Too Abhorrent to Englishmen to Render a Representation of It . . . Acceptable': Slavery as Seen by British Artists Travelling in America," in *Women's Rights and Transatlantic Antislavery in the Era of Emancipation*, ed. Sklar and Stewart, 245. For Barbara Leigh Smith Bodichon's own letters describing her travel to New Orleans, see Bodichon, *Barbara Leigh Smith Bodichon: An American Diary 1857–8*, ed. Joseph W. Reed (Routledge & Kegan Paul, 1972).
51. Greenspan, *George Palmer Putnam*, 259. Greenspan also notes that Putnam would ultimately publish some of Bremer's work (259).
52. Michie, "Reassessing the Cleverness of Frances Trollope's Social Fictions." For the way in which Trollope's rhetoric of abolition shapes the structure of Dickens's early work, see Elsie B. Michie, "Morbidity in Fairyland: Frances Trollope, Charles Dickens, and the Rhetoric of Abolition," *Partial Answers* 9, no. 2 (2011): 233–51.
53. Fredrika Bremer, *The Homes of the New World: Impressions of America*, 2 vols., trans. Mary Howitt (Harper & Brothers, 1853), 2:325.
54. Bremer quoted in Johnston, *Victorian Women*, 156.
55. Ivonne M. García, "Gothic Cuba and the Trans-American South in Louisa May Alcott's 'M.L.,'" in *The Palgrave Handbook of the Southern Gothic*, ed. Susan P. Castillo and Charles L. Crow (Macmillan, 2016), 162. In *Gothic Geoculture: Nineteenth-Century Representations of Cuba in the Transamerican Imaginary* (Ohio State University Press, 2019), see also Ivonne M. García's treatment of slavery and the gothic in representations of Cuba by writers based in Cuba as well as in the United States.
56. Bremer, *Homes of the New World*, 2:294, 297, 108. Thanks to Meri-Jane Rochelson for underscoring the confusion in Bremer's part of the dialogue.
57. Arping, "'The Miss Austen of Sweden,'" 24. Arping notes that Ralph Waldo Emerson, Nathaniel Hawthorne, Edgar Allan Poe, Margaret Fuller, Fanny Fern, Harriet Beecher Stowe, and Louisa May Alcott engaged with Bremer's work (25).

58. Arping, "'The Miss Austen of Sweden,'" 23; Åsa Arping, "A Writer of One's Own? Mary Howitt, Fredrika Bremer, Translation, and Literary 'Piracy' in the US and Britain in the 1840s," in *Gender and Translation: Understanding Agents in Transnational Reception*, ed. Isis Herrero López et al. (Éditions québécoises de l'oeuvre, 2018), 88.
59. Shattock, "Women Journalists and Periodical Spaces," 309.
60. Arping, "A Writer of One's Own?"
61. Arping, "A Writer of One's Own?," 90. Howitt didn't own the rights to Bremer's novels, either; though she and Bremer were closely identified from the beginning of Bremer's publication in English, the names of various translators appeared on Bremer's work over the years. Yvonne Leffler, *Swedish Nineteenth-Century Novels as World Literature: Transnational Success and Literary History* (LIR.Skrifter, 2020), 50.
62. Arping, "'The Miss Austen of Sweden.'" For an account in English, see Yvonne Leffler et al., *Swedish Women's Writing on Export: Tracing Transnational Reception in the Nineteenth Century* (University of Gothenburg, 2019), 97–153.
63. Åsa Arping and Yvonne Leffler, "The Wonderful Adventures of Swedish Everyday Life: Female Domestic Novels on Export in the Nineteenth Century," in *The Dynamics and Contexts of Cultural Transfers*, ed. Margaretha Fahlgren and Anna Williams (Avd. för Litteratursociologi, 2017), 67. In Louisa May Alcott's *Little Women* (1868–1869), the March family reads Bremer along with Scott and Edgeworth. In the 2018 Penguin edition of *Little Women*, the editor, Anne Boyd Rioux, glosses Bremer as a "Swedish champion of women's rights and a writer of domestic, realistic novels" (471).
64. George Eliot, "[Three Novels]," *Westminster Review* 66 (October 1856): 571–78, reprinted in *Essays of George Eliot*, with a preface and notes by Thomas Pinney (Routledge and Kegan Paul, 1963), quote on 331. This essay appears in the same October 1856 volume of the *Westminster Review* that contains George Eliot's essay "Silly Novels by Lady Novelists." See Pinney's note in Eliot, "[Three Novels]," 325.
65. Johnston, *Victorian Women*, 162, 158, 160 (quote from Bremer).
66. Maria DiBattista and Deborah Epstein Nord, *At Home in the World: Women Writers and Public Life, from Austen to the Present* (Princeton University Press, 2017), 44.

67. Bremer, *Homes of the New World*, 2:187.
68. Bremer, *Homes of the New World*, 2:185, 187, 188.
69. Bremer, *Homes of the New World*, 2:192–93. She later quotes a story by the same planter to connect it with home: "In Sweden also—in the highest circles of Stockholm—we have known ladies whose domestics bore bloody marks, and whom the police were obliged to take in charge. . . . A good thing is it that the servants of these ladies could leave them, thanks to the laws of a free country! But here, in this free country, people can, in the face of such facts, still defend slavery as a patriarchal institution, quite compatible with the laws of a free people, and with human rights and happiness!" (2:245–46).
70. Lofsvold, *Fredrika Bremer and the Writing of America*, 209.
71. Bremer, *Homes of the New World*, 2:109, Bremer's emphasis.
72. Bremer: "It was my intention, at the commencement of this work, to introduce in an Appendix at its close such of the scenes which I had witnessed, and my own experience in the slave states of America and in Cuba, as I considered necessary to be made known, but which I had not related in my letters, being unwilling to point out persons and places. The celebrated work, however, of Mrs. Harriet Beecher Stowe, 'Uncle Tom's Cabin,' and, still more, her lately published work, 'A Key, &c.' have rendered this unpleasant duty unnecessary for me; for my narratives would not have presented any facts essentially different to those which she has introduced into her story, so that I need not further prolong this work, which is already too much extended, than be remarking that my proposed narration would have principally strengthened my often-repeated observation regarding the demoralizing effect of the institution of slavery on the white population" (*Homes of the New World*, 2:653).

4. BECOMING THE "REAL UNCLE TOM": A TEXTUAL HISTORY OF THE LIVES OF JOSIAH HENSON

1. Harriet Beecher Stowe, *Uncle Tom's Cabin* (1852), ed. Ann Douglas (New York: Penguin, 1981), 618.
2. Samuel Otter, "Stowe and Race," in *The Cambridge Companion to Harriet Beecher Stowe*, ed. Cindy Weinstein (Cambridge University Press, 2004), 25.

3. Stowe, *A Key to* Uncle Tom's Cabin, 26.
4. William H. Pease and Jane H. Pease, "Josiah Henson" (revised 1982), in *Dictionary of Canadian Biography*, vol. 11: *1881–1890* (University of Toronto/Université Laval, 2003–), http://www.biographi.ca/en/bio/henson_josiah_11E.html.
5. Robin W. Winks, "The Making of a Fugitive Slave Narrative: Josiah Henson and Uncle Tom—a Case Study," in *The Slave's Narrative*, ed. Charles T. Davis and Henry Louis Gates Jr. (Oxford University Press, 1985), 112–46. Both Henson and Stowe claimed to have met one another, but, according to Winks, the details don't add up.
6. Frances Smith Foster, *Witnessing Slavery: The Development of Antebellum Slave Narratives* (Greenwood Press, 1979), 147.
7. Martin R. Delany, "Delany and Douglass on *Uncle Tom's Cabin*," in *Martin R. Delany: A Documentary Reader*, ed. Robert S. Levine (University of North Carolina Press, 2003), 230, Delany's emphasis.
8. In one sense, the edition that points most clearly to the lectures is the "revised and enlarged" version published in 1881, *An Autobiography of the Rev. Josiah Henson ("Uncle Tom"), from 1789 to 1881*, edited by John Lobb and published in London, Ontario, by Schuyler, Smith (substantially similar to the 1876 edition). This edition includes an appendix titled "Summary of 'Uncle Tom's' Public Services" that documents where Henson delivered his speeches and sermons, noting that on one occasion a church was "crowded to its full capacity" (167) and that on another "it was pleasing to witness 'Uncle Tom's' gratification on meeting the noble Earl [of Shaftesbury] again, after the interval of so many years, and the Earl's hearty reciprocity" (173). This list of speeches is followed by an account of the money Henson raised on the tour.
9. For the number of copies of *The Life of Josiah Henson* sold, see Yuval Taylor's introduction to *I Was Born a Slave: An Anthology of Classic Slave Narratives*, vol. 2: *1849–1866*, ed. Yuval Taylor (Lawrence Hill, 1999), xx; for the number of *Uncle Tom's Story of His Life* sold by 1907, see "Sketch of the Editor, 'Mr. John Lobb,'" in *Men and Women of the Time* (Routledge, 1899), reprinted in John Lobb, *Talks with the Dead; Luminous Rays from the Unseen World, Illustrated with Spirit Photographs* (J. Lobb, 1907), xix. The latter book claims that Henson, who

died in 1883, was "a frequent visitor at the séances where I have sat, and he invariably put in an appearance at the public services where I officiate. Clairvoyants often remain to inform me of his presence, and many an encouraging message he sends to me of his constant help" (32). *Talks with the Dead* also includes a "spirit photograph" of Stowe (33).

10. This quotation is from a lecture Henson gave in Dumfries in 1877: "My name is not Tom." It is the title of Hannah-Rose Murray's chapter on Henson, "'My Name Is Not Tom': Josiah Henson, *Uncle Tom's Cabin*, and Adaptive Resistance After the Civil War 1876–1877," in her book *Advocates of Freedom*, 255–91. Murray focuses on Henson's deployment of minstrelsy in his postwar tour performances, 1876–1877. She argues that he negotiated the roles of being a "living memorial" to "convince British audiences of the dangers of relying on racial stereotypes and mythologizing slavery" (260, 282).

11. Adena Spingarn, *Uncle Tom: From Martyr to Traitor* (Stanford University Press, 2018), 127.

12. For a discussion of the more general impact of slave narratives on the form of the nineteenth-century novel, see Julia Sun-Joo Lee, *The American Slave Narrative and the Victorian Novel* (Oxford University Press, 2010).

13. Winks, "The Making of a Fugitive Slave Narrative," 115.

14. Murray, *Advocates of Freedom*, 2. See also R. J. M. Blackett, *Building an Antislavery Wall: Black Americans in the Atlantic Abolitionist Movement, 1830–1860* (Louisiana State University Press, 1983). In *Bodies in Dissent: Spectacular Performances of Race and Freedom, 1850–1910* (Duke University Press, 2006), Daphne A. Brooks frames Henry Box Brown's reenactments of escape as a form of spectacular performance.

15. Stephanie J. Richmond, "Race, Class, and Antislavery: African American Women in the Transatlantic Antislavery Movement," *Journal of Women's History* 31, no. 3 (2019): 71.

16. Adams, *Performing Authorship*, 11, 12.

17. Brooks, *Bodies in Dissent*, 67. Brooks highlights speakers who transformed this framework, such as William Box Brown, who staged his own escape as "a freedom of representational form which, in turn,

allowed him to reenter the text of his own narrative and, in so doing, make new the landscape of fugitive slave autobiography" (77).
18. Murray, *Advocates of Freedom*, 6–7.
19. Lewis R. Gordon, "The Problem of Biography in the Study of the Thought of Black Intellectuals," *Small Axe: A Journal of Criticism*, no. 4 (1998): 47–48. Joseph Rezek's work gives further context for understanding Black authorship in the early nineteenth century, within an "essentializing phase" of the racialization of print, or "the point where a published book by a single author was understood as capable of representing the essential nature of an entire race of people." Rezek, "The Racialization of Print," *American Literary History* 32, no. 3 (September 2020): 419.
20. Teresa A. Goddu, "The Slave Narrative as Material Text," in *The Oxford Handbook of the African American Slave Narrative*, ed. John Ernest (Oxford University Press, 2014), 151; Lara Langer Cohen and Jordan Alexander Stein, *Early African American Print Culture*, Material Texts (University of Pennsylvania Press, Library Company of Philadelphia, 2012), 3.
21. David C. Greetham, *Textual Scholarship: An Introduction*, Garland Reference Library of the Humanities, vol. 1417 (Garland, 1992), 362, paraphrasing Michel Foucault, "What Is an Author?" (1969), in *Essential Works of Foucault, 1954–1984*, vol. 2: *Aesthetics, Method, and Epistemology* (New Press, 1998), 207.
22. Modern Language Association, "Guidelines for Editors of Scholarly Editions," revised May 4, 2022, https://www.mla.org/Resources/Guidelines-and-Data/Reports-and-Professional-Guidelines/Guidelines-for-Editors-of-Scholarly-Editions.
23. William L. Andrews, "Bibliography of Slave and Ex-slave Narratives" (2003–present), Documenting the American South, University Library, University of North Carolina at Chapel Hill, https://docsouth.unc.edu/neh/biblintro.html. The list of autobiographies that includes the 1849 and 1858 editions of Henson's lives is given as an appendix to William L. Andrews, *To Tell a Free Story: The First Century of Afro-American Autobiography, 1760–1865* (University of Illinois Press, 1986), 333–42.
24. Goddu notes that the slave narrative was "mostly produced outside antislavery" in the 1840s. Teresa Goddu, *Selling Antislavery: Abolition*

and *Mass Media in Antebellum America* (University of Pennsylvania Press, 2020), 79.

25. Robin W. Winks, *The Blacks in Canada; a History* (McGill-Queen's University Press, 1971), 183.

26. Ephraim Peabody, "Narratives of Fugitive Slaves," *Christian Examiner and Religious Miscellany* 47, no. 1 (1849): 69, 80. According to Frank Luther Mott, both Peabody and Samuel A. Eliot were members of the Examiner Club, a group "formed in 1839 to improve the level of book-reviewing" in the *Christian Examiner*. Mott, "The *Christian Disciple* and the *Christian Examiner*," *New England Quarterly* 1, no. 2 (1928): 200–201.

27. Manisha Sinha, *The Slave's Cause: A History of Abolition* (New Haven: Yale University Press, 2016), 431. From the perspective of the publishing history of the 1849 *The Life of Josiah Henson*, Samuel A. Eliot appears as a publisher and as a periodical contributor connected with the Christian Examiner network. Eliot's role in creating the 1849 edition reveals how the sociology of texts sheds light on different dimensions of a single figure. If Henson's life is evidently political in its documentation of his experience and its circulation through his public appearances, Sinha's historical perspective on the document shows it circulating in context of Eliot's public career. The Fugitive Slave Act of 1850 is important context for Stowe's portrayal of Northern complicity with slavery in *Uncle Tom's Cabin*—in James Baldwin's formulation, the panic of being caught in traffic with the devil. That Eliot could have voted in its favor and yet also have been the person who made the publication of Henson's narrative possible demonstrates the wide range of political orientations within "antislavery" politics.

28. Quoted in T. W. H., "James H. Duncan," *The Liberator* 20, no. 42 (1850): 165.

29. Andrews, *To Tell a Free Story*, 110.

30. Peabody, "Narratives of Fugitive Slaves," 74, 75, 79.

31. Nell Irvin Painter, "Difference, Slavery, and Memory: Sojourner Truth in Feminist Abolitionism," in *The Abolitionist Sisterhood: Women's Political Culture in Antebellum America*, ed. Jean Fagan Yellin and John C. Van Horne (Cornell University Press, 1994), 147.

32. Jarena Lee, *Religious Experience and Journal of Mrs. Jarena Lee, Giving an Account of Her Call to Preach the Gospel* (Printed and Published for

the Author, 1849), 83. *Religious Experience and Journal* was an expanded edition of a pamphlet issued in 1836. Gwendolyn DuBois Shaw notes that Lee's frontispiece echoes the iconography of the frontispiece in Phillis Wheatley's book *Poems on Various Subjects, Religious and Moral* (1773): "a quill in her hand and papers and books on the table beside her," which underscores the literariness of Lee's autobiography. Shaw, *The Art of Remembering: Essays on African American Art and History* (Duke University Press, 2024), 41. See also Chanta M. Haywood, *Prophesying Daughters: Black Women Preachers and the Word, 1823–1913* (University of Missouri Press, 2003).

33. Painter, "Difference, Slavery, and Memory," 147; Nell Irvin Painter, *Sojourner Truth: A Life, a Symbol* (Norton, 1997), 129.
34. See Jan Marsh on Henson's account of participating in the Great Exhibition of 1851. Marsh, "From Slave Cabin to Windsor Castle: Josiah Henson and 'Uncle Tom' in Britain," *Nineteenth Century Studies* 16 (2002): 40.
35. Vanessa D. Dickerson, *Dark Victorians* (University of Illinois Press, 2008), 58; Blackett, *Building an Antislavery Wall*, 137.
36. Delany, "Delany and Douglass on *Uncle Tom's Cabin*," 231.
37. Parfait, *The Publishing History of* Uncle Tom's Cabin, 100, 109, 103.
38. Goddu, *Selling Antislavery*, 57, 56, 79.
39. Koenigs, *Founded in Fiction*, 210.
40. Delany, "Delany and Douglass on *Uncle Tom's Cabin*," 224 (Delany's emphasis), 231, 230. Robert S. Levine frames Delany's criticism of Stowe's novel (and of Douglass's choice to ally himself with Stowe) within a larger debate between Delany and Douglass about emigration and colonization. Levine, *Martin Delany, Frederick Douglass, and the Politics of Representative Identity* (University of North Carolina Press, 1997).
41. Delany, "Delany and Douglass on *Uncle Tom's Cabin*," 231.
42. Harriet Beecher Stowe, preface to Josiah Henson, *Truth Stranger Than Fiction: Father Henson's Story of His Own Life* (John P. Jewett, 1858), iii.
43. Winks, "The Making of a Fugitive Slave Narrative." As Winks reports, "Later, when queried on the relationship between the two books, Jewett appeared to be unaware that there had been an . . . edition [of Henson's autobiography earlier] than 1852, and he asserted that

Mrs. Stowe could not have made use of Henson's work since it did not appear until 1858. . . . In c. 1882 he asserted that he had personally written about a quarter of the 1858 Henson book and that Gilbert Haven had written another quarter of it. Half of it was written by 'a Unitarian clergyman of Springfield, Mass.'" (142).

44. Parfait, *The Publishing History of Uncle Tom's Cabin*, 40; Augusta Rohrbach, *Truth Stranger Than Fiction: Race, Realism, and the U.S. Literary Market Place* (Palgrave Macmillan, 2002), 35, Rohrbach's emphasis; Mary Ellen Doyle, "Josiah Henson's Narrative: Before and After," *Negro American Literature Forum* 8, no. 1 (Spring 1974): 181, 176; John Ernest, *Chaotic Justice: Rethinking African American Literary History* (University of North Carolina Press, 2009), 92.

45. Foster, *Witnessing Slavery*, 147. See also Michaël Roy's analysis of different material forms of slave narratives in *Fugitive Texts: Slave Narratives in Antebellum Print Culture*, trans. Susan Pickford (University of Wisconsin Press, 2023).

46. Lucy Sheehan, personal correspondence, September 2021.

47. Rohrbach, *Truth Stranger Than Fiction*, 745. On books Jewett and Company advertised as antislavery literature, see Sarah Meer, "Slave Narratives as Literature," in *The Cambridge Companion to Slavery in American Literature*, ed. Ezra Tawil (Cambridge University Press, 2016), 74.

48. Goddu, "The Slave Narrative as Material Text," 152; Michael Winship, "*UTC*: History of the Book in the 19th Century U.S.," 2007, *Uncle Tom's Cabin and American Culture: A Multi-media Archive*, ed. Steven Railton, http://utc.iath.virginia.edu/interpret/exhibits/winship/winship.html.

49. "John Punchard Jewett," in *Dictionary of American Biography*, ed. Dumas Malone, Gale in Context: Biography (Tulane University) (Scribner's, 1936), 69.

50. John P. Jewett ad in *The Liberator* 52 (1856), cited in Rohrbach, *Truth Stranger Than Fiction*, 22–23.

51. Peabody, "Narratives of Fugitive Slaves," 78–79; "Father Henson's Story of His Own Life," *Methodist Quarterly Review* 40 (1858): 500. The "sympathetic source of tears" is a slight misquotation of Thomas Gray's poem "The Progress of Poesy. A Pindaric Ode" (1757): Nature reveals "her awful face" to the allegorical child and gives him the

4. BECOMING THE "REAL UNCLE TOM"   195

keys to "unlock the gates of joy; / Of Horrour that, and thrilling Fears, / Or ope the sacred source of sympathetic Tears" (3.1, ll. 93–94). Gray, "The Progress of Poesy. A Pindaric Ode" (1757), in *The Complete Poems of Thomas Gray: English, Latin, and Greek*, ed. H. W. Starr and J. R. Hendrickson, Oxford English Texts (Oxford University Press, 1966), 16.

52. Josiah Henson, *Uncle Tom's Story of His Life: An Autobiography of the Rev. Josiah Henson (Mrs. Harriet Beecher Stowe's "Uncle Tom"), from 1789 to 1876* (Christian Age Office, 1876), 158.
53. For an account of the initial British reception of *Uncle Tom's Cabin*—including visual, theatrical, and novelized adaptations—and of Stowe's own lectures there, see Audrey Fisch, "Uncle Tom and Harriet Beecher Stowe in England," in *The Cambridge Companion to Harriet Beecher Stowe*, ed. Weinstein, 96–112.
54. Josiah Henson, *The Young People's Illustrated Edition of "Uncle Tom's" Story of His Life (from 1789 to 1877)* (John Lobb, 1877). For a reading of how Lobb "laid claim" to Henson's text while "[shaping] the book for religious ends, rather than the antislavery cause," see Hannah-Rose Murray, "'It Is to a Great Extent, a New Book': Josiah Henson, John Lobb, and the Challenges of White Editorship of Black Texts," in "Black Editorship in the Early Atlantic World," ed. Nele Sawallisch and Johanna Seibert, special issue, *Atlantic Studies* 18, no. 4 (2021): 512.
55. Winks, *The Blacks in Canada*, 192.
56. Robin L. Condon, "'Finished by the Hand by Which It Was Begun': Who Wrote the *Life and Times of Frederick Douglass?*," *Journal of African American History* 99, nos. 1–2 (2014): 19.
57. Documenting the American South, University Library, University of North Carolina, Chapel Hill, https://docsouth.unc.edu.
58. Juxta: Collation Software for Scholars, https://www.juxtasoftware.org/; Stéfan Sinclair and Geoffrey Rockwell, "Voyant Tools," 2016, http://voyant-tools.org/.
59. I created a corpus from the online documents in the Documenting the American South website using only the first-person accounts (that is, I excluded prefatory and other appended material, such as the list of public presentations).

60. This calculation adjusts for length, so although both words recur about the same number of times between the 1858 and the 1876 editions, they stand out in 1858 because of the relative frequency in a shorter text and the total absence of both in the 1849 text. The word *massa* does not appear at all in *Uncle Tom's Cabin*—only the form *mas'r* does.
61. David West Brown, *English and Empire: Literary History, Dialect, and the Digital Archive* (Cambridge University Press, 2018), 109.
62. Josiah Henson, *The Life of Josiah Henson, Formerly a Slave, Now an Inhabitant of Canada, as Narrated by Himself* (A. D. Phelps, 1849), 7; Henson, *Truth Stranger Than Fiction*, 19.
63. Henson, *The Life of Josiah Henson*, 9.
64. Henson, *Truth Stranger Than Fiction*, 20.
65. Smith, "The Man Who Became Uncle Tom."
66. Stowe, *A Key to* Uncle Tom's Cabin, 26.
67. Reynolds, *Mightier Than the Sword*, 106.
68. Henson, *The Life of Josiah Henson*, 25.
69. Henson, *Truth Stranger Than Fiction*, 53–54.
70. Henson, *Truth Stranger Than Fiction*, 54.
71. Henson's choice not to dock in Ohio is presented in 1849 as his decision alone but in 1858 as made against the wishes of the "people under [him]." Henson, *The Life of Josiah Henson*, 23–24; Henson, *Truth Stranger Than Fiction*, 51.
72. Stowe, *Key to* Uncle Tom's Cabin, 27.
73. Henson, *The Life of Josiah Henson*, 42.
74. Henson, *The Life of Josiah Henson*, 43.
75. Henson, *The Life of Josiah Henson*, 41.
76. Henson, *Truth Stranger Than Fiction*, 85–86.
77. Winks, "The Making of a Fugitive Slave Narrative," 115.
78. As Winks notes, in the 1858 edition Henson erases only a reference to being arrested for debt. Winks, "The Making of a Fugitive Slave Narrative," 125.
79. W. E. B. Du Bois, *Black Reconstruction in America 1860–1880* (1935), ed. David Levering Lewis (Simon and Schuster, 1998), 13; H. A. Tanser, "Josiah Henson, the Moses of His People," *Journal of Negro Education* 12, no. 4 (1943): 630–32; Jessie Beattie, *Black Moses: The Real Uncle Tom* (Ryerson Press, 1957).

80. "Father Henson's Story of His Own Life," 501.
81. "The True Story of *Uncle Tom's Cabin,*" *New England Homestead* 3, no. 13 (1870): 110.
82. Murray, *Advocates of Freedom*, 269.
83. In late nineteenth-century Britain, Uncle Tom was an important figure for understanding both the United States as well as American discourse about the United States. Tavia Nyong'o draws on Douglass's writings about blackface to suggest that minstrelsy revealed the centrality of Black art and Black people to American culture, such that the "white attraction to Black song and dance, which fed into white supremacy as Black abolitionists well knew, was paradoxically also the grounds on which a challenge to that supremacy could be mounted, precisely insofar as minstrelsy refused to imagine an America without Blacks." Nyong'o, *The Amalgamation Waltz: Race, Performance, and the Ruses of Memory* (University of Minnesota Press, 2009), 132.
84. Winks, *The Blacks in Canada*, 193.
85. Meer, *Uncle Tom Mania*, 178; Meer, "Slave Narratives as Literature," 79.
86. Margaret Washington, *Sojourner Truth's America* (University of Illinois Press, 2011), 302.
87. Grigsby, *Enduring Truths*, 11. Grigsby's study of Truth's strategies in creating and disseminating images of herself foregrounds a crucial element of print culture elided by my book's focus on textual forms of literary celebrity.
88. Spingarn, *Uncle Tom*, 5.

5. A TRUE HISTORY OF *JANE EYRE*: THE COLLABORATIVE POSTHUMOUS CREATION OF CHARLOTTE BRONTË

1. Amanda Shaw, "'There Are Two Views Often': The Epistolary Friendship of Harriet Beecher Stowe and Elizabeth Gaskell," *Women's Studies* 51, no. 6 (2022): 684. Whitney Womack Smith traces their personal relationship in the more established critical context of the connections between Gaskell's *Mary Barton* (1848) and Stowe's *Uncle Tom's Cabin*. Smith, "Stowe, Gaskell, and the Woman Reformer," in *Transatlantic Stowe*, ed. Kohn et al., 89–110.

2. Shaw, "'There Are Two Views Often,'" 682. Mary Webb toured with her husband, Frank J. Webb, who wrote a biographical preface to the British edition of *The Christian Slave*. Eric Gardner, "'A Gentleman of Superior Cultivation and Refinement': Recovering the Biography of Frank J. Webb," *African American Review* 35, no. 2 (2001): 103. Frank Webb's novel *The Garies and Their Friends* was published in 1857. Susan F. Clark argues that Stowe's adaptation of the novel for a dramatized public reading was a "rebuttal to the critics and to the stage." Clark, "Solo Black Performance Before the Civil War: Mrs. Stowe, Mrs. Webb, and 'The Christian Slave,'" *New Theatre Quarterly* 13, no. 52 (November 1997): 341.
3. Shaw, "'There Are Two Views Often,'" 690. Shaw's account does not state whether Mary Webb visited Gaskell or not, though she notes that Gaskell refused to receive another Black orator, Miss Remond, in 1859 and that Gaskell repeatedly wrote of her support for the North during the Civil War (687–91). Mary Webb's readings advanced not only her own career but also Stowe's; as Eric Gardner argues, Webb's performance "may have authenticated Stowe's story." Gardner, "'A Nobler End': Mary Webb and the Victorian Platform," *Nineteenth-Century Prose* 29, no. 1 (2002): 111.
4. Linda H. Peterson offers a perspective on the intersection of professional and private connections among Gaskell, Brontë, and Martineau in the context of Gaskell's *Life of Charlotte Brontë*. Peterson, "Triangulation, Desire, and Discontent in 'The Life of Charlotte Brontë,'" *Studies in English Literature, 1500–1900* 47, no. 4 (2007): 901–20.
5. Lee, *The American Slave Narrative and the Victorian Novel*, 52.
6. Elsie B. Michie, "'Literary Intercourse': Charlotte Brontë, George Henry Lewes, and George Eliot," *George Eliot—George Henry Lewes Studies* 69, no. 1 (2017): 40. Michie argues that Brontë's commitment to imperfect character in *Shirley*, which has been read as a response to George Henry Lewes's criticism of *Jane Eyre*, is a reworking of Trollope's social problem novels.
7. Smith, "Stowe, Gaskell, and the Woman Reformer," 89.
8. Margaret Oliphant, "The Sisters Brontë," in *Women Novelists of Queen Victoria's Reign* (Hurst and Blackett, 1897), 5, 3. *Women Novelists of Queen Victoria's Reign* was also structured as a celebrity collab, listing

nine authors, and Oliphant's essay concludes with an image of her signature. For twenty-first-century accounts of the afterlives of Brontë's fictions, see Amber K. Regis and Deborah Wynne, eds., *Charlotte Brontë: Legacies and Afterlives*, Interventions: Rethinking the Nineteenth Century (Manchester University Press, 2017).

9. Lucasta Miller, *The Brontë Myth* (Knopf, 2003), 152. Miller also cites an episode in which Thackeray introduced Brontë as "Jane Eyre" (25). The story is drawn from an account in *Cornhill Magazine* in 1900 by Brontë's publisher George Smith, who wrote that Brontë was furious and confronted Thackeray in Smith's drawing room the next day, demanding what *he* would have thought if she had introduced him as "Mr. Warrington," dropping the words like "shells into a fortress." George Smith, "Charlotte Brontë," *Cornhill Magazine* 82 (December 1900): 791.

10. Booth, "Life Writing," 53. Novels were a small slice of the life-writing landscape. Booth emphasizes the variety of non-novel-like forms of life writing in the nineteenth century, from "magazine articles, portrait galleries, names and statements on buildings and monuments, tours to homes and shrines" to forms of "collective biography like the biographical reference work (*Dictionary of National Biography*) and the series of volumes on a category of subjects (*English Men of Letters*)" (54, 56).

11. Peterson, *Traditions of Victorian Women's Autobiography*, 324.

12. Catherine Gallagher, *Nobody's Story: The Vanishing Acts of Women Writers in the Marketplace, 1670–1820*, New Historicism, vol. 31 (University of California Press, 1995).

13. Linda K. Hughes and Michael Lund, *Victorian Publishing and Mrs. Gaskell's Work*, Victorian Literature and Culture Series (University Press of Virginia, 1999), 125; Gabriele Helms, "The Coincidence of Biography and Autobiography: Elizabeth Gaskell's 'The Life of Charlotte Brontë,'" *Biography: An Interdisciplinary Quarterly* 18, no. 4 (1995): 339–59.

14. Deirdre d'Albertis, "'Bookmaking out of the Remains of the Dead': Elizabeth Gaskell's 'The Life of Charlotte Brontë,'" *Victorian Studies* 39, no. 1 (1995): 1–31. On the myth that Gaskell constructs, see Suzann Bick, "Clouding the 'Severe Truth': Elizabeth Gaskell's Strategy in

The Life of Charlotte Brontë," *Essays in Arts and Sciences* 11 (1982): 33–47; and Meghan Burke Hattaway, "'Such a Strong Wish for Wings': *The Life of Charlotte Brontë* and Elizabeth Gaskell's Fallen Angels," *Victorian Literature and Culture* 42, no. 4 (2014): 671–90.

15. Elaine Showalter, *A Literature of Their Own*, rev. and exp. ed. (Princeton University Press, 1998), 106.
16. See Juliet R. V. Barker, *The Brontës: Wild Genius on the Moors* (Weidenfeld and Nicolson, 1994); and Miller, *The Brontë Myth*.
17. Weber, *Women and Literary Celebrity in the Nineteenth Century*, 7, 13, 30.
18. On how Gaskell's work legitimated literary tourism, see Pamela Corpron Parker, "Elizabeth Gaskell and Literary Tourism," in *Literary Tourism and Nineteenth-Century Culture*, ed. Watson, 128–38; and Booth, *Homes and Haunts*, chap. 2.
19. Deborah Wynne, "The 'Charlotte' Cult: Writing the Literary Pilgrimage from Gaskell to Woolf," in *Charlotte Brontë*, ed. Regis and Wynne, 43; Virginia Woolf [unsigned], "Haworth, November 1904," *The Guardian*, December 21, 1904.
20. Alison Booth et al., "Women Novelists Re-presented for Victoria's Jubilee," July 21, 2021, https://storymaps.arcgis.com/stories/12b5b9d93 0fc42ddacc2d8b3b10a70b5.
21. Allison Booth, "Pop Chart," n.d., Collective Biographies of Women project website, https://womensbios.lib.virginia.edu/popchart.html, accessed February 24, 2025. This part of my discussion is indebted to the larger argument in Booth, *How to Make It as a Woman*, about the treasure trove of women's biography that has been unearthed. Understanding how an author can become a market genre available to other writers can help us recognize a more richly peopled literary scene. Kimberly Braxton breaks down a perspective of Brontë's "cultural legacy" that includes a nearly five-page, single-spaced list of works "inspired by Charlotte Brontë's Life," including biographical studies; novels, poetry, etc.; plays, ballets, operas, musicals, etc.; and "film, television, radio, etc." Braxton, "Appendix: Charlotte Brontë's Cultural Legacy, 1848–2016," in *Charlotte Brontë*, ed. Regis and Wynne, 288–93. Charlotte Brontë has had good staying power.

22. Algernon Charles Swinburne, *A Note on Charlotte Brontë*, Gerritsen Collection of Women's History, no. 2785 (Chatto & Windus, 1877), 88.
23. Elizabeth Rigby [unsigned], review of *Jane Eyre* and *Vanity Fair*, *Quarterly Review* 84, no. 167 (December 1848), reprinted in *The Brontës: The Critical Heritage*, ed. Miriam Allott, Critical Heritage Series (Routledge, 1974), 111.
24. A facsimile of the dedication to Thackeray is included in Charlotte Brontë, *Jane Eyre: An Authoritative Text, Contexts, Criticism*, 3rd ed., ed. Richard J. Dunn (Norton, 2001), xiv; Barker, *The Brontës*, 606–7.
25. Gaskell also challenged a biographical account of Brontë printed from a letter Gaskell herself had written conveying secondhand information about the Brontë family. Jennifer S. Uglow observes that "Charlotte Brontë's life already fell easily into the patterns of Gaskell's fiction, with its suffering daughters, profligate son and stern father, and its emphasis on upbringing and environment, female endurance and courage, but . . . [p]art of her mission was to defend Brontë against the accusations of sensuality leveled at her novels: the story of her starved love must not be told." Uglow, *Elizabeth Gaskell: A Habit of Stories* (Faber and Faber, 1993), 399. On Charlotte as a heroine in need of defense and how "Gaskell's depictions of reformed fallen women are meant to transform existing ideals of the proper home and its female inhabitants," see Hattaway, "'Such a Strong Wish for Wings,'" 674.
26. Review of *The Life of Charlotte Brontë* by Elizabeth Gaskell, *National Magazine*, 1857, reprinted in *Elizabeth Gaskell: The Critical Heritage*, ed. Angus Easson, Critical Heritage Series (Routledge, 1991), 401, original emphasis.
27. Sean Latham, *The Art of Scandal: Modernism, Libel Law, and the Roman à Clef*, Modernist Literature and Culture (Oxford University Press, 2009), 41.
28. Gallagher, *Nobody's Story*, 124, 123.
29. My thanks to Elsie Michie for this way of seeing a doubled readerly desire.
30. Elizabeth Gaskell, *The Life of Charlotte Brontë* (1857), reissue ed., ed. Angus Easson (Oxford University Press, 2009), 381
31. Gaskell, *Life of Charlotte Brontë*, 426.
32. Hughes and Lund, *Victorian Publishing and Mrs. Gaskell's Work*, 145.

33. Review of *The Life of Charlotte Brontë* by Elizabeth Gaskell, *Saturday Review*, April 4, 1857, 313–14, reprinted in part in *Elizabeth Gaskell: The Critical Heritage*, ed. Easson, 377, but see a digital copy of the entire book review at https://www.google.com/books/edition/The_Saturday_Review_of_Politics_Literatu/RzVUAAAAcAAJ?hl=en&gbpv=0, from which I took the quote "We must acknowledge. . . ."
34. Swinburne, *A Note on Charlotte Brontë*, 88.
35. Review of *The Life of Charlotte Brontë* by Elizabeth Gaskell, *Saturday Review*, 313, reprinted in part in *Elizabeth Gaskell: The Critical Heritage*, ed. Easson, 378, 313.
36. My thanks to Daniel Mintz for this formulation.
37. Terry Castle, "Hush Hush, Sweet Charlotte," *New Republic* 214, no. 4 (1996): 33.
38. George Henry Lewes [unsigned], review of *Jane Eyre*, by Charlotte Brontë, *Fraser's*, December 1847, reprinted in *The Brontës: The Critical Heritage*, ed. Allott, 84.
39. "Cowan's Bridge" was changed to "Cowan Bridge" in the third edition of the *Life*, according to Angus Easson, *Elizabeth Gaskell* (Routledge & Kegan Paul, 1979), 143.
40. Gaskell, *The Life of Charlotte Brontë*, 57.
41. David Amigoni, *Life Writing and Victorian Culture*, Nineteenth Century (Ashgate, 2006), 2.
42. Gaskell, *The Life of Charlotte Brontë*, 60.
43. Gaskell quotes a story of Maria Brontë being roughly handled by "Miss Scatcherd" for which there is no direct analogue in *Jane Eyre*. Gaskell, *The Life of Charlotte Brontë*, 58.
44. Brontë, *Jane Eyre*, 38; Gaskell, *The Life of Charlotte Brontë*, 55.
45. Gaskell, *The Life of Charlotte Brontë*, 55.
46. "Review of *The Life of Charlotte Brontë*, by Elizabeth Gaskell," *Christian Observer*, July 1857, 489, 488.
47. Stephen, "The License of Modern Novelists," 132.
48. Lisa Rodensky, *The Crime in Mind: Criminal Responsibility and the Victorian Novel* (Oxford University Press, 2003), 173–74.
49. Stephen, "The License of Modern Novelists," 130, quoting Gaskell, *The Life of Charlotte Brontë*, 51, Stephen's emphasis.
50. Stephen, "The License of Modern Novelists," 107.

51. My emphasis. When Gaskell revised her discussion of the school under the advice of a lawyer, this pattern was repeated: she removed personal remarks about Wilson but did not substantially revise her account of the poor food and care of the children at the school—except to be more explicit about her sources. Easson, *Elizabeth Gaskell*, 148–49. Gaskell twice quotes Brontë's assertion, when Gaskell introduced the topic, that "she should not have written what she did of Lowood in 'Jane Eyre,' if she had thought the place would be so immediately identified with Cowan Bridge"; "she was not sure whether she should have written it, if she had been aware how instantaneously it would have been identified with Cowan Bridge" (apropos of the popularity of volume 2 of *Jane Eyre*). Gaskell, *The Life of Charlotte* Brontë, 51, 262. The light repetition here calls attention to the only change: how immediately, instantaneously Lowood was identified as Cowan Bridge.
52. Stephen, "The License of Modern Novelists," 130.
53. Gaskell, *The Life of Charlotte Brontë*, 57.
54. Gaskell, *The Life of Charlotte Brontë*, 51.
55. George Eliot, *Adam Bede* (1859), ed. Margaret Reynolds (Penguin, 2008), 193. As Elsie Michie describes, both Eliot and Lewes read and were moved by Gaskell's biography. See Michie, "'Literary Intercourse,'"43.
56. Stephen, "The License of Modern Novelists," 131.
57. James Fitzjames Stephen, "The Relation of Novels to Life" (1855), in *Cambridge Essays, Contributed by Members of the University* (Parker and Son, 1855), 187.
58. Altick, *Lives and Letters*, 195, 193–94, Altick's emphasis.
59. Ian Duncan, *Scott's Shadow: The Novel in Romantic Edinburgh*, Literature in History (Princeton University Press, 2007). For Duncan, "literary biography establishes the tradition according to which the author is the origin of the work, subsuming other cultural, historical, and documentary sources, which are in any case flagged within the text as his own inventions. Fictionality guarantees, as it is guaranteed by, the author's invisible, informing 'real presence,'" 276.
60. D'Albertis, "'Bookmaking out of the Remains of the Dead,'" 1.
61. Gaskell, *The Life of Charlotte Brontë*, 425–26.

62. William Caldwell Roscoe [unsigned], review of *The Life of Charlotte Brontë* by Elizabeth Gaskell, *National Review* 11 (July 1857): 127–64, reprinted in *Elizabeth Gaskell: The Critical Heritage*, ed. Easson, 424.
63. Gaskell, *The Life of Charlotte Brontë*, 426.
64. Easson, *Elizabeth Gaskell*, 136.
65. Charlotte Brontë, "Biographical Notice of [Ellis and Acton] Bell, a Selection of Their Literary Remains, and a Preface," qtd. in Gaskell, *The Life of Charlotte Brontë*, 271.
66. Gaskell, *The Life of Charlotte Brontë*, 315, my emphasis.
67. Hattaway, "'Such a Strong Wish for Wings,'" 683–84.
68. Virginia Woolf, *A Room of One's Own* (1929), in *A Room of One's Own and Three Guineas*, 2nd ed., ed. Anna Snaith (Oxford University Press, 2015), 53.
69. Woolf, *A Room of One's Own*, 36.
70. Alice Walker, "In Search of Our Mothers' Gardens" (1972), in *Within the Circle: An Anthology of African American Literary Criticism from the Harlem Renaissance to the Present*, ed. Angelyn Mitchell (Duke University Press, 1994), 404, 405, Walker's emphasis, quoting Woolf, *A Room of One's Own*, 38.
71. Saidiya Hartman, *Wayward Lives, Beautiful Experiments: Intimate Histories of Social Upheaval* (Norton, 2019), xiv. See also Tina Campt's forward-looking grammar of Black feminist futurity that demands the "performance of a future that hasn't yet happened but must." Campt, *Listening to Images* (Duke University Press, 2017), 34. Christina Sharpe directly connects Wheatley with contemporary life by drawing a line between Wheatley as she emerges in June Jordan's essay "The Difficult Miracle of Black Poetry in America: Something Like a Sonnet for Phillis Wheatley" (2002) and the photograph of "a Haitian girl child, ten years old," taken after the devastating earthquake of 2010, in order, in Sharpe's words, to "position myself with her, in the wake." Sharpe, *In the Wake: On Blackness and Being* (Duke University Press, 2016), 53. Virginia Jackson's book on the origins of American lyric in nineteenth-century Black poetry sets up a contrast between the history of how readers have engaged with Wheatley's life and the "the poetics of uncertain personhood" that characterize her poetry. Jackson, *Before Modernism: Inventing American Lyric* (Princeton University Press, 2023), 124.

72. Louisa Yates, "Reader, I [Shagged/Beat/Whipped/F****d/Rewrote] Him': The Sexual and Financial Afterlives of *Jane Eyre*," in *Charlotte Brontë*, ed. Regis and Wynne, 262, 261, 266, 265.

CODA: REFIGURING AUTHORSHIP

1. Marcus, *Drama of Celebrity*, 14.
2. See *Black Celebrity, Racial Politics, and the Press* (Taylor & Francis, 2014) for Sarah J. Jackson's account of twentieth- and twenty-first-century Black celebrity figures from a range of fields, including music, film, and sports, who "chose to challenge the existence of the mythic American ethos of equality in ways that fell outside of what was seen as 'acceptable' black expression" and in "locations seen (although technically public) as illegitimate spaces for dissent" (12).
3. Karl Berglund and Sarah Allison, "Larsson, Remade: A Computational Perspective on the Millennium Trilogy in English," *PMLA* 139, no. 1 (2024): 82–96.
4. Dan Sinykin, *Big Fiction: How Conglomeration Changed the Publishing Industry and American Literature* (Columbia University Press, 2023).
5. Platforms that depend on ad revenue, in Sarah Brouillette's formulation, work by the "maximization of profits via the expansion of casualized labor and exploitation of unpaid activity by readers and writers," which she characterizes as the *feminization* of publishing work. Brouillette, "Wattpad's Fictions of Care," *Post45*, July 13, 2022, https://post45.org/2022/07/wattpads-fictions-of-care/. In another article, Brouillette shows how a platform such as Wattpad can present as a community of care even as its business model shifts financial risk from publishers onto authors, and she expands on the role of "discourses of care and community" to this process. Brouillette, "Wattpad, Platform Capitalism, and the Feminization of Publishing Work," *Book History* 26, no. 2 (2023): 434.
6. Aarthi Vadde, "Amateur Creativity: Contemporary Literature and the Digital Publishing Scene," *New Literary History* 48, no. 1 (2017): 37. Vadde contextualizes the figure of the author as it emerges in discourse about amateur creativity, which offers a "rejection of, but also entanglement with, individualist conceptions of authorship, the

excesses of celebrity culture, the economy of prestige, and market-circumscribed attempts to monetize cultural wealth" (30).
7. Kristina Busse, *Framing Fan Fiction: Literary and Social Practices in Fan Fiction Communities* (University of Iowa Press, 2017), 36, 38.
8. Murray, *The Digital Literary Sphere*.
9. Stitch, "What's the Deal with Real Person Fiction?," *Teen Vogue*, August 11, 2021.

BIBLIOGRAPHY

Adams, Amanda. "'Here, I Could Rove at Will': Harriet Martineau, *Sartain's Union Magazine*, and Freedom in the Transatlantic Periodical Press." *Victorian Periodicals Review* 51, no. 1 (2018): 121–37.

———. *Performing Authorship in the Nineteenth-Century Transatlantic Lecture Tour*. Ashgate Series in Nineteenth-Century Transatlantic Studies. Ashgate, 2014.

Alcott, Louisa May. *Little Women* (1868–1869). Ed. Anne Boyd Rioux. Penguin Random House, 2018.

Algee-Hewitt, Mark, Ryan Heuser, David McClure, and Franco Moretti. "Around the Word 'Littérature': The English Case." Paper presentation, May 2016, LOCATION. One stage of the larger collaborative project "'Literature/Littérature': History of a Word."

Allison, Sarah. *Reductive Reading: A Syntax of Victorian Moralizing*. Johns Hopkins University Press, 2018.

Allott, Miriam, ed. *The Brontës: The Critical Heritage*. Critical Heritage Series. Routledge, 1974.

Altick, Richard D. *Lives and Letters: A History of Literary Biography in England and America*. Knopf, 1965.

Amigoni, David. *Life Writing and Victorian Culture*. Nineteenth Century. Ashgate, 2006.

Andrews, William L. "Bibliography of Slave and Ex-slave Narratives." 2003–present. Documenting the American South, University Library, University of North Carolina at Chapel Hill. https://docsouth.unc.edu/neh/biblintro.html.

———. *To Tell a Free Story: The First Century of Afro-American Autobiography, 1760–1865*. University of Illinois Press, 1986.

Aravamudan, Srinivas. *Enlightenment Orientalism: Resisting the Rise of the Novel*. University of Chicago Press, 2011.

Arping, Åsa. "'The Miss Austen of Sweden.' Om Fredrika Bremer i 1840-talets USA och litteraturhistorisk omvärdering." *Tidskrift för litteraturvetenskap* 48, nos. 1–2 (2018): 18–33.

———. "A Writer of One's Own? Mary Howitt, Fredrika Bremer, Translation, and Literary 'Piracy' in the US and Britain in the 1840s." In *Gender and Translation: Understanding Agents in Transnational Reception*, ed. Isis Herrero López, Cecilia Alvstad, Johanna Akujärvi, and Synnøve Skarsbø Lindtner, 83–106. Éditions québécoises de l'oeuvre, 2018.

Arping, Åsa, and Yvonne Leffler. "The Wonderful Adventures of Swedish Everyday Life: Female Domestic Novels on Export in the Nineteenth Century." In *The Dynamics and Contexts of Cultural Transfers*, ed. Margaretha Fahlgren and Anna Williams, 53–77. Avd. för Litteratursociologi, 2017.

Ashton, Susanna. *Collaborators in Literary America, 1870–1920*. Springer, 2003.

Bagneris, Mia L. "Miscegenation in Marble: John Bell's *Octoroon*." *Art Bulletin* 102, no. 2 (2020): 64–90.

Baraw, Charles. "William Wells Brown, 'Three Years in Europe,' and Fugitive Tourism." *African American Review* 44, no. 3 (2011): 453–70.

Barker, Juliet R. V. *The Brontës: Wild Genius on the Moors*. Weidenfeld and Nicolson, 1994.

Barrett Browning, Elizabeth. "The Runaway Slave at Pilgrim's Point." In *The Liberty Bell by Friends of Freedom*, 29–44. National Anti-Slavery Bazaar, 1848.

Barthes, Roland. "The Death of the Author" (1967). In *Image, Music, Text*, trans. Stephen Heath, 142–48. Hill and Wang, 1977.

Bassett, Troy J. *The Rise and Fall of the Victorian Three-Volume Novel*. Palgrave Macmillan, 2020.

Beattie, Jessie. *Black Moses: The Real Uncle Tom*. Ryerson Press, 1957.

Benatti, Francesca, and Justin Tonra. "English Bards and Unknown Reviewers: A Stylometric Analysis of Thomas Moore and the *Christabel Review*." *Breac: A Digital Journal of Irish Studies*, October 7, 2015.

https://breac.nd.edu/articles/english-bards-and-unknown-reviewers-a-stylometric-analysis-of-thomas-moore-and-the-christabel-review/.

Benjamin, Walter. "The Work of Art in the Age of Mechanical Reproduction." In *Illuminations: Essays and Reflections*, ed. Hannah Arendt, trans. Harry Zohn, 217–52. 1985. Reprint. Schocken, 2007.

Berglund, Karl, and Sarah Allison. "Larsson, Remade: A Computational Perspective on the Millennium Trilogy in English." *PMLA* 139, no. 1 (2024): 82–96.

Bick, Suzann. "Clouding the 'Severe Truth': Elizabeth Gaskell's Strategy in *The Life of Charlotte Brontë*." *Essays in Arts and Sciences* 11 (1982): 33–47.

Bidwell, John. "American History in Image and Text." *Proceedings of the American Antiquarian Society* 98, no. 2 (1989): 247–302.

Blackett, R. J. M. *Building an Antislavery Wall: Black Americans in the Atlantic Abolitionist Movement, 1830–1860*. Louisiana State University Press, 1983.

Bodichon, Barbara Leigh Smith. *Barbara Leigh Smith Bodichon: An American Diary 1857–8*. Ed. Joseph W. Reed. Routledge & Kegan Paul, 1972.

Booth, Alison. *Homes and Haunts: Touring Writers' Shrines and Countries*. Oxford University Press, 2016.

———. *How to Make It as a Woman: Collective Biographical History from Victoria to the Present*. Women in Culture and Society. University of Chicago Press, 2004.

———. "Life Writing." In *The Cambridge Companion to English Literature, 1830–1914*, ed. Joanne Shattock, 50–70. Cambridge University Press, 2010.

———. "Pop Chart." N.d. Collective Biographies of Women. https://womensbios.lib.virginia.edu/popchart.html. Accessed February 24, 2025.

Booth, Alison, Isabel Bielat, Lloyd Sy, and Valerie Voight. "Women Novelists Re-presented for Victoria's Jubilee." July 21, 2021. https://storymaps.arcgis.com/stories/12b5b9d930fc42ddacc2d8b3b10a70b5.

Brake, Laurel. *Subjugated Knowledges: Journalism, Gender, and Literature in the Nineteenth Century*. New York University Press, 1994.

Braxton, Kimberly. "Appendix: Charlotte Brontë's Cultural Legacy, 1848–2016." In *Charlotte Brontë: Legacies and Afterlives*, ed. Amber K. Regis and Deborah Wynne, 280–93. Interventions: Rethinking the Nineteenth Century. Manchester University Press, 2017.

Bremer, Fredrika. *The Homes of the New World: Impressions of America*. 2 vols. Trans. Mary Howitt. Harper & Brothers, 1853.

———. "Letter." In *The Liberty Bell by Friends of Freedom*, 72–76. National Anti-Slavery Bazaar, 1845.

Brontë, Charlotte. *Jane Eyre: An Authoritative Text, Contexts, Criticism*. 3rd ed. Ed. Richard J. Dunn. Norton, 2001.

Brooks, Daphne A. *Bodies in Dissent: Spectacular Performances of Race and Freedom, 1850–1910*. Duke University Press, 2006.

Brouillette, Sarah. "Wattpad, Platform Capitalism, and the Feminization of Publishing Work." *Book History* 26, no. 2 (2023): 419–38.

———. "Wattpad's Fictions of Care." *Post45*, July 13, 2022. https://post45.org/2022/07/wattpads-fictions-of-care/.

Brown, David West. *English and Empire: Literary History, Dialect, and the Digital Archive*. Cambridge University Press, 2018.

Brown, William Wells. *Three Years in Europe: Or, Places I Have Seen and People I Have Met*. C. Gilpin, 1852.

Busse, Kristina. *Framing Fan Fiction: Literary and Social Practices in Fan Fiction Communities*. University of Iowa Press, 2017.

Campt, Tina M. *Listening to Images*. Duke University Press, 2017.

Casper, Scott E. "Biography." In *A History of the Book in America*, vol. 2: *An Extensive Republic: Print, Culture, and Society in the New Nation, 1790–1840*, ed. Robert A. Gross and Mary Kelley, 458–64. American Antiquarian Society, University of North Carolina Press, 2010.

———, ed. *History of the Book in America*. Vol. 3: *The Industrial Book, 1840–1880*. American Antiquarian Society, University of North Carolina Press, 2007.

Casteras, Susan P. "'Too Abhorrent to Englishmen to Render a Representation of It . . . Acceptable': Slavery as Seen by British Artists Travelling in America." In *Women's Rights and Transatlantic Antislavery in the Era of Emancipation*, ed. Kathryn Kish Sklar and James Brewer Stewart, 221–50. Yale University Press, 2007.

Castle, Terry. "Hush Hush, Sweet Charlotte." *New Republic* 214, no. 4 (1996): 32–35.

Clark, Susan F. "Solo Black Performance Before the Civil War: Mrs. Stowe, Mrs. Webb, and 'The Christian Slave.'" *New Theatre Quarterly* 13, no. 52 (November 1997): 339–48.

Claybaugh, Amanda. *The Novel of Purpose: Literature and Social Reform in the Anglo-American World*. Cornell University Press, 2007.

Cobb, Jasmine Nichole. "'Forget Me Not': Free Black Women and Sentimentality." *Melus* 40, no. 3 (2015): 28–46.

———. *Picture Freedom: Remaking Black Visuality in the Early Nineteenth Century*. America and the Long 19th Century, vol. 20. New York University Press, 2015.

Cohen, Lara Langer. *The Fabrication of American Literature: Fraudulence and Antebellum Print Culture*. University of Pennsylvania Press, 2011.

Cohen, Lara Langer, and Meredith McGill. "The Perils of Authorship." In *The Oxford History of the Novel in English*, vol. 5: *The American Novel to 1870*, ed. J. Gerald Kennedy and Leland S. Person, 195–212. Oxford University Press, 2014.

Cohen, Lara Langer, and Jordan Alexander Stein. *Early African American Print Culture*. Material Texts. University of Pennsylvania Press, Library Company of Philadelphia, 2012.

Cohen, Michael C. *The Social Lives of Poems in Nineteenth-Century America*. Material Texts. University of Pennsylvania Press, 2015.

Coleridge, Samuel Taylor, and William Wordsworth. *Lyrical Ballads 1798 and 1800*. Ed. Michael Gamer and Dahlia Porter. Broadview Press, 2008.

Condon, Robin L. "'Finished by the Hand by Which It Was Begun': Who Wrote the *Life and Times of Frederick Douglass*?" *Journal of African American History* 99, nos. 1–2 (2014): 12–19.

Curtis, Gerard. *Visual Words: Art and the Material Book in Victorian England*. Ashgate, 2002.

D'Albertis, Deirdre. "'Bookmaking out of the Remains of the Dead': Elizabeth Gaskell's 'The Life of Charlotte Brontë.'" *Victorian Studies* 39, no. 1 (1995): 1–31.

Defoe, Daniel. *Robinson Crusoe* (1719). Ed. John Richetti. Penguin Classics, 2003.

Delany, Martin Robison. "Delany and Douglass on *Uncle Tom's Cabin*." In *Martin R. Delany: A Documentary Reader*, ed. Robert S. Levine, 224–37. University of North Carolina Press, 2003.

DeWitt, Anne. "Advances in the Visualization of Data: The Network of Genre in the Victorian Periodical Press." *Victorian Periodicals Review* 48, no. 2 (2015): 161–82.

DiBattista, Maria, and Deborah Epstein Nord. *At Home in the World: Women Writers and Public Life, from Austen to the Present.* Princeton University Press, 2017.

Dickens, Charles. *American Notes for General Circulation.* Harper & Brothers, 1842.

Dickerson, Vanessa D. *Dark Victorians.* University of Illinois Press, 2008.

Dillane, Fionnuala. *Before George Eliot: Marian Evans and the Periodical Press.* Illus. ed. Cambridge University Press, 2013.

———. "'The Character of Editress': Marian Evans at the *Westminster Review*, 1851–54." *Tulsa Studies in Women's Literature* 30, no. 2 (2011): 269–90.

Disraeli, Isaac. *Curiosities of Literature: A New Edition, Edited, with Memoir and Notes, by His Son, the Earl of Beaconsfield, in Three Volumes.* Vol. 3. Frederick Warne, 1881.

Documenting the American South. Website. University Library, University of North Carolina at Chapel Hill. https://docsouth.unc.edu.

Doyle, Mary Ellen. "Josiah Henson's Narrative: Before and After." *Negro American Literature Forum* 8, no. 1 (Spring 1974): 176–183.

Du Bois, W. E. B. *Black Reconstruction in America 1860–1880* (1935). Ed. David Levering Lewis. Simon and Schuster, 1998.

Duncan, Ian. *Scott's Shadow: The Novel in Romantic Edinburgh.* Literature in History. Princeton University Press, 2007.

Easley, Alexis. "Chance Encounters, Rediscovery, and Loss: Researching Victorian Women Journalists in the Digital Age." *Victorian Periodicals Review* 49, no. 4 (2016): 694–717.

———. *First-Person Anonymous: Women Writers and Victorian Print Media, 1830–70.* Nineteenth Century. Ashgate, 2004.

———. *Literary Celebrity, Gender, and Victorian Authors 1850–1914.* University of Delaware Press, 2011.

———. *New Media and the Rise of the Popular Woman Writer, 1832–1860.* Edinburgh Critical Studies in Victorian Culture. Edinburgh University Press, 2021.

Easley, Alexis, Clare Gill, and Beth Rodgers, eds. *Women, Periodicals, and Print Culture in Britain, 1830s–1900s: The Victorian Period.* Edinburgh University Press, 2019.

Easson, Angus. *Elizabeth Gaskell.* Routledge & Kegan Paul, 1979.

———, ed. *Elizabeth Gaskell: The Critical Heritage*. Critical Heritage Series. Routledge, 1991.

Eliot, George. *Adam Bede* (1859). Ed. Margaret Reynolds. Penguin, 2008.

———. "[Three Novels]." *Westminster Review* 66 (October 1856): 571–78. Reprinted in *Essays of George Eliot*, with a preface and notes by Thomas Pinney, 325–34. Routledge and Kegan Paul, 1963.

Eliot, Simon. "Some Patterns and Trends in British Book Production" (1994). In *Literature in the Marketplace: Nineteenth-Century British Publishing and Reading Practices*, ed. John O. Jordan and Robert L. Patten, 19–43. Cambridge University Press, 2003.

———. *Some Patterns and Trends in British Publishing, 1800–1919*. Occasional Papers of the Bibliographical Society, no. 8. Bibliographical Society, 1994.

———. "Very Necessary but Not Quite Sufficient: A Personal View of Quantitative Analysis in Book History." *Book History* 5 (2002): 283–93.

Ernest, John. *Chaotic Justice: Rethinking African American Literary History*. University of North Carolina Press, 2009.

"Father Henson's Story of His Own Life." *Methodist Quarterly Review* 40 (1858): 500–501.

Finch, Aisha K. "Scandalous Scarcities: Black Slave Women, Plantation Domesticity, and Travel Writing in Nineteenth-Century Cuba." *Journal of Historical Sociology* 23, no. 1 (2010): 101–43.

Fisch, Audrey. "Uncle Tom and Harriet Beecher Stowe in England." In *The Cambridge Companion to Harriet Beecher Stowe*, ed. Cindy Weinstein, 96–112. Cambridge Companions to Literature. Cambridge University Press, 2004.

Fisk, Catherine. "The Modern Author at Work on Madison Avenue." In *Modernism and Copyright*, ed. Paul K. Saint-Amour, 173–94. Modernist Literature and Culture. Oxford University Press, 2010.

Fludernik, Monika. "The Fiction of the Rise of Fictionality." *Poetics Today* 39, no. 1 (2018): 67–92.

Fludernik, Monika, and Marie-Laure Ryan. "Factual Narrative: An Introduction." In *Narrative Factuality: A Handbook*, ed. Monika Fludernik and Marie-Laure Ryan, 1–26. De Gruyter, 2019.

Foster, Frances Smith. *Witnessing Slavery: The Development of Ante-bellum Slave Narratives*. Greenwood Press, 1979.

Foucault, Michel. "What Is an Author?" (1969). In *Essential Works of Foucault, 1954–1984*, vol. 2: *Aesthetics, Method, and Epistemology*, ed. James D. Faubion, trans. Robert Hurley, 205–22. New Press, 1998.

Frawley, Maria H. Introduction to Harriet Martineau, *Life in the Sick-Room: Essays* (1844), 11–28. Broadview Press, 2003.

Fritz, Meaghan M., and Frank E. Fee Jr. "To Give the Gift of Freedom: Gift Books and the War on Slavery." *American Periodicals* 23, no. 1 (2013): 60–82.

Gallagher, Catherine. *Nobody's Story: The Vanishing Acts of Women Writers in the Marketplace, 1670–1820*. New Historicism, vol. 31. University of California Press, 1995.

———. "The Rise of Fictionality." In *The Novel*, vol. 1: *History, Geography, and Culture*, ed. Franco Moretti, 336–63. Princeton University Press, 2006.

Gamer, Michael, and Dahlia Porter. Introduction to Samuel Taylor Coleridge and William Wordsworth, *Lyrical Ballads 1798 and 1800*, ed. Michael Gamer and Dahlia Porter, 15–37. Broadview Press, 2008.

García, Ivonne M. "Anticipating Colonialism: U.S. Letters on Puerto Rico and Cuba, 1831–1835." In *Letters and Cultural Transformations in the United States, 1760–1860*, ed. Theresa Strouth Gaul and Sharon M. Harris, 57–75. Ashgate, 2009.

———. "Gothic Cuba and the Trans-American South." In *The Palgrave Handbook of the Southern Gothic*, ed. Susan P. Castillo and Charles L. Crow, 161–74. Macmillan, 2016.

———. *Gothic Geoculture: Nineteenth-Century Representations of Cuba in the Transamerican Imaginary*. Ohio State University Press, 2019.

Gardner, Eric. "'A Gentleman of Superior Cultivation and Refinement': Recovering the Biography of Frank J. Webb." *African American Review* 35, no. 2 (2001): 297–308.

———. "'A Nobler End': Mary Webb and the Victorian Platform." *Nineteenth-Century Prose* 29, no. 1 (2002): 103–18.

Gaskell, Elizabeth. *The Life of Charlotte Brontë* (1857). Reissue ed. Ed. Angus Easson. Oxford University Press, 2009.

Genette, Gerard. *Paratexts: Thresholds of Interpretation*. Trans. Jane E. Lewin. Cambridge University Press, 1997.

Gerland, Oliver. "Modernism and the Emergence of the Right of Publicity: From *Hedda Gabler* to Lucy, Lady Duff-Gordon." In *Modernism and*

Copyright, ed. Paul K. Saint-Amour, 195–214. Modernist Literature and Culture. Oxford University Press, 2010.

Goddu, Teresa A. *Selling Antislavery: Abolition and Mass Media in Antebellum America*. University of Pennsylvania Press, 2020.

———. "The Slave Narrative as Material Text." In *The Oxford Handbook of the African American Slave Narrative*, ed. John Ernest, 149–64. Oxford University Press, 2014.

Gordon, Lewis R. "The Problem of Biography in the Study of the Thought of Black Intellectuals." *Small Axe: A Journal of Criticism*, no. 4 (1998): 47–63.

Gray, Thomas. "The Progress of Poesy. A Pindaric Ode" (1757). In *The Complete Poems of Thomas Gray: English, Latin, and Greek*, ed. H. W. Starr and J. R. Hendrickson, 12–17. Oxford English Texts. Oxford University Press, 1966.

Greenspan, Ezra. *George Palmer Putnam: Representative American Publisher*. Penn State Series in the History of the Book. Pennsylvania State University Press, 2000.

Greetham, David C. *Textual Scholarship: An Introduction*. Garland Reference Library of the Humanities, vol. 1417. Garland, 1992.

Grewal, Inderpal. *Home and Harem: Nation, Gender, Empire, and the Cultures of Travel*. Post-contemporary Interventions. Duke University Press, 1996.

Griffiths, Julia, ed. *Autographs for Freedom*. John P. Jewett, 1853.

Grigsby, Darcy Grimaldo. *Enduring Truths: Sojourner's Shadows and Substance*. University of Chicago Press, 2015.

Gross, Robert A. "Introduction: An Extensive Republic." In *A History of the Book in America*, vol. 2: *An Extensive Republic: Print, Culture, and Society in the New Nation, 1790–1840*, ed. Robert A. Gross and Mary Kelley, 1–52. American Antiquarian Society, University of North Carolina Press, 2010.

Gross, Robert A., and Mary Kelley, eds. *A History of the Book in America*. Vol. 2: *An Extensive Republic: Print, Culture, and Society in the New Nation, 1790–1840*. American Antiquarian Society, University of North Carolina Press, 2010.

Hack, Daniel. *Reaping Something New: African American Transformations of Victorian Literature*. Princeton University Press, 2017.

Harris, Elizabeth A., Alexandra Alter, and Adam Bednar. "A Trial Put Publishing's Inner Workings on Display. What Did We Learn?" *New York Times*, August 19, 2022.

Hartman, Saidiya. *Wayward Lives, Beautiful Experiments: Intimate Histories of Social Upheaval*. Norton, 2019.

Hattaway, Meghan Burke. "'Such a Strong Wish for Wings': The Life of Charlotte Brontë and Elizabeth Gaskell's Fallen Angels." *Victorian Literature and Culture* 42, no. 4 (2014): 671–90.

Hawkins, Ann R., and Maura C. Ives, eds. *Women Writers and the Artifacts of Celebrity in the Long Nineteenth Century*. Ashgate, 2012.

Hayes, Kevin J. "Poe, the Daguerreotype, and the Autobiographical Act." *Biography* 25, no. 3 (2002): 477–92.

Haywood, Chanta M. *Prophesying Daughters: Black Women Preachers and the Word, 1823–1913*. University of Missouri Press, 2003.

Helms, Gabriele. "The Coincidence of Biography and Autobiography: Elizabeth Gaskell's 'The Life of Charlotte Brontë.'" *Biography: An Interdisciplinary Quarterly* 18, no. 4 (1995): 339–59.

Henson, Josiah. *An Autobiography of the Rev. Josiah Henson ("Uncle Tom"), from 1789 to 1881*. Ed. John Lobb. Schuyler, Smith, 1881.

———. *The Life of Josiah Henson, Formerly a Slave, Now an Inhabitant of Canada, as Narrated by Himself*. A. D. Phelps, 1849.

———. *Truth Stranger Than Fiction: Father Henson's Story of His Own Life*. John P. Jewett, 1858.

———. *Uncle Tom's Story of His Life: An Autobiography of the Rev. Josiah Henson (Mrs. Harriet Beecher Stowe's "Uncle Tom"), from 1789 to 1876*. Christian Age Office, 1876.

———. *The Young People's Illustrated Edition of "Uncle Tom's" Story of His Life (from 1789 to 1877)*. John Lobb, 1877.

Homestead, Melissa J. *American Women Authors and Literary Property, 1822–1869*. Cambridge University Press, 2005.

Howitt, William. *Homes and Haunts of the Most Eminent British Poets*. 2 vols. Harper, 1847.

Hughes, Linda K. "*SIDEWAYS!* Navigating the Material(ity) of Print Culture." *Victorian Periodicals Review* 47, no. 1 (2014): 1–30.

Hughes, Linda K., and Michael Lund. *Victorian Publishing and Mrs. Gaskell's Work*. Victorian Literature and Culture Series. University Press of Virginia, 1999.

Jackson, Leon. *The Business of Letters: Authorial Economies in Antebellum America*. Stanford University Press, 2007.

Jackson, Sarah J. *Black Celebrity, Racial Politics, and the Press*. Taylor & Francis, 2014.

Jackson, Virginia. *Before Modernism: Inventing American Lyric*. Princeton University Press, 2023.

Janssen, Flore, and Lisa C. Robertson, eds. "Nineteenth-Century Women's Campaign Writing: Broadening the Realm of Women's Civic Engagement." Special issue, *Nineteenth-Century Gender Studies* 17, no. 2 (2021).

"John Punchard Jewett." In *Dictionary of American Biography*, ed. Dumas Malone, 69. Gale in Context: Biography (Tulane University). Scribner's, 1936.

Johnston, Judith. *Victorian Women and the Economies of Travel, Translation, and Culture, 1830–1870*. Nineteenth Century. Ashgate, 2013.

Juxta: Collation Software for Scholars. https://www.juxtasoftware.org/.

Keymer, Thomas, and Peter Sabor. *"Pamela" in the Marketplace: Literary Controversy and Print Culture in Eighteenth-Century Britain and Ireland*. Cambridge University Press, 2005.

Klein, Lauren F. "Dimensions of Scale: Invisible Labor, Editorial Work, and the Future of Quantitative Literary Studies." *PMLA* 135, no. 1 (January 2020): 23–39.

Koenigs, Thomas. *Founded in Fiction: The Uses of Fiction in the Early United States*. Princeton University Press, 2021.

Kohn, Denise, Sarah Meer, and Emily B. Todd, eds. *Transatlantic Stowe: Harriet Beecher Stowe and European Culture*. University of Iowa Press, 2006.

Kooistra, Lorraine Janzen. *Poetry, Pictures, and Popular Publishing: The Illustrated Gift Book and Victorian Visual Culture, 1855–1875*. Ohio University Press, 2011.

Kraft, Elizabeth, ed. "Women and Protest." Special issue, *European Romantic Review* 32, no. 3 (2021).

Latham, Sean. *The Art of Scandal: Modernism, Libel Law, and the Roman à Clef*. Modernist Literature and Culture. Oxford University Press, 2009.

Lee, Jarena. *Religious Experience and Journal of Mrs. Jarena Lee, Giving an Account of Her Call to Preach the Gospel*. Printed and Published for the Author, 1849.

Lee, Julia Sun-Joo. *The American Slave Narrative and the Victorian Novel.* Oxford University Press, 2010.

Leffler, Yvonne. *Swedish Nineteenth-Century Novels as World Literature: Transnational Success and Literary History.* LIR.Skrifter, 2020.

Leffler, Yvonne, Åsa Arping, Jenny Bergenmar, Gunilla Hermansson, and Birgitta Johansson Lindh. *Swedish Women's Writing on Export: Tracing Transnational Reception in the Nineteenth Century.* University of Gothenburg, 2019.

Levine, Robert S. *Martin Delany, Frederick Douglass, and the Politics of Representative Identity.* University of North Carolina Press, 1997.

Lewes, George Henry [unsigned]. Review of *Jane Eyre*, by Charlotte Brontë. *Fraser's*, December 1847. Reprinted in *The Brontës: The Critical Heritage*, ed. Mirian Allott, 83–86. Critical Heritage Series. Routledge, 1974.

Lindenbaum, Peter. "Milton's Contract." In *The Construction of Authorship: Textual Appropriation in Law and Literature*, ed. Martha Woodmansee and Peter Jaszi, 175–90. Post-contemporary Interventions. Duke University Press, 1994.

Ljungquist, Kent P. "Poe's 'Autography': A New Exchange of Reviews." *American Periodicals* 2 (1992): 51–63.

Lobb, John. "Sketch of the Editor, 'Mr. John Lobb.'" In *Men and Women of the Time*. Routledge, 1899. Reprinted in *Talks with the Dead; Luminous Rays from the Unseen World, Illustrated with Spirit Photographs*, xix–xxiii. J. Lobb, 1907.

Lofsvold, Laurel Ann. *Fredrika Bremer and the Writing of America.* Lund University Press, 1999.

Logan, Deborah A. "Harem Life, West and East." *Women's Studies* 26, no. 5 (1997): 449–74.

———. *Harriet Martineau, Victorian Imperialism, and the Civilizing Mission.* Routledge, 2016.

———. "'My Dearly-Beloved Americans': Harriet Martineau's Transatlantic Abolitionism." In *Nineteenth-Century British Travelers in the New World*, ed. Christine DeVine, 203–20. Ashgate, 2013.

Lootens, Tricia. *The Political Poetess: Victorian Femininity, Race, and the Legacy of Separate Spheres.* Princeton University Press, 2016.

Lunsford, Andrea A., and Lisa Ede. "Collaborative Authorship and the Teaching of Writing." In *The Construction of Authorship: Textual*

Appropriation in Law and Literature, ed. Martha Woodmansee and Peter Jaszi, 417–38. Post-contemporary Interventions. Duke University Press, 1994.

Lynch, Deidre. *Loving Literature: A Cultural History*. University of Chicago Press, 2015.

Marcus, Sharon. *The Drama of Celebrity*. Princeton University Press, 2019.

Marraccini, Miranda. "Feminist Types: Reading the Victoria Press." PhD diss., Princeton University, 2019.

Marsh, Jan. "From Slave Cabin to Windsor Castle: Josiah Henson and 'Uncle Tom' in Britain." *Nineteenth Century Studies* 16 (2002): 37–50.

Martineau, Harriet. "Incidents of Travel." In *The Liberty Bell by Friends of Freedom*, 80–88. National Anti-Slavery Bazaar, 1848.

———. "Pity the Slave." In *The Liberty Bell by Friends of Freedom*, 182–87. National Anti-Slavery Bazaar, 1844.

———. *Society in America*. Saunders and Otley, 1837.

Matthews, Samantha. "Reading the 'Sign-Manual': Dickens and Signature." *Dickens Quarterly* 19, no. 4 (2002): 232–42.

Matus, Jill. "The 'Eastern-Woman Question': Martineau and Nightingale Visit the Harem." *Nineteenth-Century Contexts* 21, no. 1 (1999): 63–87.

Maurer, Oscar. "Anonymity vs. Signature in Victorian Reviewing." *Studies in English* 27 (1948): 1–27.

McFadden, Margaret. *Golden Cables of Sympathy: The Transatlantic Sources of Nineteenth-Century Feminism*. University Press of Kentucky, 1999.

McGill, Meredith L. *American Literature and the Culture of Reprinting, 1834–1853*. University of Pennsylvania Press, 2007.

———. "Copyright." In *A History of the Book in America*, vol. 3: *The Industrial Book, 1840–1880*, ed. Scott E. Casper, 158–78. American Antiquarian Society, University of North Carolina Press, 2007.

McGrath, Laura B. "Comping White." *Los Angeles Review of Books*, January 21, 2019.

McKivigan, John R., and Rebecca A. Pattillo. "*Autographs for Freedom* and Reaching a New Abolitionist Audience." *Journal of African American History* 102, no. 1 (Winter 2017): 35–51.

Meer, Sarah. "Slave Narratives as Literature." In *The Cambridge Companion to Slavery in American Literature*, ed. Ezra Tawil, 70–85. Cambridge University Press, 2016.

———. *Uncle Tom Mania: Slavery, Minstrelsy, and Transatlantic Culture in the 1850s.* University of Georgia Press, 2005.

Mellor, Anne Kostelanetz. *Mothers of the Nation: Women's Political Writing in England, 1780–1830.* Women of Letters. Indiana University Press, 2002.

Méndez Rodenas, Adriana. *Transatlantic Travels in Nineteenth-Century Latin America: European Women Pilgrims.* Bucknell Studies in Latin American Literature and Theory. Bucknell University Press, 2014.

Michie, Elsie B. "'Literary Intercourse': Charlotte Brontë, George Henry Lewes, and George Eliot." *George Eliot—George Henry Lewes Studies* 69, no. 1 (2017): 35–52.

———. "Morbidity in Fairyland: Frances Trollope, Charles Dickens, and the Rhetoric of Abolition." *Partial Answers* 9, no. 2 (2011): 233–51.

———. "Reassessing the Cleverness of Frances Trollope's Social Fictions." Review of *The Social Problem Novels of Frances Trollope*, 4 vols., by Frances Milton Trollope, ed. Brenda Ayres. *Nineteenth-Century Gender Studies* 5, no. 3 (2009). https://www.ncgsjournal.com/issue53/michie.html.

Midgley, Clare. "British Abolition and Feminism in Transatlantic Perspective." In *Women's Rights and Transatlantic Antislavery in the Era of Emancipation*, ed. Kathryn Kish Sklar and James Brewer Stewart, 121–40. Yale University Press, 2008.

———. *Feminism and Empire: Women Activists in Imperial Britain, 1790–1865.* Routledge, 2007.

Miller, Lucasta. *The Brontë Myth.* Knopf, 2003.

"The Miller Correspondence." *Fraser's Magazine for Town and Country* 47, no. 8 (November 1833): 624–36.

Mills, Sara. *Discourses of Difference: An Analysis of Women's Travel Writing and Colonialism.* Routledge, 2003.

Modern Language Association. "Guidelines for Editors of Scholarly Editions." Revised May 4, 2022. https://www.mla.org/Resources/Guidelines-and-Data/Reports-and-Professional-Guidelines/Guidelines-for-Editors-of-Scholarly-Editions.

Mole, Tom. *Byron's Romantic Celebrity: Industrial Culture and the Hermeneutic of Intimacy.* Palgrave Studies in the Enlightenment, Romanticism, and Cultures of Print. Palgrave Macmillan, 2007.

Moran, Joe. *Star Authors: Literary Celebrity in America.* Pluto, 2000.

Morgan, Susan. *Place Matters: Gendered Geography in Victorian Women's Travel Books About Southeast Asia*. Rutgers University Press, 1996.

Mott, Frank Luther. "The *Christian Disciple* and the *Christian Examiner*." *New England Quarterly* 1, no. 2 (1928): 197–207.

Murray, Hannah-Rose. *Advocates of Freedom: African American Transatlantic Abolitionism in the British Isles*. Slaveries Since Emancipation. Cambridge University Press, 2020.

———. "'It Is to a Great Extent, a New Book': Josiah Henson, John Lobb, and the Challenges of White Editorship of Black Texts." In "Black Editorship in the Early Atlantic World," ed. Nele Sawallisch and Johanna Seibert. Special issue, *Atlantic Studies* 18, no. 4 (2021): 512–25.

Murray, Simone. *The Digital Literary Sphere: Reading, Writing, and Selling Books in the Internet Era*. Johns Hopkins University Press, 2018.

Nichols, John Gough. *Autographs of Royal, Noble, Learned, and Remarkable Personages Conspicuous in English History*. Nichols and Son, 1829.

Nyong'o, Tavia. *The Amalgamation Waltz: Race, Performance, and the Ruses of Memory*. University of Minnesota Press, 2009.

Oakeley, Frederick [unsigned]. "Cardinal Wiseman's Essays—Periodical Literature." *Dublin Review* 34, no. June (1853): 541–66.

Okker, Patricia. *Our Sister Editors: Sarah J. Hale and the Tradition of Nineteenth-Century American Women Editors*. University of Georgia Press, 1995.

Oliphant, Margaret. "The Sisters Brontë." In *Women Novelists of Queen Victoria's Reign: A Book of Appreciations*, 1–59. Hurst and Blackett, 1897.

Onslow, Barbara. "Gendered Productions: Annuals and Gift Books." In *Journalism and the Periodical Press in Nineteenth-Century Britain*, ed. Joanne Shattock, 66–83. Cambridge University Press, 2017.

Otter, Samuel. "Stowe and Race." In *The Cambridge Companion to Harriet Beecher Stowe*, ed. Cindy Weinstein, 15–38. Cambridge University Press, 2004.

Painter, Nell Irvin. "Difference, Slavery, and Memory: Sojourner Truth in Feminist Abolitionism." In *The Abolitionist Sisterhood: Women's Political Culture in Antebellum America*, ed. Jean Fagan Yellin and John C. Van Horne, 139–58. Cornell University Press, 1994.

———. *Sojourner Truth: A Life, a Symbol*. Norton, 1997.

Parfait, Claire. *The Publishing History of* Uncle Tom's Cabin, *1852–2002*. Ashgate, 2007.

Parker, Pamela Corpron. "Elizabeth Gaskell and Literary Tourism." In *Literary Tourism and Nineteenth-Century Culture*, ed. Nicola J. Watson, 128–38. Palgrave Macmillan, 2009.

Peabody, Ephraim. "Narratives of Fugitive Slaves." *Christian Examiner and Religious Miscellany* 47, no. 1 (1849): 61–93.

Pease, William H., and Jane H. Pease. "Josiah Henson" (revised 1982). In *Dictionary of Canadian Biography*, vol. 11: *1881–1890*. University of Toronto/Université Laval, 2003–. http://www.biographi.ca/en/bio/henson_josiah_11E.html.

Peterson, Linda H. *Becoming a Woman of Letters: Myths of Authorship and Facts of the Victorian Market*. Princeton University Press, 2009.

———. *Traditions of Victorian Women's Autobiography: The Poetics and Politics of Life Writing*. Victorian Literature and Culture Series. University Press of Virginia, 1999.

———. "Triangulation, Desire, and Discontent in 'The Life of Charlotte Brontë.'" *Studies in English Literature, 1500–1900* 47, no. 4 (2007): 901–20.

Pettinger, Alasdair, and Tim Youngs. Introduction to *The Routledge Research Companion to Travel Writing*, ed. Alasdair Pettinger and Tim Youngs, 1–14. Routledge, 2020.

Pinto, Samantha. *Infamous Bodies: Early Black Women's Celebrity and the Afterlives of Rights*. Duke University Press, 2020.

Poe, Edgar Allan. "Autography." *Southern Literary Messenger*, part 1, February 1836, 205–12; part 2, August 1836, 601–4.

———. "Chapter on Autography." *Graham's Magazine*, part 1: 19, no. 5 (November 1841): 224–34; part 2: 19, no. 6, (December 1841): 273–86; part 3: "Appendix of Autographs," 20, no. 1 (January 1842): 44–49.

Pratt, Mary Louise. *Imperial Eyes: Travel Writing and Transculturation*. Routledge, 2007.

Putnam, George Palmer, ed. *Homes of American Authors; Comprising Anecdotical, Personal, and Descriptive Sketches, by Various Writers*. Putnam, 1853.

Putzi, Jennifer. *Fair Copy: Relational Poetics and Antebellum American Women's Poetry*. University of Pennsylvania Press, 2021.

Quarles, Benjamin. *Black Mosaic: Essays in Afro-American History and Historiography*. University of Massachusetts Press, 1988.

Regis, Amber K., and Deborah Wynne, eds. *Charlotte Brontë: Legacies and Afterlives*. Interventions: Rethinking the Nineteenth Century. Manchester University Press, 2017.

"Review of *The Life of Charlotte Brontë*, by Elizabeth Gaskell." *Christian Observer*, July 1857, 487–90.

Review of *The Life of Charlotte Brontë* by Elizabeth Gaskell. *National Magazine*, 1857. Reprinted in *Elizabeth Gaskell: The Critical Heritage*, ed. Angus Easson, 400–402. Critical Heritage Series. Routledge, 1991.

Review of *The Life of Charlotte Brontë* by Elizabeth Gaskell. *Saturday Review*, April 4, 1857, 313–14. Reprinted in part in *Elizabeth Gaskell: The Critical Heritage*, ed. Angus Easson, 376–79. Critical Heritage Series. Routledge, 1991. Full book review at https://www.google.com/books/edition/The_Saturday_Review_of_Politics_Literatu/RzVUAAAAcAAJ?hl=en&gbpv=0.

Reynolds, David S. *Mightier Than the Sword: Uncle Tom's Cabin and the Battle for America*. Norton, 2011.

Rezek, Joseph. "The Racialization of Print." *American Literary History* 32, no. 3 (September 2020): 417–45.

Rhodes, Jane. "At the Boundaries of Abolitionism, Feminism, and Black Nationalism: The Activism of Mary Ann Shadd Cary." In *Women's Rights and Transatlantic Antislavery in the Era of Emancipation*, ed. Kathryn Kish Sklar and James Stewart, 346–66. Yale University Press, 2007.

Richmond, Stephanie J. "Race, Class, and Antislavery: African American Women in the Transatlantic Antislavery Movement." *Journal of Women's History* 31, no. 3 (2019): 57–77.

Rigby, Elizabeth [unsigned]. Review of *Jane Eyre* and *Vanity Fair*. *Quarterly Review* 84, no. 167 (December 1848): 153–85. Reprinted in *The Brontës: The Critical Heritage*, ed. Mirian Allott, 105–12. Critical Heritage Series. Routledge, 1974.

Rochelson, Meri-Jane. *A Jew in the Public Arena: The Career of Israel Zangwill*. Wayne State University Press, 2008.

Rodensky, Lisa. *The Crime in Mind: Criminal Responsibility and the Victorian Novel*. Oxford University Press, 2003.

Rohrbach, Augusta. *Truth Stranger Than Fiction: Race, Realism, and the U.S. Literary Market Place*. Palgrave Macmillan, 2002.

Roscoe, William Caldwell [unsigned]. Review of *The Life of Charlotte Brontë* by Elizabeth Gaskell. *National Review* 11 (July 1857): 127–64. Reprinted in *Elizabeth Gaskell: The Critical Heritage*, ed. Angus Easson, 420–25. Critical Heritage Series. Routledge, 1991.

Rose, Mark. *Authors and Owners: The Invention of Copyright.* Harvard University Press, 1993.

———. *Authors in Court: Scenes from the Theater of Copyright.* Harvard University Press, 2018.

Rowland, Ann Wierda, and Paul Westover. "Introduction: Reading, Reception, and the Rise of Transatlantic 'English.'" In *Transatlantic Literature and Author Love in the Nineteenth Century*, ed. Paul Westover and Ann Wierda Rowland, 1–18. Palgrave Macmillan, 2016.

Roy, Michaël. *Fugitive Texts: Slave Narratives in Antebellum Print Culture.* Trans. Susan Pickford. University of Wisconsin Press, 2023.

Saint-Amour, Paul K. *The Copywrights: Intellectual Property and the Literary Imagination.* Cornell University Press, 2003.

———, ed. *Modernism and Copyright.* Modernist Literature and Culture. Oxford University Press, 2010.

Scholl, Lesa. "Brewing Storms of War, Slavery, and Imperialism: Harriet Martineau's Engagement with the Periodical Press." In *Women, Periodicals, and Print Culture in Britain, 1830s–1900s: The Victorian Period*, ed. Alexis Easley, Clare Gill, and Beth Rodgers, 489–501. Edinburgh University Press, 2019.

Sharpe, Christina. *In the Wake: On Blackness and Being.* Duke University Press, 2016.

Shattock, Joanne. "Women Journalists and Periodical Spaces." In *Women, Periodicals, and Print Culture in Britain, 1830s–1900s: The Victorian Period*, ed. Alexis Easley, Clare Gill, and Beth Rodgers, 306–18. Edinburgh University Press, 2019.

Shaw, Amanda. "'There Are Two Views Often': The Epistolary Friendship of Harriet Beecher Stowe and Elizabeth Gaskell." *Women's Studies* 51, no. 6 (2022): 682–98.

Shaw, Gwendolyn DuBois. *The Art of Remembering: Essays on African American Art and History.* Duke University Press, 2024.

Sheehan, Lucy, Jennifer Sorensen, and Sarah Allison. "Miscellany as Method: A Trio of Approaches to 'The Runaway Slave at Pilgrim's

Point' and the 1848 *Liberty Bell* Gift Book." *Victorian Poetry* 59, no. 3 (2021): 261–308.

Showalter, Elaine. *A Literature of Their Own*. Rev. and exp. edition. Princeton University Press, 1998.

Sinclair, Stéfan, and Geoffrey Rockwell. "Voyant Tools." 2016. http://voyant-tools.org/.

Sinha, Manisha. *The Slave's Cause: A History of Abolition*. Yale University Press, 2016.

Sinykin, Dan. *Big Fiction: How Conglomeration Changed the Publishing Industry and American Literature*. Columbia University Press, 2023.

Sklar, Kathryn Kish, and James Stewart, eds. *Women's Rights and Transatlantic Antislavery in the Era of Emancipation*. Yale University Press, 2007.

Smith, Clint. "The Man Who Became Uncle Tom." *The Atlantic*, September 8, 2023.

Smith, George. "Charlotte Brontë." *Cornhill Magazine* 82 (December 1900): 778–95.

Smith, Whitney Womack. "Stowe, Gaskell, and the Woman Reformer." In *Transatlantic Stowe: Harriet Beecher Stowe and European Culture*, ed. Denise Kohn, Sarah Meer, and Emily B. Todd, 89–110. University of Iowa Press, 2009.

Spingarn, Adena. *Uncle Tom: From Martyr to Traitor*. Stanford University Press, 2018.

Spires, Derrick R. "Aliened Americans: Pseudonymity and Gender Politics in Early Black Social Media." *African American Review* 55, no. 1 (March 2022): 33–49.

Starr, Thomas. "Separated at Birth: Text and Context of the Declaration of Independence." *Proceedings of the American Antiquarian Society* 110, no. 2 (2000): 153–99.

Stein, Jordan Alexander. *When Novels Were Books*. Harvard University Press, 2020.

Stephen, James Fitzjames. "The License of Modern Novelists" (July 1857). In *Selected Writings of James Fitzjames Stephen: On the Novel and Journalism*, ed. Christopher Ricks, 104–32. Oxford University Press, 2023.

———. "The Relation of Novels to Life" (1855). In *Cambridge Essays, Contributed by Members of the University*, 148–92. Parker and Son, 1855.

Stitch. "What's the Deal with Real Person Fiction?" *Teen Vogue*, August 11, 2021.

Stone, Marjorie. "Elizabeth Barrett Browning and the Garrisonians: 'The Runaway Slave at Pilgrim's Point,' the Boston Female Anti-Slavery Society, and Abolitionist Discourse in *The Liberty Bell*." In *Victorian Women Poets*, ed. Alison Chapman, 33–55. Essays and Studies, no. 56. D. S. Brewer, 2003.

Stowe, Harriet Beecher. *A Key to* Uncle Tom's Cabin: *Presenting the Original Facts and Documents Upon Which the Story Is Founded, Together with Corroborative Statements Verifying the Truth of the Work*. Jewett, Proctor & Worthington, 1853.

———. Preface to Josiah Henson, *Truth Stranger Than Fiction: Father Henson's Story of His Own Life*, iii–v. John P. Jewett, 1858.

———. *Sunny Memories of Foreign Lands*. Phillips, Sampson, 1854.

———. *Uncle Tom's Cabin* (1852). Ed. Ann Douglas. Penguin, 1981.

Swinburne, Algernon Charles. *A Note on Charlotte Brontë*. Gerritsen Collection of Women's History, no. 2785. Chatto & Windus, 1877.

Tanser, H. A. "Josiah Henson, the Moses of His People." *Journal of Negro Education* 12, no. 4 (1943): 630–32.

Tarr, Clayton Carlyle. "Purloined Letters: Edgar Allan Poe, Maria Edgeworth, and the Study of Chirography." *Edgar Allan Poe Review* 14, no. 2 (2013): 178–98.

Taylor, Yuval. Introduction to *I Was Born a Slave: An Anthology of Classic Slave Narratives*, vol. 2: *1849–1866*, ed. Yuval Taylor, xv–xxxviii. Lawrence Hill, 1999.

Thompson, Ralph. *American Literary Annuals & Gift Books, 1825–1865*. H. W. Wilson, 1936.

Thorne-Murphy, Leslee. "Women, Free Trade, and Harriet Martineau's 'Dawn Island' at the 1845 Anti–Corn Law League Bazaar." In *Economic Women: Essays on Desire and Dispossession in Nineteenth-Century British Culture*, ed. Lana Dalley and Jill Rappaport, 41–59. Ohio State University Press, 2013.

Thornton, Tamara Plakins. "Handwriting in an Age of Industrial Print." In *A History of the Book in America*, vol. 3: *The Industrial Book, 1840–1880*, ed. Scott E. Casper, 400–407. American Antiquarian Society, University of North Carolina Press, 2007.

———. "The Romance and Science of Individuality." Chapter 3 in *Handwriting in America: A Cultural History*, 72–107. Yale University Press, 1996.

"The True Story of *Uncle Tom's Cabin*." *New England Homestead* 3, no. 13 (1870): 110.

T. W. H. "James H. Duncan." *The Liberator* 20, no. 42 (1850): 165.

Uglow, Jennifer S. *Elizabeth Gaskell: A Habit of Stories*. Faber and Faber, 1993.

Underwood, Ted. *Distant Horizons: Digital Evidence and Literary Change*. University of Chicago Press, 2019.

———. "Distant Reading and the Blurry Edges of Genre." *The Stone and the Shell* (blog), October 2014. https://tedunderwood.com/2014/10/.

———. "Understanding Genre in a Collection of a Million Volumes." Digital Humanities Start-Up Grant Interim Performance Report, University of Illinois, Urbana-Champaign, December 29, 2014. https://s3-eu-west-1.amazonaws.com/pfigshare-u-files/1857045/UnderstandingGenreInterimReport.pdf.

Underwood, Ted, Michael L. Black, Loretta Auvil, and Boris Capitanu. "Mapping Mutable Genres in Structurally Complex Volumes." Paper presented at the IEEE International Conference, Santa Clara, CA, October 6–9, 2013. https://arxiv.org/pdf/1309.3323v2.

Vadde, Aarthi. "Amateur Creativity: Contemporary Literature and the Digital Publishing Scene." *New Literary History* 48, no. 1 (2017): 27–51.

Walker, Alice. "In Search of Our Mothers' Gardens" (1972). In *Within the Circle: An Anthology of African American Literary Criticism from the Harlem Renaissance to the Present*, ed. Angelyn Mitchell, 401–9. Duke University Press, 1994.

Washington, Margaret. *Sojourner Truth's America*. University of Illinois Press, 2009.

Watson, Nicola J. *The Author's Effects: On Writer's House Museums*. Oxford University Press, 2020.

———. Introduction to *Literary Tourism and Nineteenth-Century Culture*, ed. Nicola J. Watson, 1–12. Palgrave Macmillan, 2009.

———, ed. *Literary Tourism and Nineteenth-Century Culture*. Palgrave Macmillan, 2009.

Watt, Ian. *The Rise of the Novel: Studies in Defoe, Richardson, and Fielding*. University of California Press, 1960.

Weber, Brenda R. *Women and Literary Celebrity in the Nineteenth Century: The Transatlantic Production of Fame and Gender.* Ashgate Series in Nineteenth-Century Transatlantic Studies. Ashgate, 2012.

Weinstein, Cindy, ed. *The Cambridge Companion to Harriet Beecher Stowe.* Cambridge Companions to Literature. Cambridge University Press, 2004.

Westover, Paul. "The Transatlantic Home Network: Discovering Sir Walter Scott." In *Transatlantic Literature and Author Love in the Nineteenth Century*, ed. Paul Westover and Ann Wierda Rowland, 153–74. Palgrave Macmillan, 2016.

Westover, Paul, and Ann Wierda Rowland, eds. *Transatlantic Literature and Author Love in the Nineteenth Century.* Palgrave Macmillan, 2016.

Williams, Raymond. *Keywords: A Vocabulary of Culture and Society.* Rev. ed. Oxford University Press, 1985.

Williams, Susan S. "Authors and Literary Authorship." In *A History of the Book in America*, vol. 3: *The Industrial Book, 1840–1880*, ed. Scott E. Casper, 90–116. American Antiquarian Society, University of North Carolina Press, 2007.

Winks, Robin W. *The Blacks in Canada; a History.* McGill-Queen's University Press, Yale University Press, 1971.

———. "The Making of a Fugitive Slave Narrative: Josiah Henson and Uncle Tom—a Case Study." In *The Slave's Narrative*, ed. Charles T. Davis and Henry Louis Gates Jr., 112–46. Oxford University Press, 1985.

Winship, Michael. "Manufacturing and Book Production." In *A History of the Book in America*, vol. 3: *The Industrial Book, 1840–1880*, ed. Scott E. Casper, 40–69. American Antiquarian Society, University of North Carolina Press, 2007.

———. "*UTC*: History of the Book in the 19th Century U.S." 2007. *Uncle Tom's Cabin* and American Culture: A Multi-media Archive, ed. Steven Railton. http://utc.iath.virginia.edu/interpret/exhibits/winship/winship.html.

Winter, Alison. "Harriet Martineau and the Reform of the Invalid in Victorian England." *Historical Journal* 38, no. 3 (September 1995): 597–616.

Woo, Jewon. "The Colored Citizen: Collaborative Editorship in Progress." *American Periodicals: A Journal of History and Criticism* 30, no. 2 (2020): 110–13.

Woodmansee, Martha. "On the Author Effect: Recovering Collectivity." In *The Construction of Authorship: Textual Appropriation in Law and Literature*, ed. Martha Woodmansee and Peter Jaszi, 15–28. Post-contemporary Interventions. Duke University Press, 1994.

Woodmansee, Martha, and Peter Jaszi, eds. *The Construction of Authorship: Textual Appropriation in Law and Literature*. Post-contemporary Interventions. Duke University Press, 1994.

Woolf, Virginia [unsigned]. "Haworth, November 1904." *The Guardian*, December 21, 1904.

———. *A Room of One's Own* (1929). In *A Room of One's Own and Three Guineas*, 2nd ed., ed. Anna Snaith, 1–86. Oxford University Press, 2015.

Wynne, Deborah. "The 'Charlotte' Cult: Writing the Literary Pilgrimage from Gaskell to Woolf." In *Charlotte Brontë: Legacies and Afterlives*, ed. Amber K. Regis and Deborah Wynne, 43–58. Interventions: Rethinking the Nineteenth Century. Manchester University Press, 2017.

Yates, Louisa. "'Reader, I [Shagged/Beat/Whipped/F****d/Rewrote] Him': The Sexual and Financial Afterlives of *Jane Eyre*." In *Charlotte Brontë: Legacies and Afterlives*, ed. Amber K. Regis and Deborah Wynne, 258–79. Interventions: Rethinking the Nineteenth Century. Manchester University Press, 2017.

Zibrak, Arielle. *Writing Against Reform: Aesthetic Realism in the Progressive Era*. University of Massachusetts Press, 2024.

INDEX

Abbotsford, 59–60
Adam Bede (Eliot), 144
Adams, Amanda, 10, 80, 102
Adams, John Quincy, 45
"adaptive resistance," 102
Algee-Hewitt, Mark, 36
algorithms: discerning fiction from biography, 25–29, 105; "hard cases" for, 28–29, 105; indifference to literary subfields, 21–22, 30; patterns of feature sets, 27–28. *See also* computational perspectives
Altick, Richard D., 23, 147
American Anti-Slavery Society, 71, 75, 105
American Historical and Literary Curiosities: Consisting of Fac-Similes of Original Documents Relating to the Events of the Revolution (Smith), 47
Amigoni, David, 141–42
Andrews, William, 105
anonymity and pseudonymity, 38–40, 57, 78–79, 136, 161

anthologies, 2, 12, 42, 51, 76. *See also specific anthologies*
Anti-Pamela (Haywood), 31
antislavery discourse, 2–3; domestic lens, 93; literary forms in context of, 8, 12, 18; perspectival distance between Europe and American South, 14, 82–83, 87, 188n69, 72; transatlantic context, 5, 7, 10, 13, 43, 78, 82, 85–87, 90–91, 93, 128, 169n19. *See also Autographs for Freedom* (gift book); gift books, antislavery; print culture; *Liberty Bell, The* (ed. Chapman)
Aravamudan, Srinivas, 24
archival rediscovery, 10–11
"Ar'n't I a Woman?" speech (Truth), 107
"Around the Word 'Littérature': The English Case" (Algee-Hewitt, Heuser, McClure, and Moretti), 36
Arping, Åsa, 91–92, 186n57
Ashton, Susanna, 41

Athenaeum, 39, 76
Atlantic, The, 118
attribution, 5–6, 35, 39
aura of work of art, 48–49
authenticity, 31, 140; and handwriting, 47–49, 51, 53, 55
author, figure of: brands, 1, 8–9, 76, 158–59; as composite of constellation of texts, 162; decentralized approach to, 44, 129; emergence of across genres, 1–2, 7, 25, 32, 129; figure/text dyad, 129; at intersection of culture, commerce, and politics, 157–58; modernist conception of, 6; periodicals, identification with, 38; and persona, 5–6, 38, 102; reader search for facts about in fiction, 130–31, 134–39, 141–42; as scribe, 50; white lady authoress, figure of, 10, 72–73, 82, 85–86, 96–97. *See also* authorship; celebrity, literary; collaborative production and writing
"author-function," 41
authorship: amateur creativity, 159, 205–6n6; extratextual ideas about, 31–32; professionalization of, 59–60; reprinting linked with, 49, 177n15. *See also* author, figure of; celebrity, literary; collaborative production and writing
autobiographies, 9, 15–16; autographs as, 46; reception of autobiographies of Black authors, 103; distancing from "I" of, 83, 113–14; and figure of the author, 19, 103; textual similarities to biographies, 26–27; spiritual, 107; truth claims of, 25. *See also* biographies; Brontë, Charlotte; Douglass, Frederick; Henson, Josiah; *specific autobiographies*
autographs, 1, 12, 43, 179–80n49; as attempt to capture aura, 48–49; in commonplace books, 45; and direct correspondence with author, 51; as external indicator of personality, 55; as form of autobiography, 46; friendship albums, 65–68; as signatures, 65–69, *68*; transatlantic networks indicated by, 68–69. *See also* handwriting
"Autographs" (Disraeli), 47
Autographs for Freedom (gift book, ed. Griffiths), 13, 65–69, 161; Douglass associated with, 7, 43, 66, 77; Griffiths as editor, 43, 65, 66, 67, 77, 183n22; Mann's contribution, 67–68, *68*
"Autography" (Poe), 12, 43–44, 47, 50–57, 67, 178n17; editorship dismissed in, 56–57; as miscellany, 53; satire of authors in, 50–57, *54*; used for self-promotion, 53–57, 161

Bagneris, Mia L., 85, 177n7
Baldwin, James, 192n7

Bancroft, George, 62
Barker, Juliet R. V., 132, 140
Barthes, Roland, 39
Beattie, Jessie, 122
Beecher, Henry Ward, 112
Beecher, Lyman, 112
Bell, John, 85
belletristic prose, 19, 34
Benatti, Francesca, 40–41
Benjamin, Walter, 48–49
Berglund, Karl, 159
Bibliotheca Londinensis: A Classified Index to the Literature of Great Britain During Thirty Years Arranged from and Serving as a Key to the London Catalogue of Books 1814–1846 (Hodgson), 33–34
Bidwell, John, 45
biographies, 2, 4, 6, 7, 12, 23–4, 134, 200n21; in relation to autobiography, 19, 46, 131; collaborative production of, 58, 134; collective, 58, 134; as compilations of lives and letters, 147; imagined dialogue in, 27; literary, 131, 137, 140–41, 203n59; spiritual autobiographies, 107; in relation to the novel, 15, 23–30, 129, 139. *See also* autobiographies
Black Moses: The Real Uncle Tom (Beattie), 122
Black print culture, 103–4, 191n19; pseudonymity in, 38–39; transformation of Victorian literature, 44

Black Reconstruction (Du Bois), 122, 125
Blackett, R. J. M. 108
Blackwood, John, 149
Bodichon, Barbara Leigh Smith, 88
book history, 18–19, 33–35. *See also* literary history
book-length narrative forms, 23–35
Booth, Alison, 33, 58, 60, 64, 131, 134, 200n21
Boston Female Anti-Slavery Society, 71
Boswell, James, 23
Bowditch, William L., 75
Brainerd, David, 31
Brake, Laurel, 39
Bremer, Fredrika, 7, 14, 157; antislavery contributions, 72, 75, 188nn69, 72; contributions to *The Liberty Bell*, 72, 75; as the "Miss Austen of Sweden," 91; Stowe linked with, 93, 96–97, 182n14, 188n72; as Swedish writer, 89–92, 187n63, 188n69; Works: *Homes of the New World*, 14, 88–89
British-American Institute, 105
Brontë, Branwell, 146
Brontë, Charlotte: biographical sketches of Emily and Anne, 135, 150; as Currer Bell, 136; editing of sisters' novels, 133, 150–51; Gaskell, link with, 132, 151; Henson, link with, 127–28; imaginative development, account of, 137–40, 145–46;

Brontë, Charlotte (*continued*)
letters of, 137, 140, 147; posthumous "Brontë myth," 16–17, 31, 130–34, 200n21; posthumous figurations of, 149–55; praise for *Uncle Tom's Cabin*, 128–29; sex life as topic in reviews, 134–35; Stowe, link with, 128–29; twenty-three versions of life, 134; *Works:* "Biographical Notice of Ellis and Acton Bell," 135, 150–51; preface to *Wuthering Heights*, 150–51; *Shirley*, 128, 135, 143, 150–51, 198n6; *Villette*, 135, 137. *See also Jane Eyre* (Brontë)
Brontë, Emily, 150
Brontë, Maria, 141, 142
Brontë industry, 133–34
"Brontë myth," 16–17, 31, 130–34, 200n21
Brooks, Daphne A., 102, 190n14, 190–91n17
Brougham, Henry, 40
Brouillette, Sarah, 205n5
Brown, William Box, 190–91n17
Brown, William Wells, 74, 105, 111–12
Browning, Elizabeth Barrett (EBB), 82, 131
Bryant, William S., 37
Busse, Kristina, 160
Byron, Lord etc., 8, 15

Canada: Dawn Settlement (Ontario), 99, 105, 114, 122, 123
Casper, Scott, 58

Cassey, Amy, 66
Casteras, Susan P., 88
Castle, Terry, 140
catalogs, publisher's, 32–34
celebrity: 8–9, 157, 205n2
celebrity, literary: collaborative creation of, 1–2, 6, 8–9, 23, 39, 158–59; desire to know reality behind the legend, 17; digital literary sphere, 159–61; emergence of across genres, 1–2, 16–17, 74, 129–30; gendered and racialized expectations, 9–10, 81–86, 89–97; heightened by link between fiction and nonfiction, 124–25; as name attached to a genre, 8; networks of authors and producers, 4, 68–69, 77, 86, 91, 161; nineteenth-century treatments of, 11; nonfictional texts about celebrity authors, 12–13, 15–16, 18; as traceable to an "original," 17; political deployment of, 73; star system, 4, 100; structured by colonial perspective, 86–88; texts used in creation of, 12–13, 60, 67; in transatlantic abolitionist lecture circuit, 101–2, 190–191n17, used for political change, 157–58, 205n2. *See also* author, figure of; transatlantic context
Chapman, Maria Weston, 13–14, 75, 77, 183n22
"Chapter on Autography" (*Graham's Magazine*), 12, 53–57

Child, Lydia Maria, 6, 17
Christabel; Kubla Khan, a Vision; The Pains of Sleep (Coleridge), 39–42
Christian Age, 113–14
Christian Examiner and Religious Miscellany, 105–6
Christian Observer, 143
Christian Slave, The (Stowe), 128, 198n2
Clandestine Classics series, 154, 160–61
Clarkson, Thomas, 75
Claybaugh, Amanda, 10, 78
Clotel or, The President's Daughter: A Narrative of Slave Life in the United States (Brown), 111–12
Cobb, Jasmine Nichole, 66
Cohen, Lara Langer, 48–49, 61, 69, 103
Cohen, Michael, 66
Coleridge, Samuel Taylor, 39–42
collaborative production and writing, 1–6, 41–42, 61; asynchronous, 104; author brands, creation of, 8–9, 158–59; of biographies, 58, 134; and creation of literary celebrity, 1–2, 6, 8–9, 23, 39; editing, 6, 23, 39–40, 77; and gift books, 71, 77, 132, 161; influencer collab, 77, 161; and life writing, 148; by literary celebrities, 74–77, 130, 133, 198–99n8; as nineteenth-century form, 148; of reviews, 40–41; "social text," 104; twenty-first century platforms, 15, 159–61, 205n5; in works by and about authors, 18–19. *See also* author, figure of; authorship; editing; literary marketplace; translations; *specific anthologies*
commonplace books, 45
compendium genre, 109, 147
computational perspectives, 1–4, 11, 18–19; algorithmic criticism, 23–30; archival network analysis, 13; archival rediscovery, 10–11; bibliometric analysis of Victorian book genres, 32–33; and contemporary perspectives on the past, 157–58; data-driven approaches to literary history, 18, 21–42; on Henson's texts, 115–18, 121; Juxta software, 116, 118, 120; line-by-line comparison of Henson's texts, 116–25; probability, laws of, 24; quantitative book history, 32–33, 174n30; stylometric analysis, 40; Stylo software, 42. *See also* algorithms
Conquest of Peru (Prescott), 62–64, *64*
Cook, Eliza, 32
Cooper, J. Fenimore, 53, 59, 62, *54*
Cooper, Joseph, 115
copyright, 2–5; international, 3, 44; international, Putnam's advocacy for, 59–62; and signature of author as evidence, 48; and translation, 91; *Uncle Tom's Cabin* as test for, 3, 167n3

"counter-fictions," 31
Cowan Bridge school, 133, 139, 140–48, 203n51
"creative nonfiction," 35
criticism: algorithmic, 23–30; handwriting used to satirize authors, 50–57; racialized politics of, 103
Cuba, 72, 87–88, 90, 186n55
Curran Index, 38, 41–42
"Curse for a Nation, A" (Browning), 82
Curtis, Gerard, 47–48

d'Albertis, Deirdre, 132, 149
Dark Victorians (Dickerson), 108
David Copperfield (Dickens), 89
Dawn Settlement (Ontario), 99, 105, 114, 122
death of author, Barthes, 39; posthumous lives of Brontë, 149, 154, 179–80n49; spirit visitations by Henson, 189–90n9
Declaration of Independence, 43, 44–45, 68
Defoe, Daniel, 24, 146–47
Delany, Martin R., 100, 108, 109–10, 124, 193n40
DeWitt, Anne, 37–38
DiBattista, Maria, 93
Dickens, Charles, 7, 8, 57, 144; signature, 48; travelogue, 74, 88–89
Dickerson, Vanessa D., 108
digital humanities, 11, 26, 105

Dillane, Fionnuala, 6, 183n21
disability studies: perspective on Martineau, 79–80
Disraeli, Isaac, 47
Distant Horizons: Digital Evidence and Literary Change (Underwood), 25–26
Documenting the American South (University of North Carolina), 115, 195n59
Domestic Manners of the Americans (Trollope), 15, 89
Douglass, Frederick, 7, 9, 10, 11; in *Autographs for Freedom*, 43, 65, 66–67; criticism of *A Key*, 123, 124; criticism of "Bibles for the slaves" movement, 75; gift books sold for cause, 43; Henson contrasted to, 106–7; Stowe, alliance with, 193n40; Works: *The Heroic Slave*, 43, 66; *My Bondage and My Freedom*, 111; *Narrative*, 105, 111
Doyle, Mary Ellen, 111
Du Bois, W. E. B., 122, 125
Duncan, Ian, 148, 203n59
Dunciad (Pope), 51

Easley, Alexis, 12–13, 32, 38, 77, 78, 173n23
Easson, Angus, 150
Edinburgh Review, 38–41
editors, 6, 8, 23, 183nn21, 23; collaborative editing, 6, 23, 39–40, 77; as critics, 57; and individuality, 56

Eklund, Hillary, 95
Eliot, George, 6, 92–93, 146
Eliot, Samuel A., 105, 106, 192n26, 192n27
Eliot, Simon, 32–33, 174n30
Elizabeth Gaskell (Easson), 150
Ernest, John, 111
Essex Country Freemen, 106
Evening Post, 37
evidence, 31, 47, 55, 140; admissibility of fiction as, 133; and connection between fiction and nonfiction, 147; in Gaskell's institutional account, 140–48

facsimile: as copy of initial writing, 64; engraved, 44, 46–47, 62; in *Homes of American Authors*, 57–64, *64*; woodcuts, 46, 50, 55
factuality, 25, 29–33; interplay between fictional and factual accounts of life, 29–32, 129–31, 135–48; "partial" accounts, 145; reader search for in fictional accounts, 130–31, 134–39, 141–42; validation of first-person accounts of slavery, 29, 103, 109. *See also* nonfictional forms
Faithfull, Emily, 76
fan culture, 13; and facsimile manuscript collections, 47, 57; fan fiction, twenty-first century, 154–55, 159–61. *See also* readers
Fee, Frank E., Jr., 65–66, 67, 74–75

feminism, 72, 81, 88, 91, 131; Black feminist thought, 153–54; "white," 86
fictionality, 15, 171–72n4, 203n59; across genres, 16–17; computational perspectives on, 21–26, 28, 32; "credible" versus "plausible" narratives, 24; ethical issues, 138–39, 144–46; integrated notion of author and narrator, 141; interplay between fictional and factual accounts of life, 29–32, 129–31, 135–48; and "naively literal" readings, 130; nineteenth-century functions of, 35, 173n25; as "nobody's story," 131, 136; politics, race, and testimony in conversation with, 29, 31, 128; realist fiction, 24, 130–31, 136, 140; and rise of novel, 24; treated as a fiction by reader, 25
Fielding, Henry, 31
Fifty Shades of Grey (James), 154
Finch, Aisha K., 88
First-Person Anonymous: Women Writers and Victorian Print Media, 1830–70 (Easley), 38
Fisk, Catherine, 5–6
Flaubert, Gustave, 19
Fludernik, Monika, 25, 32, 171–72n4
Foster, Frances Smith, 100, 111
Foucault, Michel, 41, 104
founding fathers, 44–45

Fraser's Magazine, 12, 49, 51–53, 52, 57, 140
Frawley, Maria H., 80
Frederick Douglass' Paper, 100, 109–10
friendship albums, 65–68
Fritz, Meaghan M., 65–66, 67, 74–75
Fugitive Slave Act of 1850, 106, 192n7

Gage, Frances Dana, 107
Gallagher, Catherine, 24, 131, 136
García, Ivonne M., 87–8, 90
Garrison, William Lloyd, 43, 71, 77
Gaskell, Elizabeth, 16–17, 27, 91, 93, 127–29, 131–34, 136–55; Bremer, link with, 93; Brontë, link with, 132, 151; defense of Brontë's reputation, 135, 137, 152, 201n25; Stowe, friendship with, 127–28, 197n1; tragic heroine myth of Brontë, 132, 133; on "coarseness" in Brontë's novels, 149; *Works: Mary Barton*, 93, 146, 197n1; *Ruth*, 146. See also *Life of Charlotte Brontë, The* (Gaskell)
gender: and anonymous/pseudonymous writing, 38–39, 78–79, 136; in antislavery movement, 10, 66, 73, 79, 102, 183–84n27; and authorial identity, 31, 38, 78, 132–36; in imperial travel writing, 81–89, 185n40; and nineteenth-century campaign writing, 73; and racialization in celebrity, 3, 9–10, 72, 157, 205n2
Genette, Gerard, 42, 176n49
genius, idea of author as, 6, 68; handwriting linked with, 48, 55–56; and imaginative representation in Brontë, 132, 137–39; Romantic idea of, 48, 56
genre: of compendium, 109, 147; connection between celebrity and antislavery genres, 5, 7–8, 11, 16, 18, 73–74, 86–89, 111; and figure of the author, 16–17, 19, 49, 73, 79, 93, 101, 127; in miscellanies, 14, 37–38, 71; nineteenth-century perspectives on, 33–35; nonfictional literary genres, 4, 13, 22–23, 42, 151; from perspective of an algorithmic model, 23–37; from perspective of book market, 3, 7, 18. See also fictionality; nonfictional forms; novel
gift books, 6, 177n6; autographs in, 43, 66–67, 68; British, 12, 67, 177n6; and collaboratively produced, 71, 77, 132, 161; contributions to given as gifts, 76; names of contributors to as valuable, 13–14, 86; political and literary volumes, 58. See also gift books, antislavery; *Homes and Haunts of the Most Eminent British Poets* (Howitt); *Homes of American Authors* (Putnam);

Homes of American Statesmen (G. P. Putnam and Company); *Victoria Regia*
gift books, antislavery, 7, 13–14, 77; and friendship album, 66; global perspective in, 14; individual authors in multiple figurations, 71–72; letters in, 14, 36, 67–68, *68*, 75–76, 79; literary and political work blended, 43. *See also* antislavery discourse; *Autographs for Freedom*; Bremer, Fredrika; *Liberty Bell, The*; Martineau, Harriet; travelogue, antislavery
Gilbert, Sandra, 154
Girl with the Dragon Tattoo, The (Larsson), 159
Goddu, Teresa A., 103, 109, 112
Gordon, Lewis R., 103
Graham's Magazine, 12, 49, 53, 57
Gray, Thomas, 113, 194–95n51
Greek Slave, The (Powers), 85
Greenspan, Ezra, 61, 88–89
Greetham, David C., 104
Grewal, Inderpal, 87
Griffiths, Julia, 43, 65, 66, 67, 77, 183n22
Grigsby, Darcy Grimaldi, 46, 197n87
Griswold, Rufus Wilmot, 56, 69
Gross, Robert A., 44

Habermas, Jürgen, 73
Hack, Daniel, 44
Hancock, John, 45

handwriting, 12, 46, 178n17; and calligraphy, 45; as evidence, 47; genius linked with, 48, 55–56; individuality of privileged over "produced," 55–56; original act as trace of a copy, 64, *64*; Romantic ideal of, 48, 56; signatures as indexical sign of the individual, 46; susceptible to change over time, 55; transformed into print, 43–44. *See also* autographs
Handwriting in America (Thornton), 48, 55, 56
Harper's New Monthly Magazine, 61–62
Hartman, Saidiya, 153–54
HathiTrust texts, 26–28, 105
"Haworth, November 1904" (Woolf), 133
Haworth Parsonage, 132–33
Hayes, Kevin J., 55
Haywood, Eliza, 31
Hazlitt, William, 40–41
Héger, Constantin, 137
Helms, Gabriele, 132
Henson, Josiah: and authorial control, 103; as "black revolutionist," 122, 125; Britain, travels to, 108, 113; Brontë, link with, 127–28; celebrity of, 30, 102–3, 108 ,110; computational comparison of three "lives," 115–18, 121; in relation to Douglass, 11, 105, 106–7; and Dawn Settlement, 99, 105, 114,

Henson, Josiah (*continued*)
122; expanded autobiographies, 16, 99–101, 110–13; fundraising by, 16, 105, 108, 122; as international leader, 108; as lecturer, 16, 99–103, 106–7, 113–14, 160, 189n8; legacy of, 125; lives of as commercial enterprise, 100; meets Queen Victoria, 122; as minister, 100, 102, 107, 108; minstrelsy used by, 116–18, 123, 190n10; as the "original Uncle Tom," 10, 16, 30, 99–101, 122–24, 127; portrait of, 114; public persona of, 101; reappropriation of story from Stowe, 101; Stowe as foil to, 18, 100; and Underground Railroad, 121–22; versions of "lives," overview of 100; wax statue in Madame Tussaud's of, 170–71n35; at World's Fair of 1851, 122. Works: *Life of Josiah Henson*, 10–11, 21–22, 104, 105–8, 116–17; *Truth Stranger Than Fiction*, 101, 107, 110–13, 119–22; *Uncle Tom's Story of His Life*, 29, 101, 107, 113–15, 122–23. *See also Key to Uncle Tom's Cabin*
Heroic Slave, The (Douglass), 43, 66
Hertha (Bremer), 92
Heuser, Ryan, 36
Higginson, Thomas Wentworth, 75
Historical and Literary Curiosities, Consisting of Facsimiles of Original Documents (Smith), 47, 51
Hodgson, Thomas, 33–34
homes-and-haunts collections, 12–13, 57–64, 132; writer's house, 57–60. *See also* tourism, literary; writer's house
Homes and Haunts of the Most Eminent British Poets (Howitt), 12, 13, 17, 57
Homes of American Authors (Putnam), 12, 13, 17, 36–37, 43, 47; authors as contributors to, 37; celebrity created and sold in, 60, 67; descriptions of writing process in, 62–64, *64*, 161; facsimile manuscript in, 49, 57–64, *64*; as U.S. literary history, 61; writers of, 57, 61
Homes of American Statesmen (G. P. Putnam and Company), 58
Homes of the New World (Bremer), 14, 86–96, *93*; *Uncle Tom's Cabin* referenced in, 96
Hornblower, Jane E., 75
Household Words (Dickens), 8
Howitt, Mary, 7, 14, 17, 75, 187n61; as translator, 91–92
Howitt, William, 12, 13, 17, 57
Hughes, Linda K., 37, 131, 138

Illustrations of Political Economy (Martineau), 78
imperialism, 14, 123; and literary celebrity, 86–88; objectification of others, 84, 85; orientalist

tropes of, 81, 83–86; and
travelogue genre, 72, 81–86
"Incidents of Travel" (Martineau),
14, 75, 81–86
"In Search of Our Mothers'
Gardens" (Walker), 153–54
intimacy with author, creation of
sense of, 12–13, 15, 59, 80, 132,
134, 161; and letters, 51, 53,
147
Irving, Washington, 55, 59–60

Jackson, Andrew, 67
Jackson, Leon, 65, 76
James, E. L., 154
Jane Eyre: An Autobiography
(Brontë), 16–17, 31, 89, 127;
erotica versions, 154–55, 160–61;
Lowood school in, 140–48;
reviews of, 134–35, 138, 140; slave
narrative tropes in, 128. *See also*
Brontë, Charlotte
Jeffrey, Francis, 40–41
Jewett, John P., 67, 111, 112,
193–94n43
Johnson, Samuel, 23
Johnston, Judith, 87, 93
"Josiah Henson, the Moses of His
People" (Tanser), 122

Kelly, John, 31
Key to Uncle Tom's Cabin, A (Stowe),
29, 99, 101, 103, 108–10;
corrections to by Solomon
Northup, 123; corrections to by
Frederick Douglass, 123
Keymer, Thomas, 30–31

Keywords (Williams), 35
Klein, Lauren F., 6
Koenigs, Thomas, 35, 109,
173n25
Kooistra, Lorraine Janzen, 71

Larsson, Stieg, 91, 159
Latham, Sean, 136
lecture circuit, 2, 9–10; and
"antislavery wall" of formerly
enslaved Black abolitionist
speakers in Britain, 102, 108,
123, 190–191n17; Douglass as
lecturer, 9, 102; and emergence
of authorship, 160; Henson as
lecturer, 16, 99–103, 106–7,
113–14, 160, 189n8; intersection
of drama and literature in, 128;
Reddit "Ask Me Anything"
compared with, 160; Stowe as
lecturer, 127–28; transatlantic,
10; Webb's public readings on,
128, 198nn2, 3
Lee, Jarena, 107, 192–93n32
Lee, Julia Sun-Joo, 128
Leffler, Yvonne, 92
letters: in antislavery gift books,
14, 36, 67–68, *68*, 75–76, 79;
Brontë's, 137, 140, 147;
"business of," 65; epistolary
biography, 147; public-facing
concerns in private
correspondence, 128; reprinted,
178n21; as signs of credibility,
51, 140
Lewes, George Henry, 140,
149

Liberty Bell, The (ed. Chapman), 13–14, 67, 71–72, 91; autograph book, similarities with, 76; Bremer's letter printed in, 14, 75–76; celebrity contributors, 74–77; Garrison associated with, 77; Martineau's contribution, 78–87; non-abolition content in, 75; prose as primary form in, 81–82

Life and Adventures of Jonathan Jefferson Whitlaw, The; or Life on the Mississippi (Trollope), 15, 89

Life and Adventures of Michael Armstrong, the Factory Boy, The (Trollope), 128

Life and Adventures of Robinson Crusoe, The (Defoe), 24, 146–47

Life and Times of Frederick Douglass, The (Douglass), 114

Life of Charlotte Brontë, The (Gaskell), 16–17, 27, 127, 129; biographical sketches of what might have been, 149–55; "clef" structures in, 136, 151; conflation of person and character in, 141; Cowan Bridge documented in, 133, 139, 140–48, 203n51; discursive context of, 131–32; extratextual rumors challenged by, 135, 137, 152; legitimization of Brontë's impressions, 142–45; as marketable commodity, 149, 151; reviews of, 27, 133, 136, 138, 143–47; revision of, 146, 151, 203n51; suppression of Brontë's letters to Héger, 137

Life of Josiah Henson, Formerly a Slave, Now an Inhabitant of Canada, as Narrated by Himself, The (Henson), 10–11, 21–22; 1849 edition, 105, 108, 116–17; circulation of editions, 104–5; editions of, 100–101, 103; as "hard case" for algorithmic tagger, 28–29, 105; line-by-line comparison of texts, 116–25; postbellum London edition, 29; publisher, 67; as putative source for *Uncle Tom's Cabin*, 29–30, 99–101, 122–24, 127; textual analysis of, 104, 105–8; *Truth Stranger Than Fiction* version, 101, 107, 110–13, 119–22; *Uncle Tom's Story of His Life* version, 101, 107, 113–15, 122–23

Life of Samuel Johnson (Boswell), 23

life writing, 46, 86–89, 148, 199n10. *See also* autobiography; biographies; fictionality; novel; travelogue; travelogue, antislavery

liminal forms, 42

Literary Gaze, 37

literary history: data-driven approaches to, 21–42; miscellaneous texts in, 1–2; nonfiction filtered out of, 4; sociology of literature, 22, 23, 30–37, 58, 158. *See also* book history

literary marketplace, 8; "big fiction," 159; Brontë and *Jane Eyre* erotica, 154–55, 160–61; Brontë industry, 133–34; "business of letters," 65; cheap print, rise of, 9, 91–92; computational studies of, 21–22; death of author as marketable, 149, 154, 179–80n49, 189–90n9; decentralized production, 11; eighteenth-century U.S. publishing, 31; fiction and nonfiction imbricated in, 32–33; gift books as commercial literary venture, 71; gift economy, 65, 76; intimacy with author, creation of sense of, 12–13, 15, 59, 147, 161; nonfiction dominant in, 5, 33, 69; publishing platforms, 159–61, 205n5; puffing system, 61; for spiritual autobiographies, 107; transatlantic, 5, 44. *See also* collaborative production and writing; copyright; print culture
literature: limits of disciplinary subfields, 3–4, 21; "literary" texts privileged, 73–74; nineteenth-century understanding of, 19; singly authored, one-figure biography recognized as, 134; sociology of, 22, 23, 30–37; specialization, 35–36; as term, 35–36
Literature of Their Own, A (Showalter), 132

Lobb, John, 113–14, 189–90n9, 195n54
Lofsvold, Laurel Ann, 95
Logan, Deborah, 78, 81, 85
Longfellow, Henry Wadsworth, 59
Lootens, Tricia, 10, 72–73
Lost Continent, The (Cooper), 115
Lund, Michael, 131, 138
Lynch, Deidre, 23, 25
Lyrical Ballads (Coleridge and Wordsworth), 39

Madame Tussaud's wax museum, 16
Mann, Horace, 67–68, *68*
manuscript reproduction, 46–47
"Man Who Became Uncle Tom, The" (Smith), 125
Marcus, Sharon, 8, 12, 157
Marraccini, Miranda, 13, 76–77
Martineau, Harriet, 13–14, 17, 78–87, 128; contributions to *The Liberty Bell*, 72, 78–87; as "political poetess," 80; *Works: Illustrations of Political Economy*, 78; "Incidents of Travel," 14, 75, 81–86; *Life in the Sick Room*, 79–80; "Pity the Slave," 79, 86; *Society in America*, 78–79
Mary Barton (Gaskell), 93, 136, 146
Maurer, Oscar, 38
McClure, David, 36
McFadden, Margaret, 10
McGill, Meredith, 2–3, 49, 50, 61–62, 69, 178n17
McKivigan, John R., 65, 77

Meer, Sarah, 7–8
Mellor, Anne K., 73
Méndez Rodenas, Adriana, 88
Michie, Elsie B., 15, 89
Midgley, Clare, 81
Miller, Lucasta, 130, 199n9
minstrelsy, 116–18, 123, 190n10, 197n83
miscellaneousness, 1–4, 37–38; in "Autography," 53; computational perspectives on, 3–4; of epistolary biography, 147. *See also* gift book; gift book, antislavery
Modern Language Association (MLA), 104
Mole, Tom, 15
Moore, Thomas, 40
Moran, Joe, 2, 17
Moretti, Franco, 36
Morgan, Susan, 87
Mothers of the Nation (Mellor), 73
Murray, Hannah-Rose, 102, 123, 190n10
Murray, Simone, 15, 160, 161
My Bondage and My Freedom (Douglass), 111

Narrative (Douglass), 111
Narrative Factuality: A Handbook (Fludernik and Ryan), 32
Narrative of Sojourner Truth (Truth), 46
"Narratives of Fugitive Slaves" (Peabody), 105–6
Nineteenth-Century Gender Studies, 73

Nobody's Story (Gallagher), 131, 136
nonfictional forms, 4; celebrity-authored texts, 15–16; as celebrity genres, 32; "creative nonfiction," 35; dominant in nineteenth-century book market, 5, 22, 33–34, 42, 69; factual forms adjacent to novel, 15, 17, 22, 25–29, 86–89, 111–12, 129; "factual" genres lumped under, 32; fictional mode of reading, 147–48; as literary work, 23; mediated by genre, 11; as origin of novel, 29; and sociology of literature, 30–37; texts about celebrity authors, 12–13, 15–16, 18; "true" accounts, 15, 139. *See also* factuality
Nord, Deborah Epstein, 93
Northup, Solomon, 123, 124
North Star, The: The Poetry of Freedom by Her Friends, 66
Note on Charlotte Brontë (Swinburne), 135, 138
novel: blockbuster sales potential, 30–31; eighteenth-century, 33–34; factual forms adjacent to, 15, 17, 22, 25–29, 86–89, 111–12, 129; nonfictional forms as origin of, 29; periodicals imbricated with, 38; of purpose, 144; realist, 24, 130–31, 136, 140; related works that sell, 30–31; rise of as rise of fictionality, 24; roman à clef, 136, 151; share of nineteenth-century book

market, 5, 22, 33–34, 42, 69; "theological," 38; three-decker, 19, 171n39
Nyong'o, Tavia, 197n83

Octoroon, The (Bell), 85
Okker, Patricia, 6
Oliphant, Margaret, 130, 133
Onslow, Barbara, 76, 183n22
"originality," 5, 49
Oxford Historical Thesaurus, 35

Painter, Nell Irvin, 107
Pamela (Richardson), 30–31
"Pamela" in the Marketplace (Keymer and Sabor), 30–31
Pamela's Conduct in High Life (Kelly), 31
paratext, 25, 73, 176n49
Parfait, Claire, 108, 111
Pattillo, Rebecca A., 65, 77
Peabody, Ephraim, 105–7, 192n26
Pease, Elizabeth, 79
pen-and-pencil sketches, 65
Penguin Random House, 31
periodicals, literary, 4, 19, 23, 34, 37–42; anonymous reviews in, 38–40; blend of word and image, 46; novels imbricated with, 38; reprinting, 49, 61–62; signatures used to sell, 50, 65
persona: of author, 5–6, 38, 100–104
Peterson, Linda H., 79, 131

Pinto, Samantha, 9
"Pity the Slave" (Martineau), 79, 86
Poe, Edgar Allen, 12, 43, 44, 47, 50–57, 75; as editor, 12, 49, 54–55; *Works:* "Chapter on Autography," 12, 43, 44, 47, 50–57, 67, 178n17; *The Narrative of Arthur Gordan Pym of Nantucket*, 53
"political poetesses," 10, 72–73, 80
Pope, Alexander, 51
Porter, Susan F., 7
Powers, Hiram, 85
Prescott, William, 62–64, *64*, 161, 179n49
print culture, 158; antislavery print culture, 7–9, 16–18; Black print culture, 38–39, 44, 103–4; and collective creation of celebrity, 2; nineteenth-century racialization of, 191n19; periodicals; and public performance, 103–4; quantitative approaches to, 21, 23, 32–33, 37–38, 174n30. *See also* genre; gift book; literary marketplace; reprinting; travelogue
printing and illustration, developments in, 44, 46–47
Procter, Adelaide, 76–77
Prose Writers of America, The (Griswold), 69
publicity, right to, 5–6, 168n9

Putnam, George Palmer, 12, 13, 17, 36–37, 47, 161; advocacy for international copyright law, 59–62; and autographs, 49; as autograph collector, 58–59
Putnam's Magazine, 61–62

Quarles, Benjamin, 75

Reade, Charles, 144
readers: connected to writers through print forms, 3, 47, 59; "loving literature," 25, 59; "rituals of contact" with author, 57–58; search for factuality in fictional accounts, 130–31, 134–39, 141–42. *See also* fan culture
Refugee in America, The (Trollope), 15, 89
"Relation of Novels to Life, The" (Stephen), 146–47
Remond, Sarah Parker, 102
reprinting, 2, 12, 178n21; authorship linked with, 49, 177n15; and periodicals, 49, 61–62
reputation, 5–6, 77
Reynolds, David S., 118
Rezek, Joseph, 191n19
Richardson, Samuel, 30–31
Richmond, Stephanie J., 102
Rigby, Elizabeth (later Lady Eastlake), 135
Rodensky, Lisa, 144
Rohrbach, Augusta, 111, 112
roman à clef, 136, 151

Room of One's Own, A (Woolf), 152–53
Roscoe, William Caldwell, 149
Rossetti, Christina, 154
Rowland, Ann Wierda, 13, 44
"Runaway Slave at Pilgrim's Point, The" (Browning), 82
Ryan, Marie-Laure, 32

Sabor, Peter, 30–31
Saint-Amour, Paul, 5
Sartain's Union Magazine of Literature and Art, 80
Saturday Review, 138–39
Scott, Walter, 59–60
Selling Antislavery (Goddu), 109
Shadd, Mary Ann, 6
Shaftesbury, Earl of, 114, 189n8
Shamela (Fielding), 31
Shaw, Amanda, 128
Sheehan, Lucy, 82, 111–12
Shirley (Brontë), 128, 135, 143, 150–51
Showalter, Elaine, 132
signatures, 2, 5, 12, 43–69; anonymity, convention of, 38–40; artifact replaces discursive account, 46, 177n7; autographs as, 65–69, *68*; calligraphic, 45; circulation separate from author's work, 48; Declaration of Independence, 43, 44, 68; editors and publishers involved in reproduction of, 49; electronic, 46; as evidence of

authenticity, 47–48; legal, cultural power of, 45–46; mechanical reproduction of, 46–47; as proxy for author as originary figure, 50; as proxy for political support, 43; used to sell periodicals, 50, 65. *See also* autograph collecting

Simon & Schuster, 31

Sinha, Manisha, 9

Sinykin, Dan, 159

"Sisters Brontë, The" (Oliphant), 130, 133

slave narrative, 1849 review in *Christian Examiner*, 105–7; from algorithmic perspective, 28–29; circumstances of production, 100, 103–104; as documentary form, 29, 109, 110, 112; in relation to novel, 111, 128; online North American Slave Narratives archive, 105; Smith on, 11. See also *Life of Josiah Henson, Formerly a Slave, Now an Inhabitant of Canada, as Narrated by Himself, The* (Henson); *Truth Stranger Than Fiction* (Henson); *Uncle Tom's Story of His Life* (Henson)

Smith, Charles John, 47

Smith, Clint, 10–11, 118, 125

Smith, George, 128–29, 199n9

Smith, John Jay, 47

Society for the History of Authorship, Reading and Publishing, 4

Society in America (Martineau), 78–79

sociology of literature, 22, 23, 30–37, 58, 158

"Sojourner Truth, the Libyan Sibyl" (Stowe), 123–24

Sorensen, Jennifer, 82

Southern Literary Messenger, 12, 49, 50–51, 53; and manuscript "gifting," 65

Southey, Robert, 39

specialization, 35–36

speculative history, 153–54

Spingarn, Adena, 101, 125

Spires, Derek, 38

spiritual autobiographies, 107

Spooner, Lysander, 75

Spy, The (Irving), 62

Starr, Thomas, 45

Stein, Jordan Alexander, 103

Stephen, James Fitzjames, 27, 144–48

Stone, Marjorie, 75, 77, 91

Stowe, Calvin, 112

Stowe, Harriet Beecher: on antislavery as a term, 7; appropriation of Henson's story, 10, 29, 100, 109; in *Autographs for Freedom*, 66–67; Bremer's travelogue engaged with, 93, 96–97, 182n14, 188n72; Brontë, link with, 128–29; celebrity of linked with books authored by others, 31–32; copyright suit, 167n3; decentering of, 17–18; Gaskell, friendship with,

Stowe, Harriet Beecher (*continued*) 127–28, 197n1; gendered expectations of, 9–10; Henson as foil to, 18; investment in political movement against slavery, 7–8; lecture tours, 127–28; as poet, 10, 67; travelogue, 74; Works: *The Christian Slave*, 128; *A Key to Uncle Tom's Cabin*, 29, 99, 101, 103, 108–10, 123–24; "Preface" to *Truth Stranger Than Fiction*, 110–11; "Sojourner Truth, the Libyan Sibyl," 123–24. See also *Uncle Tom's Cabin* (Stowe)

Stylo software, 42

Svedjedal, Johan, 58

Swinburne, Algernon, 135, 138

Tanser, H. A., 122

taxonomies, 33–34

Tennyson, Alfred, 76–77

Textual Scholarship (Greetham), 104

Thackeray, William Makepeace, 135, 137, 199n9

"Miller Correspondence, The" series (*Fraser's Magazine*), 51

Young People's Illustrated Edition of "Uncle Tom's" Story of His Life (from 1789 to 1877), The (Sunday school book), 113–14

Thornton, Tamara Plakins, 47, 55

Tonra, Justin, 40–41

Totally Bound Publishing, 154

tourism, literary, 13, 78; autograph collections linked with, 47; "Charlotte cult" visitors to Haworth Parsonage, 132–33; imperial work of, 81, 83–86. See also homes-and-haunts collections

Traditions of Victorian Women's Autobiography (Peterson), 131

transatlantic context, 68–69; and antislavery discourse, 3, 5, 7, 10, 12, 43, 78, 82, 85–87, 90–91, 93, 108, 128, 169n19; Brontë connected to, 128; feminist network, 81, 91; social reform movements, 10, 78, 86–87, 169n19. See also celebrity, literary; gift books; politics; travelogue, antislavery

Transatlantic Literature and Author Love in the Nineteenth Century (Rowland), 44

translation, 6–7, 87, 91–92, 159, 167n3

travelogue: as celebrity genre, 7, 73–74; as commercial literary form, 86; and imperialism, 72, 81–85; included in prose fiction, 24–25; place, importance of, 87; as text "about" an author, 74

travelogue, antislavery, 7, 12, 13, 14, 69; as life writing, 86–89; as novel-adjacent, 86–89; orientalist tropes in, 24, 81, 83–86, 185n40. See also gift books, antislavery

Trollope, Frances, 15, 88–89, 128, 186n52

"true" accounts, 15, 139. *See also* biographies; factuality
Truth, Sojourner, 46, 107, 123–24, 197n87
Truth Stranger Than Fiction: Father Henson's Story of His Own Life (Henson), 101, 107, 110–13, 119–23; account of Underground Railroad involvement, 121–22
Tubman, Harriet, 125

Uncle Tom: From Martyr to Traitor (Spingarn), 125
"Uncle Tom mania," 7–8, 123
Uncle Tom's Cabin (Stowe), 2–3; *The Christian Slave* version for public reading by Mary Webb, 128; copies sold in United Kingdom, 10; copyright suit against translator of, 167n3; Delany's criticism of, 100, 109–10; Henson's narrative cited as source for, 29–30, 99–101, 122–24, 127; Henson's promotion of, 101, 108, 110; in *Homes of the New World*, 96; as illegitimate account of Henson's life, 30; publishing history, 3, 67, 108–9. *See also Key to Uncle Tom's Cabin, A* (Stowe)
Uncle Tom's Story of His Life: An Autobiography of the Rev. Josiah Henson (Mrs. Harriet Beecher Stowe's "Uncle Tom"), from 1789 to 1876 (Henson), 101, 107, 113–15, 189n8; Anglicization of

words and imperial context in, 122–23
Unconstitutionality of Slavery, The (Spooner), 75
"Understanding Genre in a Collection of a Million Volumes" (Underwood), 26–28, 105
Underwood, Ted, 25–28, 105, 172n11
Up from Slavery (Washington), 106

Vadde, Aarthi, 159, 205–6n6
Victoria Press, 13, 76
Victoria Regia (gift book), 76
Villette (Brontë), 135, 137
volume form, 2, 22, 47, 92, 161
Voyant software, 116, 122

Walker, Alice, 152
Washington, Booker T., 106
Washington, Margaret, 123–24
Watson, Nicola J., 13, 57, 73–74
Watt, Ian, 24
Wattpad, 159
Wayward Lives (Hartman), 153–54
Webb, Mary, 128, 198nn2, 3
Weber, Brenda R., 74, 132, 134
Webster, Daniel, 36–37, 59
Wellesley Index, 38
West, David, 116
Westover, Paul, 13, 44, 60
Wheatley, Phillis, 153, 193n32, 204n71
"white feminism," 86
Williams, Raymond, 35
Wilson, Carus, 143, 203n51

Winks, Robin W., 100, 114, 121, 123, 193n43
Winship, Michael, 58, 112
Winter, Alison, 80
Women Novelists of Queen Victoria's Reign, 130, 133, 198–99n8
Woo, Jewon, 6

Woodmansee, Martha, 6
Woolf, Virginia, 133, 152–53
Wordsworth, William, 39
Wuthering Heights (Brontë), 150
Wynne, Deborah, 132–33

Yates, Louisa, 154

GPSR Authorized Representative: Easy Access System Europe, Mustamäe tee
50, 10621 Tallinn, Estonia, gpsr.requests@easproject.com

www.ingramcontent.com/pod-product-compliance
Lightning Source LLC
Chambersburg PA
CBHW022046290426
44109CB00014B/1004